A. E. WAITE

MAGICIAN OF MANY PARTS

A. E. Waite by Alvin Langdon Coburn, 1922.

CONTENTS

PREFACE

AS I was coming into the world, Waite was going out; and it was my discovery of this curious, if tenuous, link between us that changed a mild interest in Waite into a fascination (an obsession, if my wife is to be believed) for the man and his work.

I discovered also that Waite was a very private man; his autobiography—*Shadows of Life and Thought*, which I have abbreviated throughout the text as *SLT*—reveals far less of his outer life than it appears to do, for Waite was more concerned to expound his mystical philosophy and to encourage others to seek for themselves the 'Way of Divine Union' than to record his personal history. In the autobiography he epitomises the image he presented to W. B. Yeats: that of 'the one deep student of these things known to me'.

But his maddening vagueness and cavalier attitude to the fine details of such episodes of his life as he *did* choose to relate masked a desire to preserve for posterity the full story—or at least the story of his adult life, for there was much about his childhood that was well enough concealed to make conjecture the principal tool for its disinterment. Not that he necessarily intended such a careful concealment, but rather that he neglected to take proper care of his papers (they were stored in damp cellars and basements) so that many of them deteriorated badly and some of the most important were completely destroyed—including everything that related to his mother's family, and all the letters he had received from Yeats.

And yet there remain so many of his papers that no biographer could justly ask for more; by chance (aided, as I like to think, by diligence) I was led first to his diaries and then to the larger bulk of his papers: personal, commercial, and esoteric. From other sources I obtained copies of his forty years' correspondence with Arthur Machen, and of his equally prolific correspondence with his American friend, Harold Voorhis. With the aid of the late Geoffrey Watkins I traced many of those who had known Waite in his later life and recorded their memories and impressions of him. All of which has taken far longer than it ought to have done, and many of those who helped me when I began my pursuit of this multifaceted man—for so he proved to be—are now themselves dead.

To those who remain I am heavily indebted. The details of Waite's American ancestry were unearthed for me by Mr Charles Jacobs of Bridgeport, Connecticut; while information on his early life was provided by Fr. Hubert Edgar, O.P., Mr Raphael Shaberman, and Fr. Horace Tennent. Much of the footwork around London was undertaken by my son, Nicholas, and Mr Timothy d'Arch-Smith gave me the benefit of his expert opinion over the question of Waite's early predilections.

Over the matter of Waite's personal life I have been greatly helped by Arthur Machen's children—Mrs Janet Pollock and Mr Hilary Machen—and by Mr Godfrey Brangham, Mr Roger Dobson, Mr Michael Goth, and Mr Christopher Watkins, all of whom supplied me with a wealth of correspondence between Waite and Machen; and by Mr A. B. Collins, Miss Marjorie Debenham, Mr C. J. Forestier-Walker, Mrs Madge Strevens, and Mr Colin Summerford, who have each provided invaluable information on Waite's two marriages and on his later life.

For the story of Waite's involvement with the Golden Dawn and with the Fellowship of the Rosy Cross I am greatly indebted to Mr Warwick Gould, the Revd Dr Roma King, Mr Keith Jackson, Mr Roger Parisious, Mrs Francine Prince, Mr John Semken, Mr Andrew Stephenson, and those anonymous survivors of the Fellowship of the Rosy Cross who wish forever to remain unknown.

Aleister Crowley's references to Waite were found for me by Mr Clive Harper and Mr Martin Starr, while I could not have charted Waite's masonic career without the constant help and encouragement of Mr John Hamill, the Librarian of the United Grand Lodge of England. I have been similarly helped by the staff of the British Library (Reference Division) and of the library of the Warburg Institute. I must also thank the many correspondents who have provided me with suggestions, clues, and obscure titbits of information during the time of my quest.

But above all my thanks are due to Ellic Howe, Lewis Richter, and the Revd Kevin Tingay: three friends and colleagues who for the past fifteen years have aided and abetted me far beyond the call of duty in my pursuit of Waite and all his works. I owe them a debt that cannot easily be repaid.

Lastly I must thank my wife, who has lived with Waite for as long as she has lived with his biographer—and has yet contrived to tolerate us both.

R. A. GILBERT
Bristol, February 1987

INTRODUCTION

WRITING to his friend Louis Wilkinson, on 7 April 1945, Aleister Crowley remarked—in uncharacteristically charitable fashion—'If it had not been for Waite, I doubt if, humanly speaking, I should ever have got in touch with the Great Order.' Inevitably he prefixed this praise with abuse: 'Waite certainly did start a revival of interest in Alchemy, Magic, Mysticism, and all the rest. That his scholarship was so contemptible, his style so over-loaded, and his egomania so outrageous does not kill to the point of extinction, the worth of his contribution.' Even this is muted criticism for Crowley; more often he heaped abuse on Waite with gusto, tingeing it with venomous personal attacks that were as unjustified as were his assaults on Waite's writing. His characterization of Waite (in his novel *Moonchild*) as 'Edwin Arthwait', 'a dull and inaccurate pedant without imagination or real magical perception', is more a reflection of his self-perception. But why should Crowley, flamboyant, indifferent to public opinion and public morals, and with a perpetual circle of sycophantic acolytes, be so exercised with the need to condemn a man he perceived as a fellow occultist?

Throughout the ten issues of his periodical *The Equinox* Crowley maintained a stream of invective and abuse against A. E. Waite, condemning the man, his works, his friends and all that he stood for. As there was virtually no public circulation of *The Equinox* these attacks seem futile and can only be explained by a wish on Crowley's part to justify his own actions. He had written to Waite in 1898, after reading *The Book of Black Magic*, and received in reply the advice to go away and read Eckartshausen's *The Cloud upon the Sanctuary*. Having read the book Crowley realized that there is a hidden, Interior Church behind the outer institutions; but when he subsequently joined the Hermetic Order of the Golden Dawn he failed to find the Interior Church—for the simple reason that it was never there. Such a Church—the Holy Assembly—would, inevitably, have required from Crowley what he did not wish to give: the renunciation of his self-centred nature. This he could only preserve by the practice of magic and it was Waite's measured analysis of the futility and wickedness of magic that so enraged him in later years.

Crowley's hostility centred on his awareness that Waite had perceived the true nature of magic and pointed to another way—that of the mystic. Unwilling to accept what he knew inwardly to be true, Crowley turned to verbiage and venom, at the same time belittling himself and ensuring that future generations of occultists should know of Waite and be curious.

And who *was* Waite? Arthur Edward Waite, the child of Anglo-American parents, was born at a time of religious upheaval and left this world as it was busily engaged in tearing apart its social fabric. He was a prolific author, but one whose books are, for the most part, unknown and unread; he was not recognized as a scholar by the academic world, but he remains the only comprehensive analyst of the history of occultism in all its many branches. Not that he approved of the term or the looseness of its connotations; to himself he was a mystic and an exponent of mysticism. He saw, what others before him had not seen, that there can be no final understanding of mystical experience without an appreciation of the traditions, outside the confines of the Church, that preserved those practices that bring mystical experience within the reach of every man and woman.

He is not easy to understand. His writing is diffuse, often verbose, and peppered with archaisms; but it has its own power and leaves the reader with the feeling that buried within the densely packed prose is a message of immense significance. This has been perceived by the more acute of his critics: Dean Inge—a scourge of sentimental pseudo-mysticism—believed that Waite had 'penetrated very near to the heart of his subject' (review of *Studies in Mysticism*, in *The Saturday Review*, 2 March 1907). But Waite refused to jettison all that was included under the heading of occultism. He saw within it, as Spurgeon said of the Talmud, 'jewels which the world could not afford to miss'; and seeing them, drew them out and displayed them for all to see—all, that is, with eyes to see.

Many readers of Waite, and most self-confessed students of 'rejected knowledge', persist in seeing him as an occultist. Usually they find him wanting: Richard Cavendish, in *The Tarot* admired his energy in pursuing esoteric lore but described as 'uncharacteristically lucid' his preface to Papus's *Tarot of the Bohemians* and killed Waite off in 1940, 'in the London blitz', thus denying him his last two years of life. Michael Dummett, in *The Game of Tarot*, speaks of Waite as having, 'the instincts, and to a large extent, the temperament, of a genuine scholar; in particular he had the scholar's squeamishness about making factual assertions unwarranted by the evidence'. And yet Waite was 'as committed an occultist as those he subjected to his rebukes'. Even more unkind—and quite unjustified—was Shumaker's comment in his important book *The Occult Sciences in the Renaissance*. 'An occultist like A. E. Waite', he said, 'whose attitude toward alchemy resembles that of Montague Summers toward Witchcraft, is temperamentally inclined to assume the possession of profound wisdom by our ancestors' (p. 162). He yet proceeded to pillage Waite's alchemical translations to illustrate his own work.

Sympathetic scholars have seen Waite in a different light. Gershom Scholem praised him for *The Secret Doctrine In Israel*: 'His work', he said, 'is distinguished by real insight into the world of Kabbalism'; although he added that 'it is all the more regrettable that it is marred by an uncritical attitude towards facts of history and philology'. That failing in Waite was the result of under-education and his achievements in the field of 'rejected knowledge' are the more remarkable when it is realized that his schooling consisted of little more than two terms at only one recognized institute.

The lack of academic training was the principal cause of Waite's peculiar literary style, which resulted in some of his work appearing far more abstruse than was really the case, and even more of it seeming to be inconclusive. A masonic friend of Waite's, B. H. Springett, referred to his enthusiasm for the significance of certain rituals and to his setting out his conclusions 'without allowing himself to be committed to any statement which the ordinary reader might construe into a definite opinion' (*Secret Sects of Syria*, p. 59). However difficult his prose might be, there were many who struggled with it successfully and came to admire both Waite and his thought. W. B. Yeats was one such; he saw Waite as 'the one deep student' known to him of Louis Claude de Saint-Martin—a mystical philosopher extraordinarily difficult to grasp. In similar vein John Masefield described Waite as 'by far the most learned modern scholar of occultism'—and this because Waite recognized the spirituality of certain of the alchemists.

Waite himself looked upon his studies of the occult (or of 'The Secret Tradition', as he preferred to call it) as of subsidiary importance—from a literary point of view—to his poetry. He was, after all, 'the exponent in poetical and prose writings of sacramental religion and the higher mysticism' (his depiction of himself in *Who's Who*). Even Aleister Crowley admired Waite's poetry: 'as a poet', Crowley reluctantly admitted, 'his genius was undeniable' (in *Campaign against Waite*, an unpublished part of the *Confessions*). Others, more favourably disposed to Waite, might hesitate to endorse that judgement, but they admired his verse for its own sake. 'Poetry of great beauty', Katherine Tynan called it; while Algernon Blackwood saw Waite's poems—'in flaming language of great beauty, yet true simplicity'—as the work of 'an inspired, outspoken mystic, nothing more or less'.

Which is how Waite wanted them to be seen. He was, above all, a mystic and wished to be known as such. That his studies of the occult are remembered when his mystical writings are neglected is a tribute to the folly of an age that exalts the irrational, not a judgement upon their merits; for it is his analysis of mystical experience and his unique approach to the philosophy of mysticism that are his true legacy. It would, however, be unrealistic to expect a swift recognition of his importance in the field of mysticism and one must rest content with the knowledge that his contribution to the history of ideas is at last becoming appreciated for its true worth.

But is the story of his life worth the telling? If for no other reason than to give an understanding of 'The Growth of a Mystic's Mind'—which is how he perceived his own career—it is; and there are other sound reasons. When writing his autobiography, *Shadows of Life and Thought*, Waite pointed out that 'These Memoirs are a record, not a confession, and it is a wise counsel after all to keep one's own skeletons in one's own cupboard', while expressing the hope that 'The *suppressio veri* has been minimised so far as possible, while the *suggestio falsi* is absent throughout.' Much that interests the student of 'rejected knowledge', however, is contained in that suppressed truth and Waite's skeletons, when released, will point their fingers at others besides himself. Indeed, it is impossible to understand the development of the Hermetic Order of the Golden Dawn without a detailed knowledge of Waite's role in its history and his relationship with its members, just as a knowledge of the wider 'Occult Revival' of the nineteenth century is impoverished without an awareness of Waite's role in its various aspects.

Then there are those who crossed his path. For varying reasons, Robert Browning, Arthur Machen, and Charles Williams all had dealings with Waite and the story of his life throws sidelights on the story of their lives also. And just as Waite was more than a mystic or maligned occultist, so there are other facets to his character and other aspects to his career: a man who could exalt in verse the love of God and of man while praising with equal facility the glories of malted milk is curious enough to be examined in his own right. If his quest for the Secret Tradition is seen as a tarnished following of occultism, and if his poetry is relegated to a minor place among the lesser poets, his progress through life nonetheless remains both eccentric and entertaining.

1

FROM THE NEW WORLD

The other day I came across an Affidavit of Theodore L. Mason, M.D., residing in State of New York, King's County, City of Brooklyn, who affirmed that in the month of September 1857 he was called to attend the wife of Charles F. Waite, who was duly delivered of a child. Captain and Mrs Waite were boarders in the house of Mrs Sarah Webb, Washington Street, City of Brooklyn.

This testimony calls for a certain interpretation. Dr Mason was probably called in at the end of the month in question, but my actual birth date was Oct. 2nd.

So, seventy-nine years later, Waite described his own birth to his inquisitive American correspondent, Harold Voorhis—who subsequently identified the boarding-house and sent Waite a description of the site:

206 Washington Street (which was on the corner of Concord and Washington Streets) in Brooklyn is now covered by the approach for the Brooklyn Bridge. It is two blocks from the Brooklyn end of the Bridge itself. The even number side of Washington Street now has not a single building on it. After the bridge approach ends—after covering about ten blocks—the remainder has been made into a rest-park. Washington Street ends nearly opposite the City Hall in Brooklyn.[1]

The time of Waite's birth can be identified with even greater precision than the place, for it is given—as 1:00 p.m. local time (5:36 p.m. GMT) on Friday, 2 October 1857—on the horoscope cast for him in March 1923 by an unknown astrologer. Why Waite, who disliked and disbelieved in astrology, should have had a horoscope cast is a question that is difficult to answer. It is equally difficult to explain why the affidavit of 1857 was sworn.

Waite himself says only that it was made 'at the instance of my paternal grandfather, that there might be some record of my nativity from a family point of view, and in case of legal difficulties on either side of the Atlantic'. More significantly he suggests that if one of his American relatives had wished to help him financially 'it was desirable to smooth his path as regards my lawful genesis and identity' (*SLT*, p. 13). This the affidavit could not do, for although there is no question that the child was Arthur Edward Waite, the document gives him neither name nor sex. Nor could it make him legitimate.

The only contemporary evidence that Emma Lovell, Waite's mother, ever married Captain Waite is an entry in Reuben Walworth's *Hyde Genealogy* of 1864.[2] There, Charles Frederick Waite is recorded as marrying, in 1850, 'Eunice Lovell of London'. The mistake over the name may have been no more than a careless transcription of a signature, but the entry is odd in other ways. Other contemporary marriages recorded in the *Hyde Genealogy* include both the month and the day—for Charles Waite only the year is given, and he is inexplicably credited with three children. Nowhere else is a third child mentioned. It is, to say the least, a remarkably unreliable record of recent events.

If Waite is to be believed, the marriage—if marriage there was—took place in the church of St Mary Abbots, Kensington, but the church registers contain no record of the event in 1850, or in any year from 1849 to 1857. Nor is the marriage recorded at the office of the Registrar General in St Catherine's House. It is, of course, possible that Emma Lovell was married in America, but if so, it was the only marriage in the Waite family for which no records survive. A final possibility is that of a marriage at sea; but why, then, did Emma Lovell pretend otherwise?

She undoubtedly met Captain Waite at sea—on her way home from Canada, according to Waite—but the Lovell family disapproved of him strongly: 'there were none too friendly feelings, either because my father was American or—more probably—not in the United States Navy' (*SLT*, p. 17). This is disingenuous, for the Lovells would have known, as Waite himself did, that the Waite family was not only eminently respectable but also distinguished.

The Waites were *not* descended from Thomas Wayte the Regicide,[3] but had settled in New England before the outbreak of the English Civil War: one Gamaliel Waite is recorded as living in Boston in 1637. A branch of the family had moved to Lyme in Connecticut before 1700, and it was from Thomas Waite of Lyme that Charles Frederick was descended. During the War of Independence the Waites supported the colonists and Marvin Waite, a county court judge in Connecticut, was one of Washington's electors in the first presidential election. The law seems to have been a favoured profession for the Waite family, culminating in the appointment in 1874 of Morrison Waite (Charles Frederick's cousin) as Chief Justice of the United States of America. (Other connections with the law were sometimes less happy: in 1680 a John Waite was a juror at the Witchcraft trials in Boston.)

Nor did the family suffer from the stigma of Dissent, for unlike most New Englanders the Waites were devout Episcopalians.[4] Evidently there were other reasons for the Lovells' disapproval—and not because of a disparity in age, for although Captain Waite was younger than Emma Lovell (he was born on 8 March 1824) it was by a matter of only eighteen months. It was, it seems, not so much a disapproval of Captain Waite as of Emma and her way of life.

Married or not, Emma Lovell remained with Captain Waite until his death.

> My mother was with him in his voyages on many occasions and crossed the Atlantic at least twelve times; on a day he had a half-share in a certain merchant ship and died in one which came to grief in mid-ocean. I heard of his sleeping on deck because of its water-logged state and succumbing to exposure in a bitter winter-tide. He was buried at sea, and I believe that the first mate brought the vessel somehow to England, where it was sold, presumably for breaking up. (*SLT*, p. 14)

Emma, however, was not with him on his last voyage: 'my sister's approaching birth being already in view, and I also, no doubt, still in arms.'

Captain Waite died on 29 September 1858, and three days later his posthumous daughter, Frederica Harriet, was born at Yonkers in New York. Initially, Emma went to Lyme:

> There is no knowing how or where the news of her loss reached her; but it took my mother to Lyme for something like twelve months while her husband's affairs were settled. It was expected that she would remain in perpetuity for want of other refuge, having regard to her narrow means; but life in my grandfather's house spelt dependence, and Lyme was an impossible proposition for a young and educated Englishwoman of the upper middle-class. (*SLT*, p. 15)

Whether she disliked the Sabbatarianism of Lyme or, as Waite suggests, 'she had no intention of becoming a "New England Nun"' Emma Lovell returned to England with her children, but to an equally miserable situation. Neither her mother nor any other of the Lovells welcomed her arrival: 'Events of after years shewed in a plenary sense that there was never a homeward coming desired or looked for less' (*SLT*, p. 16). If the Lovells had disapproved of Emma before she met Captain Waite, their attitude to her now—returning with the fruits of her relationship—bordered on hostility. It was, perhaps, not a surprising reception on the part of a pious middle-class family, bearing in mind the prevailing public standards of morality at the time, and the story of her marriage at Kensington may have been invented by Emma to shield her children from the distressing truth about their legal status.

In Waite's case the deception failed. That he knew of his illegitimacy seems clear from the content of the long dramatic poem, *A Soul's Comedy*,[5] which he published in 1887. The hero of the poem is an orphan whose life parallels that of the author: he has the same experiences of boyhood, undergoes the same emotional turmoil, and suffers from the same religious doubts. He is also illegitimate—the child of an illicit marriage between a brother and his half-sister. In turn, the hero himself has an illicit affair and fathers a son who is also modelled on Waite: he has the same name, Austin Blake, that Waite adopted as a pseudonym for some of his early poems. Nor do the parallels end here: the hero's parents meet at Lyme (where he is born), and his second self is conceived and born in

1857. What effect the poem had upon Mrs Waite can only be guessed at. If she chose to identify herself with the hero's mother the implications were appalling; for Waite, cruelly and with unnecessary embellishment, had woven into the story episodes from Emma Lovell's own past.

She was born on 18 August 1822, the second daughter of the second marriage of Francis Lovell, 'who had made his money in India', retired early, and come to live at Sloane Street, Chelsea. Little else is known of him. (Waite is always maddeningly vague about names, dates, and places in his autobiography, arguing that 'my business throughout [is] with the lineage of the soul, rather than with earthly generations' and that 'things external signify little enough, except as they help or hinder the inward life' [*SLT*, pp. 14, 35].) On 8 December 1810 a Francis Lovell of St Pancras married Elizabeth Ottley at St George's, Hanover Square,[6] and this may well have been the first marriage of Emma's father. Mr Lovell had three children by his first wife: a son, Francis, who became a physician, and two daughters: Eliza, who married a Mr Gordon, and Mary Ann, who emigrated to Australia. By 1820 he had remarried and proceeded to add six more children to his household in Sloane Street. Of the three sons of the second marriage George, the eldest, 'is a name only', while the second, William, was described by Waite as living 'quietly till about fifty years of age'; Waite further recalled that he once, only once, had a meeting with his sister after her return from America—albeit on neutral ground, in the garden of a public house near Chalk Farm Road.

The third son, Edward, had a more adventurous life in which Emma was involved: he 'had drifted over to Canada, where he must have wasted himself and his substance. Before her American cruises, my mother was there for a season, presumably in his care; but a curious cloud covers the circumstance which led to this Canadian visit. There were stories about the careless life led by my Uncle Edward, stories of rye whiskey, its crude and potent qualities; and it might be that his sister Emma was sent out for his rescue and reform.'

But there may have been other reasons than solicitude for a wayward son in the decision to pack her off to Canada.

> There is a problem also respecting my mother herself, then—I presume—in the early twenties. It will never be solved now; but something occurred either as the result of speculation or an inscrutable gift, to reduce her capital by half; and my maternal grandmother may have sent her to one of the colonies, thus removing her from some inimical influence and hoping perhaps that she might marry and settle down abroad. (*SLT*, p. 17)

Whatever the 'inimical influence' was, Waite took it up and turned his mother's flight from the first family of her twice-married father into an episode of his fictional heroine's history. And whatever the real reason for her Canadian journey, Emma Lovell returned and met Captain Waite.

He at least had the good grace to die honourably and, for all her rejection, Emma Waite could yet look upon her sisters with a degree of wry satisfaction. Harriet, the elder, married Augustus the brother of Charles Dickens, and might have expected fame and fortune, but instead lost in succession her sight and her husband—who fled to America with Bertha Phillips, an erstwhile friend of his wife's, and made a living by lecturing on his brother's works. Embittered by this desertion Aunt Harriet lived with her mother in Bayswater, refusing to meet her elder sister for many years and dominating Mrs Lovell, who was 'rather a negative personality, easily influenced, easily over-ridden and anxious probably to have peace at any price in her own home circle'. Waite remembered his aunt by her absence: 'During all the years of my childhood she never crossed our threshold, nor was my mother invited to enter their sacred precincts' (*SLT*, p. 41).

The youngest sister, Julia, was less hostile. She had married the 'fine-looking, open-handed, roystering Frederick Firth', but he too deserted his wife and went to America, leaving her to bring up three children alone. Eventually he returned, but Aunt Julia refused to see him, 'having formed other arrangements for herself and the little ones' (*SLT*, p. 18). Perhaps her unlucky experience of marriage made her more sympathetic towards her sister, for Waite recalled occasional visits, more especially after 1872 when his mother moved to Bayswater and he had reached an age at which the fact that his cousins were all some years older than himself mattered little.

Frederick, the eldest of his cousins, Waite described as 'worthless', but he remembered the two girls, Louie and Elsie, with affection. He maintained his friendship with them in later years, but when he called on Elsie, the younger sister, at her home in Chiswick in 1937 he had not seen her for over twenty years: he found her 'scarcely recognizable' and discovered that she could 'remember next to nothing about our past family history'.[7] He had no interest in his cousins' children, and when he once saw two of Louie's daughters he 'thanked my guiding stars that we need never meet again' (*SLT*, p. 104).

Waite remained curiously detached from all his relatives—both Lovells and Waites—throughout his life, largely because of his mother's isolation from them, and the consequent absence of any sense of family identity or of family roots had a profound effect upon him. As he grew into his extended adolescence his social diffidence increased and his tendency to introspection intensified. But alienation from a wider family was not the only factor in the shaping of Waite's character; his mother sought consolation in religion and this had an even deeper effect upon her son.

2

'THE CHURCH OF ROME I FOUND WOULD SUIT'

IN HER religious observation Emma Lovell was typical of the English middle-class—'a Church-going woman of a quiet Anglican type' (*SLT*, p. 19)—and when she returned from America she maintained her religious respectability, however suspect she may otherwise have been in her family's eyes. The small Waite family settled from the first somewhere between Kentish Town and Hampstead, for Waite recorded that 'my earliest recollections are round about Haverstock Hill, for there grows up before me a spacious Protestant Church, where Mr Hathaway was a curate or priest-in-charge, and where on one occasion it was [Mrs Waite's] lot to make the responsions as sole congregation at Morning Prayer'.[1] But the Church of England proved unable to provide the spiritual consolation that Emma, faced with the open hostility of the Lovell family, so urgently needed.

She sought it instead from the Church of Rome, to which she turned in the summer of 1863. Whether from chance—Waite says that 'we were walking out, once on an afternoon, when it pleased God to send us rain in Summer, and we were driven into the refuge of a Church' (*SLT*, p. 19)—or after careful consideration will never be known, but on 8 October 1863 Emma Waite and her children were received into the Roman Catholic Church by a Dominican Friar, Father Austin Rooke.[2] The memory of this *sub-conditione* baptism remained with Waite: 'I can just remember being taken, on a day, into some kind of Baptistry—as it seems to me—on the north side of the Sanctuary, possibly a Lady Chapel, and being there re-Christened conditionally, in case some Protestant minister had missed his mark in flipping water from thumb and middle fingers.' (*SLT*, p. 19).

The decision to convert would not have been taken lightly: Roman Catholics had been freed of their political disabilities only so recently as 1829, and the establishment of the Catholic Hierarchy in 1851 still aroused passionate debate. Waite himself never understood what led his mother to take a step that alienated her still further from her family.

My mother was not in any considerable sense a woman led by emotions, even a woman of sentiment, and still less a person of intellectual life. I do not know how she came to change her form of so-called Faith; and when I saw him once on a day in my first twenties it did not strike me that Father Rooke could be called a persuasive man, or one who would awaken personal devotion, even in susceptible girls. (*SLT*, p. 20)

Before her reception she had watched the laying of the Foundation Stone of the Dominican Priory at Haverstock Road, and it may be that the splendour of the occasion impressed her sufficiently to lead to her seeking out the Church.

Whatever the immediate cause of her conversion, Emma Waite 'never doubted for one moment that she had done the right thing' and if there had been any doubts on the question of respectability they were allayed by the presence of the Dominican nuns in Fortess Terrace, whose Superior was the Revd Mother Mary Catherine Philip Bathurst, a convert herself and an aristocrat. In such company Emma Waite felt 'as if a seal of legitimacy were placed upon the whole business'. And if the conversion was momentous for his mother, it was equally so for Waite, who later said of it: 'I do not believe in my heart that there has ever been greater guidance than that which took me into the humble Dominican Church of Kentish Town.' (*SLT*, p. 19).

They did not remain long under the care of the Dominicans, but 'drifted northward from Kentish Town and passed under the spiritual providence of the Passionists at St Joseph's Retreat, Highgate',[3] where, in due course, Waite made his first confession, received his first communion, and was later confirmed. True to form he gives no dates for any of these events and it has not been possible to trace them in the archives of St Joseph's Retreat, but his first communion was probably in 1865, and if his confirmation was at the age of twelve it would probably have taken place late in 1869.

From the beginning Waite was an ardent Catholic. At St Joseph's he served as an altar-boy, although 'in a shy and nervous manner, for I was ever conscious of an awkward gait in childhood, and of the strictures and privations of poverty'. In spite of this, serving at the altar gave him his 'love of the Altar and of all that belongs to Rites. It gave me the sense of the Sanctuary, of a world and a call therein' (*SLT*, p. 22). Nor did the Church neglect his education, although Waite is characteristically vague about his schooling.

Of the first school he says only 'with whom and where it was—in what street not far away—I carry no notion', although he recalls himself in wholly negative terms as 'backward, nervous, self-conscious and self-distrustful'—a condition reinforced, no doubt, by the frequent unsettling moves from one temporary home in Kentish Town to another.[4] During the early part of 1870 he attended the Bellevue Academy under its Principal, George White, a prolific author of both educational and religious works, whom Waite unkindly described as 'a vast, loosely incorporated and impassioned man, who was affirmed credibly to eat six eggs at his early dinner on Fridays' and whose time was spent 'fretting and fuming and raging over an academy of third-rate day-boys'.[5]

Later in the year he transferred to the school of a Mr Kirkby in Upper Park Road, Belsize Park, at first as a day-boy and later as a boarder. Here 'presumably I must have learned something, but in truth I know not what, and must have been under this nondescript guidance for six or seven months, when the pupils of both classes were electrified by an astonishing and untoward occurrence. The amiable and excellent Mr Kirkby had vanished in a certain night, making off with any ready cash that he found in his sisters' purses. I went home with my strange story and never heard what became of him' (*SLT*, p. 37).

After this fiasco the family moved to Bayswater—not so much to be near Mrs Lovell in Ledbury Road as to enable Arthur to attend St Charles's College, a Catholic boys' school housed at that time in a tall building adjoining the church of St Mary of the Angels. The College had been founded in 1863 by Cardinal Manning's nephew, William, and by 1870 it had gained a considerable academic reputation while endeavouring 'to bring education within the reach of all who desire a sound and high course of instruction for their sons at a moderate cost'.

Waite claimed to have spent three years as a day-boy at St Charles's College, but he does not appear on the Class Lists until 1872, and although his name is on the register for January and February 1873 there is no record of his attendance or progress during that term (it was probably at this time that he 'fell ill with scarlet fever'). He would also then have reached fifteen years of age, and thus become a senior student with a consequent increase in school fees from 12 to 15 guineas a year. It was already proving difficult for Waite's mother to pay for her son's education and it seems likely that by 1873 she could no longer afford to keep him at school.

What Waite was doing during the time between the flight of Mr Kirkby and his entry into St Charles's College is not clear: perhaps it was then that he learned French from his mother, for it was during his time at the College that he 'learned Latin and Greek and forgot most of the French she had taught me'.[6] He also recalled vividly Father Rawes the Prefect of Studies, 'with his rather feeble body, his flaming countenance and the remanents of an uncared-for-tow-coloured mop'. It was almost certainly Father Rawes who encouraged Waite in his earliest literary efforts and who, perhaps, suggested to him that he had a vocation to the priesthood.

Waite unquestionably felt drawn to the *idea* of priesthood. In an interview in 1896 he described himself as having been 'intended for the priesthood', and in later life he saw his role in his Fellowship of the Rosy Cross as pre-eminently that of a priest; but in adolescence three factors held him back. One was his endemic self-distrust ('more than all it was the dreadful narrowness in all my ways of life that kept me stunted, alike within and without') and almost constant illness; the second was a gradual loss of faith; and the third (though he was not conscious of it until much later in life) an abhorrence of the idea of celibacy.

Occasionally, however, he did make half-hearted forays towards a vocation. While staying at Deal during the winter of 1881 he helped a young server to realize his dream of becoming a missionary priest and wondered, on his own part, 'just for one moment whether it might be possible after all to do with Rome, however far apart from a Hostel of the Lord in Deal. It came to nothing.' (*SLT*, p. 75). But whatever his early dreams and anxieties, they were overshadowed by tragedy.

In September 1874, two weeks before her sixteenth birthday, his sister Frederica—weakened by scarlet fever—died from 'general debility'. Her mother never recovered from the loss, and Waite himself was more profoundly affected than his own account leads one to believe.

> At fifteen years of age my sister Frederica died; and I suppose that my cousin Firth and myself alone saw her body interred at Kensal Green. She passed away without the benefit of Sacraments, in the haste of going away. The sorry dream of being was now a more sorry nightmare, while as to my poor Mother the hopeless days of mourning went on for years. I was much too dead myself for any reality of grief; but the dull, the vapid, the unprofitable had turned sour in my heart and head.[7]

Since his own recovery from illness Waite had been working as a clerk, probably in a solicitor's office, in a position obtained for him by James Mellor Smethurst, an elderly barrister who became his cousins' guardian after their mother's death. Waite says nothing of his clerical career, other than to indicate that it lasted for no more than two years—'at nineteen the halter of clerical work had long since removed its yoke'—and to complain that 'it was narrow and dull and opened no prospects'. The death of his sister increased the emptiness of his life. He was increasingly estranged from his mother—'there was nothing in common between us and there was no sympathy'—and further illness, in the late autumn of 1875, removed the chance of a university education: 'Once at this time the clouds seemed to open out, and there was a prospect of sunshine for a moment. A friendly hand was stretched forward to assist him in graduating, after a humble fashion, as an unattached student at Oxford, but in the end the scheme fell through. It was another disappointment to be survived.'[8] He even considered suicide: 'There came a time indeed when I carried laudanum as a possible way of escape. Was it a private pose offered to myself, I wonder, or did I think for a moment that self is evaded thus? In any case, the potion was not drunk' (*SLT*, p. 85).

A pose it almost certainly was, for although Waite protests his loss of faith unceasingly in his autobiography—'There was nothing so dead for me as the life of the Latin Church. The Oblates of Mary Immaculate at Kilburn filled my soul with emptiness, and I fared no better with the Oblates of St Charles Borromeo at Bayswater' (*SLT*, p. 58)—he not only maintained his church attendance but became a strident apologist for the Faith.

His early reading had been restricted to picture books, fairy tales, adventure stories and the poetry of Mrs Hemans, but during his adolescence it became catholic in a very broad sense:

From the *Fundamental Philosophy* of Balmes, a Spanish theologian after the scholastic manner, to Hamilton and Stuart-Mill; from the ascetic writers of the Latin Church to the last issue of the *National Reformer*, or the last pamphlet of Bradlaugh; from an antiquated commentary on Genesis, through Pye and Hitchcock on geology, with something from the *Connection of the Physical Sciences*, a little from the *Plurality of Worlds*, and more from pleasant old Brewster, so forward to the works of Charles Darwin and the first criticisms of Mivart—thus ran the bizarre circle of [my] serious reading.

The effect was that he 'read himself speedily into religious chaos'.[9] Order, however, rapidly supervened and from reading controversial works Waite turned to writing letters and essays in the same vein. By 1877 he was contributing a series of 'Essays for Idle Hours' to a Catholic weekly, *The Lamp*—possibly at the promptimg of Father Rawes, who was himself a regular contributor. In one of these essays, *Outcomes*, Waite made a violent attack upon the Reformation:

Centuries had taught the children of this world the lesson that this Church could not be crushed out with fire and sword. The spirit of evil is persevering, and it therefore turned about for other means, and by a masterstroke of fiendish ingenuity they devised a plan for setting up a secular religion in the place of the priestly 'Sacerdotalism' and a human Christianity in place of the divine Christianity of the Church. To answer their vile ends, the whole spirit of Christianity was altered or distorted, its most distinctive features struck out and only a few broad truths retained . . . Such a heresy which began by denying half the truths of God, was not likely to improve with time. The Satan who had inspired had a far deeper intention than he who began it, or the princes who fostered it . . . In the present day it is developed—we do not say finally—into Pantheism, Agnosticism, Materialism, Idealism and every species of infidelity, every phase of Atheism.

Nor was his purple prose confined to Catholic journals. In one of the many small literary journals of the time, *The Idler*, he assailed one of its contemporaries and compared it unfavourably with the gutter-press of the day: '[*The National Magazine*] has less brains, less intelligence, less enlightenment; more coarseness, more hopeless bigotry, more imbecile fanaticism.' Waite was moved to this outburst by the 'No Popery' stance of the *National Magazine*'s editor—who had at least the good grace to print Waite's ironic letter of protest on behalf of 'the Church [of] which with pride and joy I am myself a member':

But as Popery *must* be abolished, (Mr Harding [the editor] uses no conditional terms) to save Protestantism, this law will have to be brought into force, all the millions of existing Catholics must be *exterminated*. This is the logical outcome of your correspondent's words. Military inquisitors and the rabid rabble of an infuriated populace must burst into quiet English homes, and drag their inmates to the dungeon and the gibbet. The priest must be torn from the altar, and, for the sake of the next generation, the white robes of the acolytes, whose pure boy-faces gleam at the altar through clouds of incense, must be stained with blood.[10]

Other letters of the same period were more temperate. In 1877 Waite defended Catholic dogmas in the *Kilburn Times*: 'If the children of the Church believe her to be the repository and teacher of the truth, they are in conscience bound to accept her dogmas as the truth. If the Church claims to be the repository and teacher of the truth, to be logical she must assert the truth of her decrees.' In the *Hendon Times* he engaged in an argument over the character of Thomas à Becket, displaying a considerable knowledge of historical sources, while upon the readers of *The Universe* he urged the need for 'evening classes for Catholic young men and women.' 'There are', he said,

many such Protestant institutions in London, but it must be confessed that we Catholics are rather backward in this particular . . . [Catholics] must either give up (and how hard this is) their laudable wish of improving their education, or they must have recourse to the Protestant institutions, which are numerous and often offer many allurements (medals, certificates, queen's prizes); and they are thus laid open to many temptations—to the evil effects of bad example and bad company, which otherwise they might have avoided. And can nothing be done? I am loth to think so.

Much as he might encourage others, however, he took no action himself, and in time he *did* lose his faith—though by a process of gradual erosion rather than through any sudden rejection following his sister's death, and the Church of Rome always remained for him, for all that he had left it, the only valid form of institutional Christianity. The Reformed Churches he loathed: the kindest comment he could bring himself to make about them was a description of them as 'a lean method of observance and worship which finds the soul in nudity and cares for it without clothing it'.[11] His uncompromising attitude is perhaps best summed up by one of his aphorisms from *Steps to the Crown*, in which he says: 'Protestantism is not so much a dereliction of creed as a virus of atmosphere' (I. 2. xxxvi).

England, however, was an overwhelmingly Protestant nation and it was a Protestant ethos that was reflected in the popular literature of the time—the 'penny dreadfuls'—that had enraptured Waite as a boy and continued to enchant him throughout his adult life. The Catholic boy proved as susceptible to blood and thunder as his Protestant fellow.

3

DANGEROUS RUBBISH: PENNY DREADFULS AND A WORLD OF DREAMS

'ONCE on a golden day', Waite recalled, 'a little book of *Arabian Tales* was brought to me or my sister . . . by my unofficial guardian, a Mr William Walker, of happy memory' (*SLT*, p. 27). This family friend had been deputed by the Dominicans to oversee the spiritual welfare of Mrs Waite and her children, but by his gift he unwittingly laid the foundations of a love of fantastic tales that would, in time, lead Waite into paths that the Church shunned and utterly condemned. The *Arabian Tales* brought Waite into a world of hidden cities, sorcerers, and enchanted princesses, but for heroes he was obliged to wait until 1869 and his discovery of *The Boys of England*.

Pre-eminent among 'old boys' books', *The Boys of England* was launched in 1866 by Edwin J. Brett, as a weekly offering its youthful readers an endless diet of serial stories of chivalry and impossible derring-do, all of them illustrated by lurid woodcuts. It captivated Waite, as did its host of imitators, and he 'became very learned on the periodical press for boys by walking to and fro in the district and glueing my eyes on the contents of newspaper shops' (*SLT*, p. 34). But parental disapproval was never far away. *Black Rollo, the Pirate King* and *The Skeleton Crew* proved too much, and 'my unofficial guardian, in combination with my careful mother, put an end to my reading of the alleged "dangerous rubbish". Rubbish of course, but not for me a danger, who had no inclination towards running away to sea, no chance of taking to the road without a horse or of entering the Lists of Chivalry. Rubbish once again, but it was something to enter the world of adventurous romance even from the backstairs, or from London purlieus.' (*SLT*, p. 35)

For this addiction, however, there was to be no cure. The Christmas of 1870 brought with it the extra number of *The London Journal* and Pierce Egan's *The Horrors of Hoathley Hall*—adding a supernatural element to the high adventure of *The Boys of England*. The spell was now complete. Waite 'read as much as I could of dangerous rubbish' and reflected, at the end of his life, 'that I should never have entered those other occult paths, and come out of them to proceed further, had I not—amidst my last attempt at schooling—come across the

Shadowless Rider, his League of the Cross of Blood, and the *Forty Thieves of London*, who were led by Black Hugh' (*SLT*, p. 36).

Not that he left the 'Penny Dreadfuls' behind. By the age of twenty years he was writing his own. The earliest, *Tom Trueheart; or, the Fortunes of a Runaway*, appeared in *The Idler* in July 1878. The hero, an orphan, is in the charge of a wicked uncle and an odious tutor who seek to rob the boy of his inheritance. His only friend is his faithful dog, Nelson, who helps him to get the better of his enemies in the course of a brawl. However,

In his excitement, our hero had quite forgotten his uncle, who now approached him, and laying his hand heavily on his shoulder, while his voice trembled with suppressed passion, hoarsely said:—'What you have done today is that which you can never repair, and what years of remorse, nor groans of sorrow cannot wash out. In making an enemy of me you have done what you will repent of to the last hour of your life, for my revenge will fall so heavily upon you, that it MUST crush you.'

Tom shuddered at the bitter hate which his tones expressed as much and more than his words.

His uncle then left him and went in the direction of the house, calling on the tutor with an oath to follow him.

The Reverend Jonas Creeper obeyed, casting as he passed a look of fiendish malignity on our hero, who met it fearlessly. Nelson gave a low growl which quickened his steps considerably, and he hastened up the steps of the verandah four at a time.

Alas, this first episode was also the last, for *The Idler* failed and the fate of *Tom Trueheart* must remain for ever unknown.

The story was followed by *Hamet the Moor, a Romance of Old Granada* (in *Green Leaves*, May 1879), *Paul Dactyl, or the Travelling Merchant's Story* (in *The Story Teller* for 1878), and by a series of tales written in the 1880s but never published. One of them, *The Invisibles*, was set up in type for a projected fourth volume of *Horlick's Magazine* in 1905, and this Waite preserved with typed copies of other delights such as *The Princes of the Night*, *The Scarlet Mask*, and *The Black Brothers*. They are, however, 'improved' and for the most part rather restrained in manner—although one, at least, does have an appropriate excess of blood. In *The Fall of the House of Morland* occur such passages as this:

'See, see,' I cried, 'It has life: it is moving.'

My father started back horror-struck, for the assassin had risen—risen upon his hands and knees, and was crawling towards us. The mask had fallen from his face, revealing features of appalling hideousness. I shrieked with terror as I gazed upon it.

'Here, here is fatality,' cried my father, 'The death-blow only reveals their faces.'

'It means us harm, father. Beware, beware! Surely that cannot be human. Let us fly.'

There was a yell; the monster had leaped upon us and had clutched my father. From its own torn and bleeding side it had wrenched the dagger, and raised it aloft. My love for my parent gave a man's strength to my frame. I seized and held the descending arm, striving for possession of the weapon.

A moment only the contest lasted. The assassin's arm dropped, the pallor of death overspread his countenance, and he fell back upon the grass. He uttered some words in a language which I did not understand, and was dead.

This, however, is an exception, and unlike *Tom Trueheart*, these later tales cannot stand beside *The Boys of England* or the true 'Penny Dreadfuls' of Thomas Peckett Prest.

But if Waite could no longer publish such stories, he could yet write about them from the vantage point of an almost unrivalled knowledge of the genre, gained in large part from his own ever-increasing collection of the tales, for the British Museum Library proved to be a great disappointment to him in this respect: so much so that in 1887, in his first study of 'Penny Dreadfuls', he condemned the inadequacy of the library catalogue in no uncertain terms: 'The lists in the reading room are full of errors; tales which were not only completed but have been re-issued are labelled ''No more published'' because the museum copies are imperfect, and other periodicals are declared to have suspended issue when, as a fact, they have continued to exist for a considerable period subsequently.'[1]

That study, *By-ways of Periodical Literature*, is important for its early recognition of the historical significance of popular literature. Waite urged upon his readers the need to preserve this 'vast and perishing literature' which 'a little care will rescue from complete oblivion'. If not, he said, then 'in a few years the names of these productions will be totally, as they are for the most part now, unknown'. His pleas would undoubtedly have fallen on more attentive ears if his own text had not been bowdlerized.

At the time, *Walford's Antiquarian Magazine* was ostensibly edited by its publisher, George Redway, but in reality the editor was Arthur Machen, and it was due to Machen's sensibilities—heightened by the contemporary prosecution of Vizetelly for publishing Zola's novels—that Waite's intemperate language was curbed. Thus, G. W. M. Reynolds, 'the high priest of cheap periodical fiction', became 'hard-working' rather than 'unscrupulous' and was no longer 'a writer for the people in the worst sense of the phrase; that is, his works, written obviously to expose and exaggerate the misconduct of the aristocracy, were, in moral and manner, so objectionable that they were quite unfit for introduction into any respectable household.' One cannot help but suspect also that would-be collectors would have sought more eagerly for novels that were 'unhealthy always, and often flagrantly vicious' than for those that were merely 'eccentric'.

Collectors, however, did arise, and when Waite visited the foremost of them 'Barry Ono' (i.e. F. V. Harrison) in 1927 he was amazed at Mr Ono's 'vast and astonishing' library. His own collection had been sold some years previously, in 1920, to a truly unscrupulous bookseller named John Jeffery. Jeffery kept them until 1933, when he placed them in auction: this gave Waite the satisfaction of seeing them sell at an average of 2*s* per volume[2]—but not before he had begun an ambitious study of the whole genre, entitled *Dealings in Bibliomania*.

In 1923 he suggested to Wilfred Partington that the essay might be suitable for anonymous publication in the latter's *Bookman's Journal*, adding, with a characteristic lack of false modesty, 'It is true that I am an expert—and there is indeed no other—on the subject of Penny Dreadfuls. I know all the first editions and all the dates; things which amateurs have not dreamed of have passed through my hands.'[3] Partington toyed with the idea for some years, finally agreeing that something could be done with the manuscript in 1930, but by then it was too late: the *Bookman's Journal* faced serious financial problems and in 1931 it ceased publication. Waite made little effort to interest other publishers, and with the appearance in 1938 of Montague Summers's *The Gothic Quest* (followed in 1940 by its companion volume, *A Gothic Bibliography*) all hope of publishing *Dealings in Bibliomania* came to an end.

One reason for Partington's indecision over the book was Waite's insistence upon anonymity. In his later years he had become anxious that the public should see him solely as he described himself in *Who's Who*, as 'the exponent in poetical and prose writings of sacramental religion and the higher mysticism'. They might, he thought, experience some difficulty in reconciling his role as a mystic with that of enthusiast for *The Boys of England* and *Varney the Vampire*. His friends, however, had no such qualms.

While Waite was busying himself with *Dealings in Bibliomania*, Arthur Machen was writing *The Grande Trouvaille* for R. Townley Searle, who wanted it as an introduction to the third catalogue of rare books issued by his 'First Edition Bookshop'. In March 1923 it appeared—revealing to the world Waite's passion for the 'Penny Dreadful'. It was an entertaining story:

Once upon a time—it is the fairy tale beginning, and therefore a very good one—I was walking up Pentonville with my old friend, A. E. Waite. It was a grey afternoon; one must always choose a grey afternoon if one would walk fitly up Pentonville. I think we were setting out on a journey to explore Stoke Newington, with the view of determining whether Edgar Allan Poe's school were still in existence. This was a matter which had engaged us both, at odd intervals, for years, and we had set out many times on the adventure, but had always wandered away on quite alien trails and on haphazard quests; and to this day the matter remains so doubtful that I am not quite sure whether Waite and I ever discovered the school in the dim English village which Poe describes in 'William Wilson'. The fact was that both of us had so many interests, which led us astray. Waite, perhaps, thought that he might find the Holy Grail, disguised, disgraced and dishonoured in some back shop of a back-street; while I have always had the great and absorbing desire of going the other way. The other way? That is the secret.

Anyhow, on this long-ago afternoon we were lounging up the weary-all hill of Pentonville, when Waite stopped suddenly. I looked at him in some curiosity. There was a singular expression on his face. His eye—I think—became fixed. His nostrils—to the best of my belief— twitched.

Otherwise, there was an odd fixity about his position. I believe that in a certain kind of sporting dog this attitude is called 'making a point'. I did not say anything: the Order generally known as the Companions of the Eighties knows how and when to preserve silence, but there was, I fancy, an interrogative expression in my eyebrow. Frater Sacramentum—I mean A. E. Waite—stood still to gaze for a moment or two, staring eagerly at the opposite side of the road—the right hand side, as you go up to the Angel—and said at last:—

'Machen, I feel that I must go into that shop over the way. I know there's something there for me!'

And so we crossed over. It was a small and quite undistinguished shop on the side of the grey hill. I think it sold inkpots, pens and pencils, exercise books, comic songs on long sheets, the evening paper, and the miscellaneous. I couldn't imagine what Waite could expect to find there.

We went in. Somewhere at the back of the shop there was a row or two of dingy, greasy, tattered old books; and a fire glowed in Waite's eye as he beheld them. The scent held.

'Have you any old bound volumes of boys' stories?' he asked the ancient man of the shop. 'There were two or three left,' said the man, a little astonished I thought at the enquiry. There used to be a small lending library here, he explained, and he had taken over the stock.

And, to cut the story short, Waite went out into Pentonville, which, I am sure, had now become for him not grey but radiant, with a copy of 'The Old House in West Street' under his arm.

Perhaps I should explain. My friend Waite, besides taking over all mysticism, occultism, alchemy and transcendentalism for his province, has a hobby, like most good men. In his case, this hobby is the collecting of 'Penny Dreadfuls' of ancient date: the forties and early fifties are, I believe, the golden age of this adventure. And amongst those 'Penny Dreadfuls', as they are affectionately called, one of the choicest prizes is 'The Old House in West Street'. And Waite had got it for eighteen pence or half-a-crown: a greasy, old bound volume of the old weekly parts, vilely printed on wretched paper with amazing woodcuts: and yet a find, a delight.

Then if recollection serves, we had some gin. It was an occasion.

Machen gives no date to the episode, but it must have taken place early in their long friendship, for in his essay of 1887 Waite was able to describe *The Old House in West Street* in far greater detail than any other title that he mentioned: 'This was the most voluminous of Prest's acknowledged productions, and in appearance it is superior to its predecessors. Some care, indeed, seems to have been spent on it; the type is painfully small, but very clear. It is printed in double columns, and was issued, like all Lloyd's publications, in penny numbers, each containing an illustration. It reached to 104 numbers and was completed in August, 1846.' He adds, 'it is written in Prest's usual style of absurd melodrama, at once stilted and extravagant. The work is now very scarce, and is said to command a fair price in the market.'

It is, in fact, an extremely rare book, and Machen was quite right: its discovery was indeed 'an occasion'.

4

THE 'TIRESOME VERSE-RECITER'

'PENNY DREADFULS' were for Waite, as was fiction in general, a 'byway' of literature—for him the 'highway' was poetry. As a small boy he had read Mrs Hemans and was captivated by her sentimental verse—although more probably by *Casabianca* than, as he claimed, by her *Siege of Valencia*; but poetry in general had no hold over him, and it was not until he was seventeen, in the months following his sister's death, that he conceived the burning ambition to be a poet. His barren evenings had been spent 'with nothing to do but dream and read therein' until, quite suddenly, 'a change came over the face of things when I found, on a day or a night, that I, even I, could write verses. Yes, it was a lifting of clouds, and by the light in which they dissolved there was granted me a rainbow gift of dreams. From that moment presumably I read nothing but poems and the lives of those who had achieved a name in rhyme. A hunger and thirst after glory in the craft of song possessed my whole being.' (*SLT*, p. 48)

He could never explain in later years what gave him this passion for poetry. It remained for him a question 'for an answer to which he has vexed himself vainly and often'. And just as 'the impulse to make verses' was inexplicable, so it was incurable:

I went up and down in the great city and wandered in and out. There was a fever of verse upon me. I took care of the sounds, as it seems to me, and the sense took care of itself, till there came some rough lessons. Because I was seventeen and because at eighteen Shelley had written *Queen Mab*, it was obviously right and fitting that thus early there should be given to the world somehow a thing 'ecstatic and undemonstrable', denominated *Zastroni*. Described as a lyrical drama, it was surely a wilderness of nonsense far prolonged (*SLT*, p. 50).

The name was a marriage of Shelley's *Zastrozzi* and Lytton's *Zanoni*, and when it was complete, Waite took *Zastroni* to Father Rawes, who, whatever he may have thought of the poem, 'did what he could to encourage me with earnest kindly words, adding that it was long as yet before I could dream of print'.

As Fr. Rawes had predicted, *Zastroni* was never published, but other poems, preserved in Waite's scrapbook of 'Early Verses', were. The earliest seems to have been 'A Dirge' for his dead sister, written before the end of 1875 and printed in an unidentified journal:

> Clods of earth are piled above thee,
> Dust is now thy fair young form;
> We who mourn thee, we who love thee,
> Have consigned thee to the worm.
>
> Round thy grave the shadow creepeth,
> And the summer breezes blow;
> There the drooping snowdrop sleepeth,
> There the yew and myrtle grow.
>
> But thy pure soul, heavenward soaring,
> Far beyond the furthest star,
> Now is at God's throne adoring,
> Where the radiant angels are.

If *Zastroni* was of similar quality it is, perhaps, all to the good that it 'perished, with other *ludibria* and note-books'.

A rather more polished epitaph, entitled 'Sleep', followed in 1876 and was also printed, probably in *The Lamp*:

> Thou wilt not see the woodbine creep,
> Upon the lattice bars;
> Thou wilt not hear the waters sweep,
> Beneath the silver stars.
> Thy rest is calm, thy rest is deep,
> The dust is on thy eyes;
> The dust remains for us who weep,
> Thy soul is in the skies!

But Waite's energies were directed increasingly towards longer poems. Recuperating from illness at Ramsgate, in the winter of 1875 he spent his days at Dumpton Gap, 'and stood on a ledge of cliff for an hour or more, with the sea beating under, or contemplated rock and weed, when tide was out, from narrow caves. I was looking for plots of poems, mostly great of length, and hankering still after the Lyrical Drama' (*SLT*, p. 52).

And not in vain, for he promptly wrote *The Seeker, a Lyrical Drama*, and *The Fall of Man, a Miracle Play*. They are, at best, of uneven quality but both were published, under the pseudonym of Philip Dayre, although the journals in which they appeared have not been identified.

Waite was well aware of his literary shortcomings and suffered miserably from 'an acute consciousness—so common in such apprenticeships—of a sheer disparity between ambition and ability'. In an attempt to reduce this disparity he wrote to Robert Browning 'for advice and guidance', but refrained from sending any samples of his work. Perhaps because of this reserve, Browning replied:[1]

June 27th, 1876

Sir,—I am sure I have read your letter with great interest and sympathy; and if I thought I could do you the least good by reading your poems, I would comply with your request. I assure you that, even in the event of my opinion—whatever it is worth—proving favourable, it would not have the least effect in procuring you any publisher with whom I have acquaintance. Every publishing establishment has its professed 'Reader', who reads, or does not read, but decides on the acceptance or rejection of a manuscript—and manuscript poetry has little chance of finding favour in his eyes.

The preferable course—if you want remuneration for your work, the only course—is to send one or more of your pieces to a magazine. But, if you permit me to advise you, do *anything* rather than attempt to live by literature, anything good and reputable, I mean. An ungenial situation—such as you seem to have retired from—would send you to your studies, and, subsequently, to a proper use of them—with a sense of relief and enjoyment you will never obtain from 'singing' all day long, when 'song' is turned into the business of life. Pray take in good part what I am bound to say when an applicant is as modest and intelligent as you seem to be, and believe me,

Yours very sincerely,
Robert Browning

The advice was sound and Waite followed it—at least to the extent of sending his poems to *The Lamp*. And although there was no financial necessity—Emma Waite's 'circumstances were materially improved' after her mother's death in 1874, and Waite himself received, in 1876, a small legacy from his paternal grandfather—he may have returned to his 'ungenial situation'. Certainly, he said of Browning's letter (writing in the third person) 'the closing note of warning struck deeply into his heart, and he sought to profit by the advice. A change in the direction of his energies did not, however, bring much profit or happiness'; but against this must be set the image of his manner of working depicted in his early poem , 'The Student':

I work in the midnight, seen only by stars,
  Which shine through the darkness so mournfully sweet,
While the moon sometimes looks through the black lattice-bars,
  And her pale beams fall down at my feet.

Forgotten, forgetting, and therefore content,
  Behold me at work on a work of my own,
Neither asking nor seeking for help to be lent:
  What I do I am doing alone!

You may wonder to see me thus night after night,
With patience unflagging, refusing repose,
Till the stars, my companions, grow pale in their light,
And the roses of morning unclose.

The World does not heed me, nor know me—not one
Can I call of its great ones a helper or friend;
In the midst of a crowd I am truly alone,
And my days in a solitude spend.

His output was growing, and with it his confidence. From sending poems to literary magazines Waite turned to publishing small broadsheets himself. The first of these, *The Maiden and the Poet*,was issued from 12 Atkinson Terrace, Kilburn—where Waite and his mother were living in 1876—at a price of 'One Half-penny'. It was followed by *A Serenade*, priced this time (in imitation of R. H. Horne, the 'farthing poet') at 'One farthing'; but before his farthing poem appeared, Waite's increasing self-confidence had led him to write again to Browning, this time enclosing a number of his poems. Browning's reply was reassuring.

Feb. 5, 1877

My Dear Mr [Waite]

I must beg your pardon for having delayed a little my thanks for your poems, and my reply to the letter which accompanied them. Perhaps the difficulty of a proper reply may have hindered me somewhat. I really wish, most sincerely, to be of what service I am able: but, first of all, in no mock-modesty, I want you to understand that I am by no means a thorough judge in this matter. What I like and look for in poetry comes out, possibly, in an after-stage of experiences; and the want of it, earlier in life, may be as necessary as that leaves should precede fruits on a tree: on the other hand, the existence of qualities which fail to seem conclusive proof of the right faculty in a poet, may be a rarer fact than I have noticed or sufficiently sympathized with. I *do* see in you very decided literary accomplishment, and no inconsiderable mastery of the mechanical part of verse-writing (there is hardly a slip except the rhyme of 'universe' with 'us' on the first page), and your musical 'ear' is very good indeed. When one—after forming this opinion of your productions—goes on to consider that they have been helped (according to your own account) by very scanty education—I think I am not wrong in finding them very remarkable indeed—most assuredly they justify me in supposing that you are quite equal to any situation in which a decided literary skill is required. Now, if I fail to discover as much positive novelty of thought or fancy as I suppose is demanded in the poetry of a 'coming man',—remember that I cannot help my own tastes, nor the standard of excellence which I acknowledge—that the dispensers of reputation generally differ with me altogether—and that, since you please to refer to my own case, I am often told I am 'no poet at all', precisely because what I accept as a law of musical expression is not taken into account by the generality of critics. Yet, with all these drawbacks to the worth of my opinion, I should be forced to say, 'Don't try to publish yet.' It is possible that 'success in poetry' may come out of future exertions; there is nothing here against such a hope; but, in the meantime, I would—with a real interest—

urge on you to show that the true spirit inspires you by continuing to try and obtain some employment which, while it leaves you at liberty to prosecute your studies, gives you the all-in-all sufficing privilege of independence. Surely, some such employment may be found—and you must know that what you esteem a great prize, 'poetical success', would be worthless, indeed, were it to be picked up at first stooping down in the public way. Why, pray, should your 'handwriting' remain unclerkly ('*bad*', it is not) simply for want of a week's practice at 'drawing circles against the sun', as the sailors say? Five minutes practice with a pencil at mere circle making could remedy whatever is wrong soon enough. Finally, don't forget—while you count over what may be very real disadvantages of every kind—the immense set-off you may boast—youth, energy and however low anybody may reckon them—assuredly talents. Be a brave fellow, and see what you can do with these! You will greatly gratify your true well-wisher.

Robert Browning

It did not occur to Waite that Browning's praise may have been diplomatic and that the *real* message of the letter was the injunction 'Don't try to publish yet'. This advice Waite ignored, and in the summer of 1877 he published, at his own expense, *An Ode to Astronomy and other Poems*, 'a minute quarto pamphlet of verse, written at divers times—one hundred copies of a few pages only' (*SLT*, p. 56). He did not choose to alter the rhyme that had jarred on Browning's ear, and yet—to his surprise—'the tiny edition got sold, so I gained something in shillings rather than lost a cent by this initial venture'. Among the purchasers was Fr Rawes, who read the 'Ode to Astronomy' to the assembled pupils of St Charles's College. What they made of this decidedly mediocre poem is not recorded.

Encouraged by his success, Waite continued to pour out verse, but the major literary periodicals—both heavyweights like *The Athenaeum* and lighter monthlies such as *Belgravia*—utterly ignored him, and the publications in which, as he modestly says, 'some things got into print', were modest indeed.

Then, as now, the easiest road into print for fledgling poets was that of co-operation, and throughout the 1870s 'amateur' periodicals flourished. A few of them—including *The Golden Pen*, which was edited by Waite—circulated in manuscript, but the majority were printed, and, on the whole, printed and designed rather well.[2] Waite contributed short poems to most of them, and two of them he favoured with his long, and clearly derivative, 'Lyrical Dramas'. *The First Sabbath*, modelled closely on P. J. Bailey's *Festus*, appeared in *Echoes from the Lyre* while *The Poet's Magazine* printed his Byronic 'Fairy Romance', *The Enchanted Wood*.[3]

Nor was this all. In 1877 an attempt had been made to establish an 'Amateur Conference', but the first meeting, at Stratford-on-Avon, was a disaster and nothing came of it. Waite, however, took up the idea and in the following year was instrumental in founding The Central Union—an 'association of authors and others' that met monthly, for the purpose of mutual criticism, over a period of some two years. For the whole of that time Waite acted as secretary, wrote the Union's prospectus, and edited the first (and only) issue of its unofficial organ, *The Central Review and Amateur News*.[4]

Firmly established—among his fellow 'amateurs'—as a poet, Waite now undertook a more ambitious project, announcing for publication in February 1879 *Lucifer; a dramatic Romance, and other Poems*. When this 'pamphlet of 64 quarto pages' finally appeared, in late spring, it had shrunk to 48 pages, shedding two of its projected 'Three dramatic Poems' (only 'The Heart's Tragedy in Fairyland' remained), and *Lucifer* had been relegated to page 29, having given way on the title-page to *A Lyric of the Fairyland*. Many of the poems betray the influence of Waite's reading. 'The Wanderer's Life-Song', for example, owes more than a little to Poe:

> And we wander now and listen
>   To some ocean's murmur deep,
> Though we see no waters glisten,
>   Though we hear no wavelets leap.
> Thou who rulest, thou who reignest
>   O'er the shadowy world unknown!
> We have hoped when hope seemed vainest
>   And toiled on with many a groan;
> Say, when we embark in silence
>   Bearing neither scrip nor store,
>   Shall we ply the weary oar,
> Shall we reach the happy islands
>   Seen by seers in days of yore,
>   Or upon some rocky shore,
> By no gleam of glory lighted,
> Wander cheerless, cold, benighted,
>   Lost for evermore?

The amateurs praised the book, but professional critics (anonymous, for while Waite preserved all the reviews he did not identify the journals in which they appeared) took a harsher view, which was not entirely justified. Certainly, the poems exude pessimism, doubt, and even despair; but they are not so poor in either structure or content as to merit condemnation as 'often crude and formless', nor did Waite deserve to be told that 'he cannot grasp a thought and hold it firm' or that 'the prevailing characteristic of his ideas is a certain flabbiness, not to say pulpiness'. Another reviewer praised the sequence of sonnets with which the book ends, but added, 'both rhyme and rhythm must have greater care bestowed upon them, and morbidity must be avoided if Mr Waite is to produce anything worthy of after-remembrance'.

Undaunted by these strictures, Waite wrote for a third and last time to Browning, enclosing a copy of the book. Browning replied with yet more advice:

June 22nd, 1879

My Dear Sir,

I have been so wholly engaged for some time past, that it was impossible for me to read your poems as carefully as I wished, and now that I have read every line, I must try and be as honest and serviceable as your accompanying letter seems to require and to deserve. You have so many of the faculties of a poet, as I told you before, that you may be safely advised—in the assurance of having them ready for employment when a proper occasion arises—to let them be unemployed *now*, when your business is to *live*—learn life: at present all these yearnings and regrets are an accepted and recorded fact in the experience of every youthful susceptible nature, and in once more expressing them, however musically, you either invite attention from natures like your own, and so only too familiar with them, or from the opposites of these, natures to which your complaints are incomprehensible—a surprise or an annoyance. Of course there was a time when, at least in literature, there would have been 'novelty' indeed in the avowal of such aspirations and such disappointments as fill your volume: but now we all want—whether or no we get it—an experience from those who have passed through and surmounted altogether—or even partially—the discoveries we made at 'one-and-twenty'. *What* may you not do in the next ten years?—I hardly care *how*, so long as it is earnestly and conscientiously done—which will answer your own doubts, and enable you to help others who are at your present stage of attainment! I say this the more freely that you mean—as you manfully say—to continue in any case to practise the composition of poetry: if so, I would suggest that you confine yourself for the present to what is called 'objective' poetry: take a fact, of any kind, and describe it scrupulously, letting it produce its own effect: do not occupy yourself with your own feelings concerning things in general,—how you wish them to be and regret to find them. By giving us one *fact*, you give us perhaps what we can explain, as we were hardly fitted to do at the age which happily is still yours. Shall I apologize for this rough liberty of advice to one whom I would gladly serve? I think not—you will believe I am your affectionate well-wisher.

Robert Browning

On this occasion Waite allowed Browning to guide him. He had come to realize that Browning was a shrewd judge of character as well as of poetry, and Waite recorded that he 'profited by the advice he received; that he set himself to 'learn life'; that he held over his 'faculties of a poet' until many lessons had been put to heart; that the term of years mentioned by Robert Browning brought strength to those faculties; and that 'the "spark from heaven" has possibly at length fallen'. He did not stop writing his poems, but only a very few would be printed in the 1880s, there would be no more privately printed pamphlets, and nothing substantial would appear until 1886 and *Israfel*. And that was to be a very different work indeed.

5

'LOVE THAT NEVER TOLD CAN BE'

DURING much of the Victorian era the majority of periodicals for children were overtly, almost aggressively, religious in tone, although there were exceptions, among the most prominent of which was James Henderson's *Young Folks' Paper.*[1] Its most famous contributor was Robert Louis Stevenson—both *Treasure Island* and *Kidnapped* first appeared in its pages—but the bulk of its contents came from less eminent authors, among whom was A. E. Waite. In the mid-1880s Waite wrote a series of essays for *The Young Folks' Paper*, on such obscure subjects as 'Ever-burning Lamps', 'The Phoenix', 'Legends of the Rainbow' and even on 'Electricity in Domestic Life', and contributed a number of poems to the 'Literary Olympic': a feature of the paper devoted to the budding literary talents of its readers. In these columns Waite gained sufficient recognition as an aspiring poet to be included among the biographical 'Portraits' in the Christmas Supplement of 1885; but before his rise to limited fame in *The Young Folks' Paper* he had been nurtured by one of its contemporaries.

A poem by Waite, 'An Exhortation', had appeared in April 1878 in *Aunt Judy's Magazine*,[2] to be followed at intervals by some of his better efforts until August 1884 when 'The Sea Fowl' was printed in one of the last issues of the magazine before its closure in the following spring. He had been introduced to *Aunt Judy's Magazine* by an eccentric clergyman who was a family friend of the editor, Horatia Gatty, and who was to prove a formative influence during Waite's early adult life. He was an accomplished writer of both prose and verse and he undoubtedly helped Waite in his career; but it was not in the field of literature that he proved of greatest service.

Greville John Chester[3] was born at Denton, in Norfolk, on 25 October 1830. In 1858, after his graduation from Balliol College, Oxford, and his subsequent ordination, he was appointed Vicar of St Jude's, Moorfields, at Sheffield, where he astonished the population with both his extreme high-churchmanship and his extraordinary missionary zeal. He would stand, with his curate, 'in their surplices at the entrance to the church and solicit the passers-by to come in', and he later celebrated the first harvest festival ever held in Sheffield. But his 'greatest and most lasting moral success' was considered to be 'The influence that he gained over young men—youths at an age when the turning is commonly made, either to the right hand for good or to the left for evil.'

All this came to an end, however, in 1867 when he retired from the role of parish priest—apparently because of ill-health—and took up a new career as traveller and amateur archaeologist. He first visited the United States of America, where he travelled extensively before returning home to give a markedly hostile account of the country and its people—whom he heartily detested—in his book *Transatlantic Sketches* (1869). After his adventures in the West he made regular winter excursions to the Middle East, exploring and excavating in Egypt and Palestine (sometimes on behalf of the *Palestine Exploration Fund*), returning to England each spring with a fresh haul of antiquities; most of these he presented to the Ashmolean Museum at Oxford.

He also took to writing novels, one of which—*Julian Cloughton; or, Lad-life in Norfolk* (1880)—illustrates his great and continuing interest in young men, in whom he seems invariably to have inspired a profound devotion that occasionally manifested itself in curious ways. Writing to the *Sheffield Daily Telegraph* after Chester's death, on 23 May 1892, a Mr Harry Hems related the following anecdote:

> One summer evening, in Old Park Woods, Mr Chester and I—then a lad—were together, and he was giving me a lesson in geology when another lad, all in tatters, came along. At sight of the rev. gentleman he suddenly became all aglow with excitement, and rushing at him, threw himself down, and began kissing his feet and legs. I learned afterwards that our late friend had sheltered and nursed this youth after some serious accident, and this was their first meeting afterwards. I have seen men in the East cast themselves down and kiss another's feet, but this was the first and last time I ever saw it done in phlegmatic England.

He was to inspire a similar, if less flamboyantly expressed, devotion in the young A. E. Waite.

Chester, whom Waite considered to be 'the first good friend that I ever made among seniors', came into his life 'about 1877' when Waite was twenty years old, having 'heard of me first because he knew Firth, my cousin, and insisted that I should be brought to see him. It was done accordingly, not a little against my cousin's will'. Waite described Chester as 'a travelled man of forty and a talismanic eccentric whom it was a boon to know' and 'assuredly one in a thousand, one also who must have been handsome in youth and was now of a notable presence, a fine passionate man. He was ever and continually in a righteous rage about something, the convention in most cases being that it was for the public good' (*SLT*, p. 59).

He commented further: 'If Chester made real friends with anyone, that person—whoever—had cause to count it as an epoch in his tale of life', adding, but without elaboration, 'It was such in my own case and, even to this day, he and his eccentricities, his rampant prejudices, his love of his own way and his generous heart are lively and precious memories' (*SLT*, p. 60). All of which describes a personality the very antithesis of the gauche and naïve young man he befriended, for 'The truth is that I was not much more than twelve at sixteen years and had not reached intellectual puberty when I lived to be twenty-one' (*SLT*, p. 52). But for all his self-perceived immaturity Waite was drifting into emotional turmoil in the shape of a 'romantic frienship' and he would need all of Chester's sympathetic and experienced guidance to draw him back from a potentially destructive relationship.

From the beginning of his career as a poet Waite had attempted verse dramas, but they had been invariably badly constructed and far too short for their themes to be developed. Recognizing these weaknesses Waite began, in the autumn of 1881, to sketch out 'a long tale, a tale with a happy ending' that would, so he hoped, suffer from none of them. The first draft of the 'tale' was completed within twelve months, but it was to be another five years before *A Soul's Comedy* was published.

The structure and style of the poem are modelled on those of Bailey's *Festus*, while the title was clearly intended to be associated with Browning's *A Soul's Tragedy*; Waite, however, gives his own explanation of the title in a prefatory note: 'A tragedy in its ancient and legitimate sense depicts the triumph of destiny over man; the comedy, or story with a happy ending, represents the triumph of man over destiny. It is in this sense that the spiritual history of Jasper Cartwright is called a Soul's Comedy' (*A Soul's Comedy*, 1887, p. vi).

The plot, with its themes of unwitting incest, treachery, illegitimacy, and final redemption, is wholly Waite's own and is based to a degree on his somewhat bitter perception of his parentage. Both the major and minor heroes (Jasper Cartwright and his illegitimate son, Austin Blake) are self-portraits, while the intertwined sub-plot—the story of the obsessive love of Jasper for the young acolyte Gabriel—is a working out of Waite's feelings and experiences at the time he began the first draft.

In the complex plot of the poem Waite, as the hero Jasper Cartwright, first sees Gabriel when he enters by chance St Joseph's Retreat ('the Roman Church which stands on Highgate Hill') and watches the Mass:

All around
Were men, like fairy kings, in robes of gold,
And boys in white who held long torches up,
While two were swinging censers full of smoke,
And flame and fragrance. One was like a saint,
His hair all gold. About the Church they came
In long procession; there his eyes met mine,

And since I love him, may I choose him now
To be my faithful friend? (*A Soul's Comedy*, p. 48)

The acolyte waits for Jasper when the Mass is ended:

And so he led me to the porch which look'd
Out on the silent night. And still he held
My hand, and said, You are a stranger here,
Do come again! This is the One True Church,
And all who join it will be happy on earth,
And go to Heaven as well.—Will you be here?
I asked. O, always, he replied, I serve
Before the altar! Will you be my friend?
Said I. He answer'd, I will love you always,
If you will only come. So then we kiss'd,
And parted.(*A Soul's Comedy*, pp. 49-50)

His love for Gabriel is reiterated in other passages, with increasing frequency after the young acolyte dies, and culminates in a long, impassioned and obsessional hymn to the dead Gabriel—of which these verses are typical:

Is thy heavenly bliss complete?
Hast thou now no more desire
For the love we thought so sweet
Ere thy soul ascended higher?
Thy blue eyes are deep, and deep
Their expression lies therein;
They their inward counsel keep,
All their secrets shut within.

Who sprinkles the lilies that bind thy brow
With the dews that keep them cool and bright?
Who folds thy garments white?
What hand caresses and tends thy tresses,
And clasps thy golden girdle now?
Who washes thy feet that are white and fair,
And dried them with his hair? (*A Soul's Comedy*, pp. 170-1)

But the real Gabriel was not dead.

Waite gives no clue to Gabriel's identity, but clearly he had no connection with Highgate, for by 1881 St Joseph's Retreat was ten years in Waite's past. Equally clearly he had a real existence, for twenty-five years later—and fourteen years after Greville Chester's death—Waite published another *Gabriel* poem in which both his own feelings and Chester's awareness of them are set out more openly than in the ambiguous *A Soul's Comedy*:

> Then, knowing that none except yourself above,
> With me below, will penetrate our love,
> However plainly stands the written word,
> Let me conceal no more, whose heart is stirr'd
> To tell outright what then I spoke alone
> Either to you, apart in undertone,
> Or but in parables to other men.[4]

He describes his first sight of Gabriel and his realization that his feelings must remain unspoken:

> As in your ear then, plainly let me tell
> When first it was we look'd on Gabriel,
> At mass or vespers, guarded, earnest, blythe,
> A white-robed, censer-bearing acolythe;
> Only a face amidst an incense cloud—
> Silent within the chants which swell'd so loud.
> Lovely he was, as human beauty goes—
> The lily's lustre, the faint blush of rose,
> Met in his face; his lips were chaste as fair
> And a dim nimbus was his auburn hair,
> While his eyes had caught, as in a net,
> All the dark glories of the violet.
> Youth though he was, in our two hands we could
> Have ta'en his face to kiss as lovers should,
> But on his earthly presence had come down
> So high a sense of vision and of crown,
> That out of any place where lovers lean
> And whisper, he, with his uplifted mien,
> So bright uprose that, like the ground he trod,
> We knew him seal'd and set apart to God.

From acolyte Gabriel has risen to be 'perchance, a consecrated priest', while Chester—who alone knew Waite's feelings and helped him to come to terms with them—has died:

Well, you are dead, and God is strong to save,
But certain secret matters to my grave
I carry heavily concerning you,
Who were through all so good and more than true;
Still in your heart make them a safe retreat,
If you can do so, at the judgment-seat.

And this poem, unlike *A Soul's Comedy*, tells the true story:

Old friend, whate'er our early verse may tell,
Here is the mystery of Gabriel.

but the past is lost to Waite for,

Oh, you are dead, and he has gone away!

That going away was Waite's salvation, and he had engineered it himself—for the acolyte Gabriel was the young server whom he had met in 1881 during his autumn at Deal. All he says of the boy is that he was 'the intelligent son . . . of a widowed Irish woman, poor and slatternly', who 'served at the altar in a miserable Catholic Church' (*SLT*, p. 74). The priest-in-charge of the church was Fr James Scratton,[5] 'an eccentric elderly gentleman' and 'a ceremonial ne'er-do-well' who could offer no help to Waite over his 'difficulties': 'there was never a poor pitiful cleric more well-intentioned and more completely incompetent'. Nor would he help his server when the boy wished to study to become a missionary priest; it was left to Waite—who thought that 'Heaven might help those who sought to help others'—to act in his place, when 'against all expectation [I] managed to have the lad placed' (*SLT*, p. 74).

Of itself this is insufficient to prove the identity of the young server with Gabriel, but there is more: among his bound manuscripts Waite preserved a series of poems written in 1882—they are entitled 'Fragments of Rejected Scenes from Jasper Cartwright'.[6] One section 'A Poet's Letter to his Friend', begins,

There is an acolyte at Deal this day
Whose face hath struck me; I discern a soul's
Fine texture, where fragility alone
And bashful modesty, attract in eyes
Less partial.

In a later passage the poet remarks that:

'We spoke last night together. The boy seems
Thoughtful beyond his age, and earnestly
He told me his ambition was to be
A priest.'

Waite helps the boy to realize that ambition, but anticipates with anguish the day of his ordination, when he will see him for the last time:

Farewell, and ever after it farewell!
Henceforth devoted to the cause of Christ,
In lands remote His cross and crown thou'lt bear.

There is enough in these 'fragments' clearly to identify the poet with Waite, and he never felt able to publish them—but he was equally unwilling to destroy them.[7]

It is probable that Chester encouraged Waite to help the boy, if only to remove his physical presence; he also brought Waite out of his state of morbid introspection and broadened his social horizons, taking him out 'to dine for the most part, but on rare occasions to breakfast', even making a brief excursion to Paris (*SLT*, pp. 66, 67). Chester further impressed upon Waite the extreme importance of embracing the heroic virtue of chastity, and in subsequent poems (as well as in the unpublished 'fragments') the theme of chastity is prominent.

In *Israfel*[8] which was written after *A Soul's Comedy* but published earlier, the figure of Israfel is an idealized amalgam of an angelic being and the acolyte Gabriel; Waite's human love for Israfel/Gabriel is shown sublimated and transformed, and expressed in terms of an almost mystical experience, as when:

We have seen his face, and the memory of its beauty dwells for ever in our minds—it constrains us towards the perfect life; like a magnet, it draws us to the summits of heroism and sacrifice. It has been revealed to me in vision that by a voluntary act we may transfer the merits of a noble and virtuous existence to the most chaste and starbright soul of Israfel, who will shine in the eternal world with the imputed merit of both our lives (*Israfel*, pp. 11–12).

Israfel is described invariably in terms of sexual purity: 'he stands with face transfigured in a virgin's robe'; 'he is a white virgin whose spotless maidenhood is our common faith, our pious hope, our bond of brotherhood in the charity of the New Life'; 'His chief emblem is the Unicorn, in which inviolate chastity is typified' (pp. 13, 28, 31). But if Waite's soul was transformed, the Old Adam was sleeping rather than dead, for it is repression, not sublimation, that is implied by the claim that 'the sight of his passionless beauty' has 'frozen all lust within us' (p. 21).

And celibacy was quite definitely not a state to which Waite was called; nor was it one of which he really approved in others. When writing on asceticism in his most important work on mysticism, *The Way of Divine Union*, he recognized that 'every mystical saint of the Latin Church was a great ascetic', but he saw too that 'Celibacy . . . accomplished a most peculiar work—of which as yet we understand too little—by the transfer of repressed and starved sexuality to a spiritual plane'; and even though he was aware that just such a transfer was one of the more important elements in the awakening of his own mystical consciousness, he condemned the state because 'the erection of celibacy into a counsel of perfection . . . in certain directions threatened to poison the well-spring of one of the Church's own sacraments' (pp. 151–3). The whole question of the sanctity of sex in marriage and the more immediate problem of the relationship between sexuality and mystical experience he discussed at length in *The Secret Doctrine in Israel* (1913), but by then he spoke with the voice of experience: at the time of writing *Israfel* he had yet to experience the 'talismanic attraction of any daughter of woman'.

Within a few years of the publication of *Israfel* and *A Soul's Comedy*, however, the whole tenor of his poetry had changed. *Lucasta*, which appeared in 1890, is an exaltation of married love, dedicated to his wife, but it remains lyrical poetry for poetry's sake: his later works are quite different. *A Book of Mystery and Vision* (1902) and *Strange Houses of Sleep* (1906) are no longer collections of simple verse but attempts at conveying to the world at large the essence of his own mystical experience—although the manner of expression is more appropriate to the characters in the esoteric verse dramas which form a significant part of the text. These would undoubtedly have bewildered his early readers in *Young Folks' Paper*, just as they infuriated such unmystical critics as G. K. Chesterton, who said of *A Book of Mystery and Vision*:

There are certain general characteristics in Mr Waite's work which are extremely typical of the current tendencies of mysticism, and which demand an emphatic protest. First, for example, there is his endless insistence, prominent in his verses and especially prominent in his preface, on the fact that only a few can enter into his feelings, that he writes for a select circle of the initiated. This kind of celestial snobbishness is worse than mere vulgarity. When we hear a man talking at great length about the superiority of his manners to those of his housekeeper, we feel tolerably certain that he is not a gentleman; similarly, when we hear a man insisting endlessly upon the superior character of his sanctity to the sanctity of the multitude, we feel tolerably certain that, whatever else he may be, he is not a saint. A saint, like a gentleman, is one who has forgotten his own points of superiority, being immersed in more interesting things.[9]

And this mystical elitism, thought Chesterton, is not poetry. Nor is it reality:

And then the mystic comes and says that a green tree symbolizes Life. It is not so. Life symbolizes a green tree. Just in so far as we get into the abstract, we get away from the reality, we get away from the mystery, we get away from the tree. And this is the reason that so many transcendental discourses are merely blank and tedious to us, because they have to do with Truth and Beauty, and the Destiny of the Soul, and all the great, faint, faded symbols of the reality. And this is why all poetry is so interesting to us, because it has to do with skies, with woods, with battles, with temples, with women and wine, with the ultimate miracles which no philosopher could create.

In those terms Waite could never again be a poet, for after the resolution of his traumatic inner conflicts, poetry was no longer an end in itself but only a means to an end: he was achieving a delayed maturity, and at the same time becoming increasingly self-aware, and venturing eagerly on to the shifting sands of occultism. It was a new world for Waite; a world that held out the promise of providing the means to create something more significant than mere verse.

6

'WHILE YET A BOY I SOUGHT FOR GHOSTS'

AT THE time of his sister's death, in 1874, Waite had no doubt as to the reality of life after death: her soul, 'heavenward soaring', would be with the angels in the presence of God. But as his faith slowly ebbed away in the years that followed he became increasingly sceptical of the Church's teaching on the posthumous state of the soul, and increasingly pessimistic about the very possibility of survival. His doubt is reflected in an untitled sonnet written in 1878, which concludes with these lines:

> Though Life has parted us, let Death unite
> Just one short moment!—and with that—adieu!
> For, gazing into the eternal night,
> No torch nor starlight come to help us through.
> How joyless there for both if we should meet
> In Death's dark maze, roaming with weary feet!

A Lament from the same year, ends even more bleakly:

> What is life itself but madness?
> What is death but endless night?

Amidst all this gloom and despair the awareness of death was ever present, for by 1879 Waite and his mother had moved to Victor Road at Kensal Green, a road, as he says, 'a little above the entrance to a Catholic part of Kensal Green Cemetery' and close enough for his mother to mourn perpetually almost within sight of her daughter's grave. But if Waite mourned, it was not over Frederica's grave but while he 'walked in dreams and dreamed in endless walks' (*SLT*, p. 67); and it was on one of these walks that he found a way of escape from his doubts:

My wanderings had taken me once to the crowded purlieus of Edgware Road, and in the side-window of a corner pork-butcher's shop I had seen displayed to my astonishment a few copies of the *Medium and Daybreak*, a journal devoted to Modern Spiritualism. Having long contemplated the columns of the front page, I went in to purchase a copy, taking care to address him whom I assumed to be the master rightly, a tall, broad, expansive personality, with goodwill inscribed upon him. My youth and nervous hesitation must have drawn him towards one shewing thus an early interest in subjects which were evidently near to his heart. He told me of trance orations, of spirits assuming material forms, of dead men coming back, and probably gave me two or three elementary pamphlets, brought forth from a drawer beneath one of his counters. It is remembered to this day that I emerged from that talk with a vague feeling that all this was like a story of which I had heard previously; that it was not strange and new; that it was rooted in the likelihood of things rather than abnormal and far beyond the ken (*SLT*, p. 57).

Thus predisposed—and in 1878, when this revelation occurred,[1] he was eager for his doubts to be overthrown—Waite took up Spiritualism with enthusiasm.

The Spiritualist movement had begun in America, at Hydesville in New York State, in 1848, although for some four years before then visionary accounts of the Spirit World had been issuing from the entranced Andrew Jackson Davis, the 'Poughkeepsie Seer'. In the year of European Revolution the little American town had been disturbed by the alleged spirit of a murdered pedlar, who began to communicate by means of persistent rappings that occurred in the presence of two young girls, Kate and Margaret Fox. On the basis of the rapped messages evidence of the murder was discovered and the girls became celebrities. Soon others, too, received messages purporting to come from the dead, at first by means of raps or table-turning, later by way of automatic writing and trance utterances, and the movement spread rapidly throughout the United States. As mediums—the persons supposedly acting as intermediaries between the worlds of the living and of the dead—proliferated, the movement began to take on the rudiments of formal organization and by 1852, when it appeared in England in the person of Mrs Hayden, the first visiting American medium, Spiritualism as a definable sect was well established.

England proved as susceptible to spiritualist phenomena as the United States, and although English mediums were at first few and far between, by the 1870s they were to be found in abundance, producing all the more spectacular effects of their American counterparts: direct voice messages (in which the medium spoke with the voice of the communicating spirit), levitation of objects, and materializations of the hands, faces, or whole forms of the departed. Such phenomena usually occurred under strictly prescribed conditions at seances, meetings at which the sitters—either those seeking messages from dead relatives, investigating intellectuals, or the merely curious—sat around a table, linked hands with the medium and with each other, extinguished the lights—and waited. As a rule their patience was rewarded with phenomena, often spectacular and not always easy to explain, despite the frequent detection of trickery among both professional and amateur mediums.

Both 'real' phenomena and exposures of fraud were faithfully reported in the spiritualist journals and in the multitude of books devoted to the subject, for the devotees were eager to present a respectable face to the world and to establish their 'Science, Philosophy and Religion of continuous life, based upon the demonstrated fact of communication, by means of mediumship, with those who live in the Spirit World'[2] as an acceptable faith. Indeed, it was largely through the propaganda of the journals that potential converts were gained: Waite among them.

Before he began to attend seances Waite immersed himself in spiritualist literature, until 'there came a time when I could almost say that I was acquainted sufficiently with the whole output of Spiritism, so far as England, America and France were concerned' (*SLT*, p. 60). He soon acquired a remarkable knowledge of the subject for he had, as he says, 'a considerable faculty in my studies for extracting the quintessence of books, and it remained with me' (*SLT*, p. 61)—a fact borne out by the enormous number of notes and shrewd comments made in his manuscript commonplace book, *Collectanea Metaphysica*. He also came to know many of the most prominent spiritualists of the time; men such as James Burns, the Revd William Stainton Moses, John James, and E. Dawson Rogers.[3] But the chief attraction of Spiritualism remained its ability to revive his faith in an afterlife, albeit at the cost of further alienation from the Catholic Church:

It remains to be said that the horizon opened by Spiritism, as of another world and its prospects, and of the possibility in earthly life of belonging in a sense to both, led me further away from the notion of an Infallible Church which offered Hell opened to Christians in place of Eternal Hope. I beheld on the further side, in the so-called hither hereafter, a place where men can dwell and healed by slow degrees of all their hurts can find new life in new and other work, world without end, because of endless worlds (*SLT*, p. 62).

His first direct experience of a medium was with the Revd Francis Ward Monck[4]—popularly but inaccurately known as 'Dr' Monck—who had produced remarkable materializations at his seances in the early 1870s, but who had also in 1876 been exposed as a fraud and gaoled. Waite met him in 1878:

I made casual acquaintance with Dr Monck, the notorious cheating medium, . . . I came across [him] keeping a noisome shop on the other side of a foot-bridge spanning the railway lines at Westbourne Park. It was shortly after his imprisonment, and he had married a dreadful creature picked up in that neighbourhood and from whom he ultimately fled to America, evading as best he could, with some negative help in my presence, a crowd of the woman's sympathisers. He must have gone as a steerage passenger, and I heard from him once afterwards, announcing his safe arrival' (*SLT*, pp. 76–7).

He was not impressed by Monck, who was for Waite 'a feeble and foolish being, who told me his criminal story and seemed to have faith in his own supposed powers. There was talk of shewing me curious things; but it came to nothing, no doubt through my own apathy: it was difficult to tolerate a pseudo-medium whose effects had been seized and proved to contain the hocus-pocus of common conjuring' (ibid. p. 77).

Other mediums proved more satisfactory. In 1885 he attended a series of seances in the company of a friend, Captain Cecil Dyce, an ex-Indian army officer, older than Waite, who was the cousin of a school-friend from St Charles's College.[5] Dyce was not a believer in Spiritualism, being 'ribald and sceptical' although 'also curiously drawn', but Waite was inclined to accept the apparent evidence of his own senses. Referring to his experiences some twenty years later he remarked:

> If anyone asked me whether I have seen intelligent writing produced between locked slates under circumstances which fairly exclude the suggestion of trickery, I should reply that I have; and if he questioned me further, whether in dark seances, when the so-called medium has been held in my arms, I have witnessed the levitation of inert objects, I should again reply that I have (*Studies in Mysticism*, pp. 133–4).

What he did not add was that when these events occurred he was seeking, and half-believed he had received, a message from his sister.

The first seance was with William Eglinton,[6] a young medium who had produced amazing materializations during the 1870s but who by the mid-1880s was concentrating on slate-writing (the production of alleged spirit messages on sealed or locked school slates); among his sitters for this form of communication had been W. E. Gladstone, who was convinced that the phenomena were genuine. Waite and Dyce visited Eglinton on 19 October 1885 and Waite afterwards wrote out a full account of the sitting, although the final leaf of the manuscript is unfortunately in such poor state as to be almost wholly illegible. Eglinton proved to be a prepossessing young man: 'His speech and manner are refined, his temperament is genial; in short, he impressed me favourably, being so different to other mediums I have seen.' The medium was, however, somewhat put out by the slates that his sitters had brought with them: 'We produced our slates, when he frankly told us it was very unlikely we should get anything written in them. The point to be noticed here is that he asked us if we had brought slates, but when he saw how they were tied and sealed, he expressed the above opinion. However, he was willing to try and we might succeed.' The medium then explained to them 'why we should probably get no writing on our own slates—viz. because the conditions were new and the slates not magnetized.'

Using two of Eglinton's own slates—one single and one double, which had been locked by the sitters—the seance began, with first one and then the other slate being held against the under-side of the table at which they were sitting. For half-an-hour or more nothing happened, perhaps because Waite was wary:

> Immediately the slate was under the table, Eglinton began to talk in a rapid manner as if to engage our attention. This excited my suspicion and I kept my eyes on his hand which held

> the slate. I should say that one-third of it was always in view. The conversation fell and Mr E. asked us to talk as preoccupied silence was an unhealthy condition. We did so, but I kept a sharp look-out notwithstanding. Nothing occurred.

Eventually, however, 'Just as the medium was himself beginning to despair, the spasmodic contortion which had previously thrilled his frame increased, and an answer was written. I distinctly heard the writing, then three raps with the point to show that it was finished. The question was answered partially.'

Waite had brought with him a copy of Zollner's *Transcendental Physics* and his question was a request for the author's name to be written. Presumably part of the name appeared: to the cynic it was probably that part visible on the spine of the book, but Waite gives no further details. More, however, was to follow: 'After this the slate was cleaned and again put under the table when I asked verbally Is the spirit of my sister present and able to communicate? or words to that effect. Writing occurred as before, the answer was yes. I then asked for her name to be written but this was not done.' All in all it was an unremarkable performance.

They next visited Messrs. Williams and Husk, two professional mediums from whom Waite at least did not expect great results. The sitting-room used for the seances Waite found to be 'the most exceptionally lurid in its furniture that I have ever seen. The walls have red paper, the curtains and suite are a dull red; a red chinese umbrella of vast proportions depends extended from the ceiling; in a word it is just the apartment in which the terrible Scarlet Woman might be expected to be found. There is nothing to excite suspicion in it beyond the unmitigated bad taste which thus rampantly displays itself.' He also noted that 'from six to a dozen people usually attend; an instrument called Fairy Bells, a large and small musical-box, some paper trumpets, are the stock in trade of these marvel-mongers.'

When the seance commenced 'the musical box is lifted, the instruments pass from head to head of the sitters; voices sound in all directions; spirit jokes are cracked in broken voices, and all the well known series of thaumaturgic commonplaces follows.' None of this impressed him and he concluded that 'the best argument for the genuineness of the majority of these manifestations is that the small sum charged for admission divided among confederates would be too small to make it worth anyone's while to keep a suite of rooms all the year round.'

The most successful seance was on 3 March 1886 'with a private, non-professional medium of great power, Mr Rita,[7] who came to us in a friendly manner, without remuneration, which indeed he does not accept'. All began well: musical instruments were levitated, a musical box 'was set playing apparently by spirit agency', raps were heard, and spirit lights appeared, one of which 'disappeared close to my own face with a slight smell of phosphorus'. Then the phenomena began to centre on Waite. 'I was the object of some attention on the part of the spirits, partly because I was next the medium, but I suppose also because of the mediumistic powers with which all these beings seem to credit me'. 'Charlie', one of the spirit 'controls' of the medium, 'volunteered the statement that I should make a very good medium' and then 'materialized twice over the table, holding the slate which cast its phosphorescent light upon the drapery and ghostly countenance. I think he turned in succession towards all of us, and then ascended towards the ceiling, vanishing in darkness'.

Even more impressive was

> the sudden materialization of a beautiful face between myself and the medium, which came apparently to myself alone, and was seen [by] only one other sitter who was in the same range of vision, so to speak. It was draped in white like a nun; the mouth was not visible, the seat of expression was in the eyes, which were large, dark, luminous, and full of the most solemn significance and sweet intelligence. I caught all this in an almost momentary glimpse—a glimpse too brief for me to feel in any way sure that the general resemblance to my dead sister which I traced in it was more than a trick of imagination.

He added, with astonishing naïvety, 'moreover, as often in the most genuine materializations there was a faint phantasmal resemblance to the general contours of the medium's own features, but transfigured out of all knowledge'. Rita, he thought, was genuine, for 'In this seance, the essential element of fraud was wanting—i.e. there was no gain likely to accrue in any way financially or otherwise to the medium'.

It did not occur to him at the time that enthusiastic, unsolicited testimonials could be extremely beneficial to Mr Rita. Later, he revised his opinion and in his autobiography described Rita as 'the last kind of person in looks whom one would be prepared to trust on sight. The ordinary observer would have termed him a shifty customer' (*SLT*, p. 78).

Undoubtedly Waite had a deep need to believe in survival, and the seances seemed to reassure him; but as his own thought matured his attitude to survival became less simplistic, although he recognized the importance of objective proof for others. In his autobiography he stressed that 'authentic Spiritism is a demonstration, solely and only, of an alleged fact that the dead return at times in the communications of the séance-room and give proofs of their identity'. As to the nature of such proof:

> The *sine qua non* on the question of Spirit Return is whether and when disembodied mind communicates through any given medium with the mind incarnate, delivering that which the channel cannot know, while the sitter himself does not, but which he proves to be true subsequently. If Spiritism is to be justified beyond reasonable challenge, here lies the one test of truth which truly signifies (*SLT*, pp. 210, 211).

Shortly before his death, in 1942, he urged upon the secretary of the London Spiritualist Alliance—who had come for a private interview with him—the need to publicize proven cases of survival: 'The most important and desperate need of the time is the proving of Survival. If only a Spiritualist would begin a chronological production of attested cases of evidence. I should like to see one old and one new case of evidence of Survival each week in *Light*.'[8]

For himself it no longer mattered—Spiritualism had long since given way to mysticism.

Even by the late 1880s, when he was contributing to *Light*, already one of the leading spiritualist journals, Waite was expounding the merits of mystical as opposed to psychic experiences. In 1890 he delivered a lecture to the London Spiritualist Alliance on 'The Interior Life from the Standpoint of the Mystics'[9] and dismayed his spiritualist audience by insisting on the superiority of the 'transcendental'—the inner experiences of the mystic—over the merely 'phenomenal', which included the phenomena of the seance-room. And just as he startled the cultured readers of *Light*, so he confused the more simple-minded readers of its rival, the *Medium and Daybreak*, with his curious allegorical fairy-tale 'Prince Starbeam', which had been published serially in its columns in 1889. This odd romance had not the remotest connection with the concerns of everyday spiritualists, and a heavy-handed attempt to interpret it in their terms, by a pseudonymous critic 'Ossian' (almost certainly the editor, James Burns), only increased their confusion.

But even as his active involvement with the spiritualist movement faded, Waite maintained his academic interest and continued to write on both Spiritualism and on psychical research in general (he read all the relevant journals as a matter of course for his regular *Periodical Literature* feature in *The Occult Review*); he did not, of course, commit himself to a specific belief:

> There are, broadly speaking, two theories based on the acceptation of the facts after ninety per cent of the alleged phenomena have been removed from the consideration. One of these has determined that certain organizations of mankind can, owing to some psychological or psycho-physiological peculiarity, become the mediums of communication between man and the worlds of unseen intelligence, usually that world which the same theory peoples with disembodied human spirits. The alternative explanation sets aside the idea that there is any operation of intelligence outside that of the person designated as the medium, and concludes that the phenomena which take place in his presence are the product of his own psychic nature externalised, so to speak. Between these theories it is not necessary to exercise a decided choice in the present instance; the evidence is so inconclusive that any selection would merely indicate a particular mental predilection (*Studies in Mysticism*, p. 134).

Not that he doubted the phenomena, or the reality of life after death; he was simply not convinced that the one necessarily followed from the other. In an interview with *The Christian Commonwealth* in 1914 he affirmed his belief in survival and described his own concept of life after death:

> Until we are withdrawn in perfect union of nature, I believe that we shall abide in successive

worlds, our relations with which will be instituted and maintained by successive vehicles. As to the state or world into which we shall enter at death, psychical research and its concomitants have produced the beginnings of a demonstrative theory, and we must look in that direction for an answer. But the question is better left. It is much better to be striving after the state of union than to study the possibilities of intermediate worlds.[10]

All this, however, would be a prelude to our perfect Union with God, which is man's ultimate goal. To the question 'Have you had any personal experience . . . that the so-called dead are still living and active?' he gave no answer. After thirty years his seances were no longer convincing.

He did record, some years later, a remarkable case of clairvoyance. In February 1919 his daughter Sybil was at Ramsgate, dangerously ill with septic double pneumonia, but with careful and intensive treatment she slowly recovered. During her illness Waite commuted between London and Ramsgate, staying with friends when he could not return to the coast. On one such occasion, on 22 March,

I was able to attend hurriedly an important London Meeting and stayed perforce for a single night with Frater Paratum Cor Meum [i.e. G. Barrett Dobb] at Edenbridge. Though an exceedingly keen, tireless and successful business man, it may interest Spiritists to learn that he was not alone highly psychic but held frequent communications with an unseen Guide, claiming—I believe—to have been a North American Indian. I used to hear about this Guide occasionally, in my detached manner; but after dinner or supper, on the night in question, we were sitting by ourselves, with the inevitable pipes, when the Guide, I suppose, was mentioned, and Frater Paratum decided to get into communication for help on a matter of his own, and one important to himself. The Guide came, and in what seemed to be a cavalier manner brushed aside my friend's anxieties and sent a message to myself. It said that at that moment Sybil was sitting up for the first time in her room at Ramsgate. This ended the communication, and the fact was duly verified on my return home (*SLT*, p. 205).

His diary gives further details, recording that the psychic message 'was about 9 p.m.' and that the nurse's report, which he received on the 24th, confirmed this: 'she was up in her room, probably at the time it came'.

Waite himself had no such clairvoyant ability. In March 1936, while he was staying at Maida Vale, he awoke one night 'suddenly with a voice—which seemed to be Sybil's—calling, as if for help, and I feared that she might have had some accident alone at Betsy Cottage'. In great anxiety he telegraphed to Broadstairs, only to learn that all was well. 'Such', he said, 'is my kind of psychism.'[11]

Messages received through genuine psychics he respected—as with one Harry Gordon who visited Waite at Ealing in 1919 and 'obtained strange communications with a little table in our dining-room'—and he even suggested that some psychics may have a religious role to play: 'I feel that we stand here on the threshold of things unrealized, that the day may come when a consecrated and ordained "automatist" assisted by a dedicated circle—in the plenary sense of these expressions—will obtain records from a "dissociated personality" or from "the other side", and that they will carry an authentic note.' At the same time he disapproved strongly of treating Ouija Boards as toys, condemning them as 'about the last plaything to be put into the hands of children'.[12]

Forty years after his first lecture on mysticism to the London Spiritualist Alliance Waite spoke to them again on 'The Relationship between Mysticism and Psychical Research' on 10 April 1930. He accepted the possibility of spirit communication but reaffirmed the supreme importance of mysticism and of the goal of Divine Union. How his audience reacted is not recorded, but the Association clearly liked and admired him; so much so that in 1938 it was suggested that he might become editor of *Light* in succession to George Lethem who was in ill-health. The immediate reason for the suggestion was, however, somewhat bizarre, as Waite noted at the time:

> The Council of the Sp[iritualist] All[iance] knows of no-one to succeed [Lethem] and Phyllis [i.e. Mercy Phillimore, Secretary of the Association] was asked to see a certain medium through whom Stainton-Moses is said to communicate. He—I—advised that I should be consulted. But I know less of likely people. If the advice really came from S.M., was it intended to see whether I would serve? This is a moot point. Was it subconsciously in the mind of Phyllis? She at least thought of me once in connection with the editorship. I made my position plain on the score of sincerity, and it seems not far apart from hers.

He also recognized the major problem: 'Whether my own health and age would let me make the experiment are other questions' (Diary, 28 July 1938). The Council evidently answered those questions in the negative and the editorship eventually went elsewhere, to C. R. Cammell, the poet and biographer of Aleister Crowley.

Waite would unquestionably have been a most unsympathetic editor. Latterday spiritualists with their frequent emphasis on reincarnation irritated him, and, according to his daughter, by 1938 'he had long lost interest in the L.S.A. having known so much deception'.[13] His lack of enthusiasm for the more uncritical aspects of Spiritualism had long been clear to the faithful: when his 'digest' of the writings of Andrew Jackson Davis was re-issued in 1922 an American critic wondered, 'whether or not this book was compiled for the purpose of giving the enquiring public an intelligent conception of the writings of A.J. Davis, or is it an effort to mislead and confuse the enquirer, and as Shakespeare put it, "damn with faint praise" the greatest prophet and seer of all time'.[14]

It was probably a just criticism, for although Waite recognized the importance of Davis's work and felt it desirable that there should be a digest of 'the essential parts of his doctrine, philosophy and testimony to the world of spirits and the natural law therein' (*Harmonial Philosophy*, p. xi) he did not find the preparation of the book a congenial task. His personal antipathy to 'the seership and writings of Davis' were clear to others as he worked on the book throughout 1916. Mercy Phillimore recalled that

He used to come fairly often to our library to borrow and consult the Davis books. This was at our old rooms in St Martin's Lane. The Davis books were housed in a room on the top shelf close to the ceiling. He usually came late in the afternoon. The room was lighted by low-hanging, shaded lamps. He would climb dangerously to the top of a none-too-robust ladder, and perched, high up in the dimness, would browse on the books; from time to time deep groans would amuse us, groans to remind us of how bored he was.[15]

And yet however boring Spiritualism might be, it had helped to restore his faith and—even more important—it had helped him to open 'that Gate which opens on the Path of Love'.

7

DORA AND THE COMING OF LOVE

MR RITA had made a deep impression upon Waite at the seance with Cecil Dyce, and when the offer of a further sitting was made Waite took it up eagerly. What happened at that second seance is not known, for only the first paragraph of Waite's manuscript account of it has survived; enough, however, to record who was present:

> I think it was on the Saturday following [i.e. 7 March 1886] that I was invited to a seance with the same medium at Captain James, Gt Hereford Road, Bayswater—present our host, the Revd Mr Newbold, General Maclean, Miss Peck, Mr Stuart Menteath, Miss Menteath and myself, in addition to the medium Rita, who arrived last of all, whereupon we immediately took our seats.

It was a momentous day when Waite met 'Mr Stuart Menteath' for 'out of those meetings followed things which changed my life' (*SLT*, p. 78).

Waite's memory of that first meeting was vague—he remembered neither the month nor the year, thinking that it was in the 'Summer, possibly of 1885'; but he was clear as to what followed: 'In the autumn we renewed acquaintance under the same auspices and Stuart-Menteth, for some obscure reason was drawn in my direction'. Undoubtedly Stuart-Menteath (there was no consistency of spelling, even in the family) 'cultivated my acquaintance more especially in connection with his ambition to form a circle for private seances, in the hope that an unprofessional medium would develop therein', and eventually Waite was invited to dinner, 'so that we could talk things over and compare points of view'. Perhaps he was invited for social reasons also: 'Possibly I was invited in the first instance to meet or renew acquaintance with a friend of Evelyn Ogilvie Stuart-Menteth, the older girl. In this case the second guest was Caroline Corner, who was supposed to be concerned with psychic things and who had written a little volume called *Beyond the Ken*, as thin and invertebrate as she herself proved to be, wherever, in the first instance, we chanced to meet' (*SLT*, pp. 78, 79). This ungallant dismissal of a fellow writer omits to mention her essay on 'Nuremberg'—printed in *Walford's Antiquarian Magazine* in 1887—which Waite cheerfully pillaged three years later for his own brief note on the city in *Young Folks.*[1] Towards the Stuart-Menteaths he was less cavalier.

Granville Stuart-Menteath he remembered as 'a slight, small man with almost yellow hair and beard, his shy and nervous manner contrasting somewhat with a fixed assurance over psychical matters.' He recalled also that 'it was not for months that I learned he was once in Holy Orders and had even a country living, I think, in the Lake District. But his congenital self-mistrust made it a misery to take services and led to sad mistakes, omissions and so forth therein. He was a widower, with two sons and two daughters, these latter being respectively eldest and youngest in a family of four' (*SLT*, p. 79). At the time they met the Revd Granville Thorold Stuart-Menteath was forty-eight years old (he was born on 6 June 1838); he had been educated at University College, Oxford, ordained in 1861 and subsequently appointed Curate of Brent-Pelham in Hertfordshire. In 1865 he had married Susan Ogilvie Oliver who produced for him his four children, Evelyn, Charles, Edward and Mary. It was presumably after his wife's death in 1881 that he took up Spiritualism.[2]

Soon after Waite's first visit to the Stuart-Menteath household at Grittleton Road the weekly private seances began. 'It was', Waite recalled,

the most haphazard gathering that was ever formed on earth for Psychical Research. We sat at a mahogany dining-room table and hoped for something to happen; but nothing did. It was understood, however, that perseverance over such matters was a virtue that was rewarded in the end, so Menteth and I whiled away the dark hours with moderate aids to reflection in whiskey and soda and Old Judge tobacco.

Eventually 'a time came when objects moved in the dark and faint raps were heard', but they were clearly fraudulent, although Waite declined to identify the culprit. It mattered little to him, for by this time 'there was another and very different link which drew me to the Stuart-Menteth household and bound me to all its ways. This was Miranda—her sacramental title at that time among us—otherwise, Theodora—then moving in her grace to the threshold of twenty-one' (*SLT*, p. 80).

Waite remained extremely coy about giving any information concerning Dora, although he was happy to wax lyrical over her appearance: 'there was no earthly loveliness to compare with that of Miranda in her red-gold aureole of waved hair, flowing down almost to her ankles, and her star-born eyes which heaven's grey-blue had glorified'—for which he may be excused, as 'it was my first talismanic attraction towards any daughter of woman' (*SLT*, p. 81). He was, alas, not alone in his love for her. She was intended for Stuart-Menteath who, as Waite recognized, would inevitably marry her whatever her own feelings might be:

It was as if a star had spoken in silence, addressing no-one but registering a fact to come, in the aloof way of some stars. So it was and would be in the sequence of future events. And this reposed in my mind, as it might in hers, without concerning the mind. It was partly as if an esoteric sense within me was aware in advance of what would fall out in due order at the right moment. How it stood therefore between Theodora and myself was neither concealed nor told, that I know of, in respect of Stuart-Menteth: it transpired only (*SLT*, p. 81).

'How it stood' *after* would be concealed rather more carefully.

Despite Waite's reticence and fondness for pseudonyms, Dora's identity is easy to establish, although it is less easy, indeed virtually impossible, to answer with certainty the questions of how, when, and why she came to be a part of the Stuart-Menteath household. Annie Lakeman—Dora, Theodora, Miranda, Melusine; whatever Waite chose to call her—was born at Hendon on 21 February 1864, the daughter of a gardener, William Lakeman, and of his wife Sarah, who was a domestic servant: an unlikely background for the future wife of a scion of the minor nobility. It is possible that Dora was acting as a governess to the two younger Stuart-Menteath children who were, in 1886, twelve and fourteen years of age; but if this was the case she chose to conceal the fact on her marriage certificate where no occupation at all is entered. But if there are doubts as to Dora's occupation there are none at all concerning her father.

William Henry Lakeman was born in 1829, probably in Devon (Waite says it was a 'Devonshire family'), although his entire adult life was spent in the outer suburbs of London. From Hendon in the north he moved to Thornton Heath, on the southern outskirts of the city, where he set up the Queensbury Nursery about the time of Dora's marriage. Other nurserymen who knew Lakeman believed him to be a retired clergyman (probably a confusion with Granville Stuart-Menteath), and remembered the nursery well:

Mr Lakeman was a clergyman, who took up growing Border Carnations, first of all as a hobby, then later he started showing and worked up quite a good name. Queensbury Nursery was only two garden plots, with a greenhouse where he rooted his cuttings but he issued a Catalogue and attended some of the Flower Shows (including Chelsea) where he booked his orders, and also he used to advertise in the Garden Magazines.

If not a large concern, Queensbury Nursery was at least a successful one, to the satisfaction of its proprietor, who was, no doubt, equally satisfied with his daughter's marriage.[3]

Dora, however, seems to have had little in common with her husband: she had no interest at all in spiritualism and little enthusiasm for Granville's hobbies of cycling and photography, but she *was* enthusiastic about poetry, even to the extent of admiring *Israfel*, the publication of which had coincided, more or less, with her first meeting with Waite. Above all she loved fine clothes and gracious living, neither of which could be expected from an impecunious poet but which Stuart-Menteath could supply in abundance. (By the terms of a settlement made in 1865 at the time of his first marriage, and through a subsequent Trust, Granville

Stuart-Menteath received the income from properties in Chelsea, Hounslow, and Battersea and was able to purchase a cottage at Polruan in Cornwall and Toftrees, a large house on the Thames at East Molesey, to which he moved with Dora shortly after their marriage.)

But if mercenary considerations had helped Dora to decide in favour of Stuart-Menteath, she was to find that his bounty did not extend to a society wedding—rather the opposite. On 29 June 1887, for no other reason than that it was the church nearest to Grittleton Road, the Revd Granville Thorold Stuart-Menteath, priest of the Church of England, married his Anglican bride at St Peter's Park Baptist Chapel. It may, of course, have been an early example of practical ecumenism—Stuart-Menteath did, on subsequent occasions, open church bazaars and distribute Sunday-School prizes for the minister, the Revd J. Mitchell-Cox—but convenience seems a more simple, if more cynical, explanation.

Waite was resigned to the marriage but he could not bring himself to be present: 'It was seen to on my part that whosoever might be present, at what function soever by which the seals were set, I at least was far away, with the sounds of the sea and the sounds of the light and the night-time to drown intoning chants, if chants there happened to be' (*SLT*, p. 113). In all probability he went to Worthing to visit a friend who was herself about to be married. He had met Amy Hogg during the previous summer while staying at Worthing with his mother. There, through her attendance at the Roman Catholic church, 'my mother became acquainted with some elderly Anglo-Indians, Mr and Mrs Hogg, who had a daughter named Mysie, a tall pallid girl, well-shapen but with little attraction in her looks. I had occasional talks with her and found that she had no horizon beyond that which was proffered and provided by Latin doctrine and practice.'

There was, however, an elder sister of less restricted views and less constraining ways. Amy Hogg 'was living in London and mixing much with authors, artists and actors. It was understood that she and I would prove to be kindred spirits, if chance brought us together as well it might, since she was always a possible visitor to Worthing and her parents for a few days, or so long as she could stand the place' (*SLT*, p. 105). Which was not for long, since she was very much one of the *avant-garde* and seen as such by her friends. One of them, Jerome K. Jerome, recalled that 'she lived by herself in diggings opposite the British Museum, frequented restaurants and aerated bread shops, and had many men friends: all of which was considered very shocking in those days' (*My Life and Times*, p. 115).

When, eventually, she came down to Worthing, Waite took long walks with her, on which they discussed 'occultism, Spiritism, psychical research and the rest'. She had little interest in such topics but determined to introduce Waite to one of her Bohemian friends who *was* a fellow enthusiast. And so 'it was from Amy Hogg that I first heard of Arthur Machen, in special connection with her firm resolve that he and I should meet as soon as possible when I returned to London' (*SLT*, p. 106). Their meeting, however, was somewhat delayed, for while Waite was still at Worthing, Machen had gone home to Monmouthshire; they corresponded before the end of the year but it was not until Machen's return to London that they met 'one dark morning of January 1887 under the great dome of the Museum'. It was a most happy occasion, the birth of a deep and enduring friendship: fifty years later Waite recalled that 'we were friends and great intimates from the beginning' and when Waite died in 1942 Machen wrote of his loss to Oliver Stonor: 'To lose Waite is for me to lose a considerable part of life.'[4] In the same letter he described Waite and himself as being 'utterly at variance on fundamental things, and yet with a strong underlying sympathy'. They were alike and unlike in almost equal measure.

Arthur Llewellyn Jones-Machen was born at Caerleon, Monmouthshire, on 3 March 1863, the only child of the Revd John Jones-Machen, Rector of Llanddewi. Machen was a lonely, introverted child but his loneliness, unlike Waite's, was chosen rather than thrust upon him: he had a settled and secure home life, his roots lay deep in his native county, and he received a sound, rounded education at Hereford Cathedral School. And yet, just as Waite's hopes of Oxford had been dashed, so had Machen's, brought to an end by a drastic fall in his father's income. In 1880 he went to London in a vain attempt to be a medical student, but failed utterly and returned in the following year to try his hand at journalism. Then he began to experience the misery of enforced loneliness, exacerbated by poverty and alleviated only by long explorations of the dreary new suburbs of West London. While he was wandering through Turnham Green, Gunnersbury, Willesden, and Harlesden, Waite also 'walked among the lanes of Middlesex' and 'dreamed in winding tracks which are now suburban streets' through Mill Hill, Acton, Hayes, and Perivale. They might almost have passed each other unknown.

Gradually Machen adapted, writing for himself, translating and cataloguing for George Redway the publisher,[5] and punctuating his employment with brief visits home—his parents were by now too poor for him to stay for long away from London. He began to socialize, made friends, and met Amy Hogg, who in turn brought him to Waite. The friendship was cemented from the start and celebrated, much in the manner of characters in Machen's fiction, by frequent visits to taverns and music-halls. 'Do you remember', Machen asked Waite half a century later, 'how we had beer at the old vanished Bell in Holborn, and went to see *Faust* at the Lyceum?', and further, 'how long ago we explored Bermondsey, and how the Bermondsey barmaids, on our calling for gin, would offer us "Two Two's"?'[6]

There was, of course, a more serious side to their friendship. Both men were deeply immersed in the literature of occultism; for Waite it was the raw material of the critical studies he was beginning to write and the stuff out of which his own beliefs were slowly and painfully taking on systematic form, while for Machen compiling catalogues of new and secondhand occult books was a significant part of his work for Redway—it also gave him the technical background for his early fantastic stories. But their two approaches to magic and all other forms of occultism were quite different. Machen was fascinated but condemned it all—he was rooted firmly in the Church of England and never really deviated from his traditional Christian Faith—whereas Waite sought a common reality behind both occultism *and* the Church. Whatever the specific question at issue they would never be in agreement, but would always argue over it furiously and joyously. When writing to Waite about their disputes over the Holy Grail, Machen reminded him:

> Was there not a tacit convention that we should avoid mere argument? If this still stands: good: if not: have at you for *all* your opinions as to the Church and the Heresies! From them all, so far as I understand them, I wholly and heartily dissent: in the hypothesis of the Holy Assembly I do not believe: in the Popish Church as the *sole* custodian of the Faith or Sacraments I utterly disbelieve! I am ready if necessary to maintain theses on all these points, when and where you will.[7]

At the time of their meeting both men were involved with George Redway, Waite as an author and Machen as editor of *Walford's Antiquarian*, in which capacity he persuaded Waite to produce essays for the journal, although in a matter of months it would come to an end. After the demise of the *Antiquarian* they continued to work together on Redway's behalf, compiling between them the seven issues of *George Redway's Literary Circular*, and when Waite's *Handbook of Cartomancy* was published (pseudonymously) in 1889, Machen's delighful advertising puff, *A Chapter from the Book called The Ingenious Gentleman Don Quijote de la Mancha*, was bound up with it.[8] It was at just such brief essays that Machen excelled; he never enjoyed the labour of writing and marvelled at Waite's capacity for it. He wrote about Waite's industry in a letter of October 1887, to Harry Spurr, the publisher: 'The *High Class Gypsy* has been in once or twice; I believe he spends most of his time in that Resort of the Learned Vagabonds, the British Museum, slogging away at his Lives of the Alchemists; to be published by us. I fancy it will be a good thing.'[9]

But this was after an eventful summer. Dora was married in June and Waite sent her as a wedding present a copy of *A Soul's Comedy* inscribed 'To Miranda, with love from Arthur Edward Waite'; it would be a full year before he could bring himself to use her married name. In August Machen and Amy Hogg were married at Worthing, probably with Waite in attendance; he did not stay, for he needed to return to London to set about the business of marriage on his own part.

Of the two witnesses at Dora's wedding, one was her sister Ada, and it was to her that Waite now turned. On 7 January 1888 'I married the beloved Lucasta [his pet name for her; it derives from Lovelace, whose poems Waite admired]; and I think that no man in this possible world of ours had a better helpmeet, rooted in spiritual faith of the simplest and most assured kind' (*SLT*, p. 114). Nor a more unlikely and long-suffering 'helpmeet'. Ada Alice Lakeman had all the plainness that her older sister lacked, and was as reserved as Dora was forward. In *Belle and the Dragon* she is the Dormouse, 'for there was said to be no assignable limit to her capacity for sleeping' (p. 19) and when awake she was of such 'unassailable taciturnity' that 'as she never spoke willingly, and seldom answered anyone except upon extreme pressure, this silence became itself a kind of eloquence' (p. 20). She also possessed a serene indifference, both to Waite's occult pursuits and to his poetry (when his anthology of fairy poetry was published in the summer of 1888, he gave Ada a copy of the pocket edition, reserving the larger and more sumptuous version for her more appreciative sister). She remains a curiously nebulous figure, but Waite was undoubtedly fond of Ada, and if high passion and high romance were alike absent from the marriage her inert personality ought to have led to a life of placid contentment. But there remained Dora.

Whatever Ada's reason for marrying Waite, it was not for his money. Initially they lived with his mother, 'but as happens so often with mothers, the best included, it proved impossible'. They then moved to a home of their own in Ashmore Road (but not a whole house: 'certain rooms only in the first floor') and Waite continued to scrape a living as a writer—albeit with little encouragement from his wife, who was now more concerned with their daughter, Sybil (born on 22 October 1888), although when reporting the birth Ada dutifully recorded Waite's occupation as that of 'poet'.

As more books and commissioned articles were published and Waite became involved with journalism proper, their circumstances improved and they moved away from furnished rooms, taking a house at Hornsey and then, in 1891, purchasing Eastlake Lodge, a large semi-detached house in Harvard Road, Gunnersbury. It was a suitable home for a poet, being on the edge of the consciously *avant-garde* community of Bedford Park; it was also within easy reach of East Molesey and the Stuart-Menteaths—which proved just as well, for early in 1892,

> Lucasta and I had fallen desperately ill, with a bout of influenza as it was in those old days, when the complaint was first generally described by that name. For a whole month we could scarcely move or speak, while Sybil also was in bed, with a recurring attack of so-called continued fever. There is no question that Evelyn Stuart-Menteth saved our three lives, nursing us day and night, hardly taking off her clothes and sleeping anywhere to insure proximity, because of our hourly needs (*SLT*, p. 129).

Evelyn was, in fact, the *only* practical member of the Stuart-Menteath household. A somewhat beefy young woman, she was a competent artist who illustrated three of Waite's books and designed the covers for a number of others.

As with all of Granville's children (including Ludivina, his daughter by Dora) she remained unmarried and her only memorial is the figure of the Dragon in *Belle and the Dragon*, Waite's curious fairy tale—a 'ludibrium' he called it—about the Stuart-Menteath family ('The Ravens of Ravendale') and their doings at Toftrees. Central to the story is the desire of the heroine Melusine (Dora) to become a 'great poetess' in the manner of the Mystic (Waite); and what she achieved in fiction she achieved also in fact. Or so it seemed.

In December 1894 the *Pall Mall Gazette* described a recently published poem as 'a work of real merit and genuine poetical feeling', and *The Tablet*, in May 1895, praised the same poem for its 'word-pictures, often of considerable beauty'. What they were praising was *Avalon: a poetic Romance*, ostensibly by Dora Stuart-Menteath but in reality almost entirely written by Waite himself—as might have been guessed from the tone of other, less precious reviews: the *Glasgow Herald* called it 'a high-toned, high-coloured, excessively wordy, and wearily-preachy performance', while *Church Bells* saw only that 'a slender streamlet of poetry trickles through monotonous sands of superfluous verbiage'. Dora's contribution to the work cannot be identified as the manuscript is entirely in Waite's hand, but the prefatory 'Argument' could have been written by no one save Waite.[10]

Avalon is the story of an alchemist—representing the earthly man—who seeks the elixir of life and dies in the quest, while his daughter—who stands for the Soul—follows her successful quest of Spiritual Love. From Waite's 'Argument' it is also obvious ('clear' would be a quite inappropriate word) that the heroine, Angela, is also Dora:

> She is also the higher womanhood in search of the higher manhood, typified by Arthur. Arthur in one aspect represents the archetypal man, the divine pattern from which the race has defected, and in this sense he is not wounded, but in another he is the inner greatness of humanity which is wounded by the imperfection of mankind. Under either aspect he is now withdrawn and unmanifest, abiding in restful, spritual Avalon, the world of the within. The love of Angela for the hidden King is the desire of Psyche after Pneuma. The Holy Grail is the divine principle of healing, by which man is made whole. And this can be love alone, but it is love spiritualised, elevated, and directed to perfection. So is the gift sought without by Angela in reality to be found within, whence she attains it in vision only, or otherwise in the inner world. And the true manhood, the archetype, the divine pattern is within also, and so Arthur is likewise reached in vision (pp. vi–vii).

All concerned knew that the poem was not Dora's but Waite maintained the public deception and only once, in 1931 when he thought of reprinting it, did he refer to it in his diary, and then as 'the old concealed poem'. With the poem in print Dora was, for the moment, content.

And during these years Machen, too was content. Happily married to Amy and lifted from poverty by legacies from his Scottish relatives, he could write in earnest—much for the journals, including Waite's *Unknown World*, but little for the publishers until *The Great God Pan* in 1894 and *The Three Impostors* in the following year. These stories of corrupting evil were a great success with the *avant garde* but were attacked by reviewers of the establishment as unwholesome and degenerate. Waite received a copy of each book as a matter of course, but Dora also read and enjoyed *The Three Impostors*, presumably enjoying the idea of outlandish and improbable adventures in prosaic London streets. In due course she, Waite, and Machen would have their own adventures in those same streets; less improbable adventures, admittedly, but decidedly unconventional.

The prelude to them came in the form of a tragedy. Machen's wife was never in good health and in 1894 her illness was diagnosed as cancer; she grew steadily weaker until in the summer of 1899 she died. Machen's grief was not lessened by its being expected and was so intense that he could never after bring himself to write directly about Amy's death. Even Waite says of it only that 'she was reconciled to the Latin Church—that of her childhood—before she passed away', and this to Machen's 'great satisfaction' (*SLT*, p. 156). Her dying is recorded more poignantly by Jerome:

> The memory lingers with me of the last time I saw his wife. It was a Sunday afternoon. They were living in Verulam Buildings, Gray's Inn, in rooms on the ground floor. The windows looked out on to the great quiet garden, and the rooks were cawing in the elms. She was dying, and Machen, with two cats under his arm, was moving softly about, waiting on her. We did not talk much. I stayed there till the sunset filled the room with a strange purple light (*My Life and Times*, p. 116).

Machen was supported in his dereliction by Waite. He had not sought help, but Waite recognized the need and the coming change in Machen:

> Amy was older than her husband by quite a few years, and much as he felt her loss there is a not unreal sense in which—consciously or unconsciously—it acted as an open entrance to a new epoch. Another phase of life, almost a new world, was destined to unfold about him. He had been a man of comparatively few friends and seemed almost to envy me, or at least to wonder at my ever-widening circle of acquaintance. They seemed now to pour in upon him, and by no means solely because he had written the *Great God Pan*' (*SLT*, p. 156).

These 'friends' came through Waite, but not until Machen had passed from a state of shock in the immediate aftermath of Amy's death to a state of dreadful despair: 'A horror of soul that cannot be uttered descended on me on that dim, far-off afternoon in Gray's Inn; I was beside myself with dismay and torment; I could not endure my own being' (*Things Near and Far*, p. 134). To escape from this state Machen put his theoretical knowledge of occultism to practical use, and after using a 'process' that seems to have been some sort of magical auto-hypnosis ('I may tell you that the process which suggested itself was Hypnotism; I can say no more'[11]), he achieved 'a sort of rapture of life which has no parallel that I can think of, which has, therefore, no analogies by which it may be made more plain' (*Things Near and Far*, p. 137).

Perhaps he found the 'process' in Waite's *Book of Black Magic* of 1898, for Waite might almost have had Machen in mind when he wrote:

> It would, however, be unsafe to affirm that all persons making use of the ceremonies in the Rituals would fail to obtain results. Perhaps in the majority of cases most of such experiments made in the past were attended with results of a kind. To enter the path of hallucination is likely to insure hallucination, and in the presence of hypnotic and clairvoyant facts it would be absurd to suppose that the seering processes of Ancient Magic—which are many—did not produce seership, or that the auto-hypnotic state which much magical ritual would obviously tend to occasion in predisposed persons did not frequently induce it, and not always only in the predisposed. To this extent some of the processes are practical, and to this extent they are dangerous (p. vii).

The danger in Machen's case he fully recognized and averted it by steering him into the relatively harmless waters of the Hermetic Order of the Golden Dawn. The story of the Golden Dawn is reserved for a later chapter and here it is enough to recount Machen's reaction to it.

He was initiated into the Order, as Frater Avallaunius, on 21 November 1899—the last member to have had the original form of the Order's 'Obligation' administered to him—and progressed to the Grade of Practicus, at which point he stopped. Nothing within the Order seemed of value to him and he found that it 'shed no ray of any kind on my path', but Waite had done his work well: Machen had pulled back from the destructive path of Black Magic and would soon leave all of occultism for a new career on the stage.

He had also met within the confines of the Golden Dawn 'a dark young man, of quiet and retiring aspect, who wore glasses' and who told him 'a queer tale of the manner in which his life was in daily jeopardy' (*Things Near and Far*, p. 148): a living counterpart, to all intents, of the Young Man in Spectacles who figures so prominently in *The Three Impostors*. But even this extraordinary parallel between his real and his imaginary worlds faded from memory. In 1942, in his last letter to Waite, he remarked, apropos of the 'dark young man', 'I have no notion of whether he be alive or dead. I have forgotten his very name.' As it happened, the Young Man in Spectacles had died in 1939: his name was W. B. Yeats.

8

FRATER AVALLAUNIUS AND 'THE ROAD OF EXCESS'

MACHEN'S sojourn in the Golden Dawn lasted no more than twelve months and came to an end shortly before January 1901, when he exchanged theatrical rituals for the Theatre and began his eight-year association with the Shakespearean repertory company of the distinguished actor-manager F. R. Benson, to whom he had been introduced by Christopher Wilson, the company's musical director.[1] Almost immediately he discovered that magic was not so easily left behind, for he was called upon to provide a conjuration for one of the company's productions at Stratford. He appealed for help to Waite, who promptly obliged by compiling a 'Conjuration to be used in Theatres' of some one hundred words of Latin gibberish—although he had no idea for which play it was required (in fact, *Henry VI, Part 2*). Waite noted in his diary (11 April 1901) that 'Bensonian magic is preposterous, for the operator is caused, despite all precedent & ignoring all dangers to stand outside the circle. F[rater] Avallanius burning to have the Black Art performed satisfactorily has set himself to remedy the mischief of all this ignorance, and hence this request.' He added, complacently, that his own conjuration 'has the merit of being much wickeder than the Grimoires, for Black Magic, as I have already shown, is not nearly so black as it is painted'.

It is doubtful if Machen spoke the conjuration himself in 1901 as he is not known to have played the part of Bolingbroke the Conjuror until he took it up as his final role before leaving the Benson Company in 1909. At that time, he told Oliver Stonor in 1932, 'I wrote three or four pages of high class incantation, with matters not generally known contained therein'. If he had kept Waite's conjuration it was, no doubt, included.

Machen did not tour with Benson all year and every year; he often played in smaller companies in and around London, so that Waite, who was now working in the City, saw him frequently. They met usually at the Café de l'Europe, where they drank in the company of Christopher Wilson, The Shepherdess (Vivienne Pierpont, the actress), and others of Machen's Bohemian friends, some of whom had been enrolled by him into the 'Rabelaisian Order of Tosspots'. This curious society had been created by Machen at Stratford in April 1901 (under the Welsh name of 'Sasiwn Curw Dda') with the rather unnecessary aim of encouraging his fellow Bensonians to drink. It was not restricted to actors—although only founding members could assume the title of Lords Maltworm[2]—and Machen was anxious for Waite to join; so much so that Waite was made a member a mere two days after first hearing of the Order. On 6 October 1902 he was given the official name of Master Basil, the honorary title of Lord Tosspot, and the role of archivist of the Order; as befitted a drinking society the minutes he kept were both scrappy and all but illegible.

In addition to the 'Rules and Reasons' of his Rabelaisian Order, Machen had devised a ritual for what he termed 'Hermetic Marriage'—a disreputable parody of the marriage service that he reserved for the amusement of his more intimate friends: Waite, the Shepherdess, Christopher Wilson, and an unidentified actress whom they called 'the Page Bertholde'. Waite says that the Hermetic Marriages 'took place incontinently with no banns or preaching, and independent of the consent or knowledge of the parties', and he told Machen that his 'Rite of Hermetic Marriage was a Rite of Belial, at which he made much ado' (Diary, 13 and 17 October 1902). All this was said, of course, with his tongue in his cheek—where it presumably remained when he transcribed the ritual and added his own comments.

'The Hermetic Ritual of Frater Avallaunius'[3] seems to have been a series of Latin versicles and responses, accompanied by much drinking; but Waite's manuscript is illegible to such a degree that it is difficult to decipher the verses, although his comments, giving parallels from Kabbalistic sources, can be read. 'The use of the chalice', he says, 'belongs to a recondite order of infernal symbolism. It is not merely the affirmation of two principles in the Atziluth world but in a veiled yet discernible manner it propounds the frightful doctrine that the masculine principle emanates from the good principle and the feminine from the evil principle. It is in fact, the occult theory of monosexualism based on a blasphemous distortion of the sacred text.'

Succeeding verses involve further distortions and blasphemies—not, however, to be taken seriously. He sums up the Rite in this way:

> The rite puts asunder what God has joined together. It then unites them in a bond of defiance to the command that they should fill the Earth. It takes the male from the female and the female from the male and then promises a spiritual union between the female parts with the suggestion or the inference that there is a more fruitful union still possible between their male parts.

If the words had been translated into literal deeds it would have been an extremely curious rite.

Machen and Waite, however, were both very much concerned with female partners. Long before the advent of Machen's 'Hermetic Marriage'—probably in 1900—Waite had introduced Dora to Vivienne Pierpont and persuaded her to join them for their drinking evenings at the Café de l'Europe. Dora was far from unwilling to escape from Molesey and the ageing Granville and the four set out to enjoy themselves. How they did so is told in a highly cryptic fashion in *The House of the Hidden Light*, an extraordinary book written jointly by Machen and Waite.

No work of either author has been the subject of so much eccentric speculation and ill-informed comment as has this one, largely because very few people have ever been able to see it. Only three copies were printed (of which two only, together with a set of corrected proofs, have survived): one each for Machen and Waite and one for Philip Wellby, Waite's friend and publisher. Of those few who *have* seen the book, Adrian Goldstone and Wesley Sweetser, Machen's bibliographers, believed it to have been issued for members of the Golden Dawn—as did Gerald Yorke, who owned the copy they saw, and W. R. Semken, a friend of Waite's who had read Waite's copy. They were all mistaken, but not to the extent of Ithell Colquhoun, who gave a long, ignorantly learned analysis of the book in *Sword of Wisdom*, her biography of S. L. McGregor Mathers. In the course of this analysis she argued that the names in the book were applied to offices rather than to individuals and concluded that the text concerned, in part, 'sexual congress with praeternatural beings' (p. 288). An entertaining point of view, no doubt, but far from the truth. Speculation on what Miss Colquhoun would have made of Machen's 'Hermetic Ritual' gives one considerable pause for thought.

The text of the *House of the Hidden Light* is in the form of thirty-five letters between Filius Aquarum (Machen) and Elias Artista (Waite), preceded by 'The Pastoral' (Waite's introduction), and two analyses of the letters, 'The Aphorisms and Maxims of the Secret Mystery' and 'The Versicles and Responses of the Secret Order'. The letters are all headed with fantastic, allegorical addresses—'From a Valley of the Shadow', 'From the Passes of the East', 'Under a New Star in Serpentarius'—and the whole work is written in a mock-antiquated style, deliberately and misleadingly verbose. It is yet possible, by a conscious and considerable effort of will, to penetrate to the meaning of the book as it is set out in 'The Pastoral':

> Wherefore two brothers, hereby and herein, having been advanced, by a glorious and singular dispensation, a certain distance through the degrees of a true experience, have, with deep affection and humility, assumed an office of admonishment, firstly, one to another, and afterwards, by reason of the great, increasing urgency, to such of the great concourse of the elect as in this present have been born out of due time with the ears to hear. And hence it is that there is undertaken in the manner hereafter following such a declaration of the Light as has seemed possible, opportune, needful and making for salvation to many. Yet, being pledged to one another and to the Greater Masters, that they should not speak openly, because such gifts are to other some unseasonable, they have written after the manner of the Philosphers with a prudent

affectation of the letter, so that these things are to be understood only by the appeal to a second sense, which, for the increase of facility, has been made to interpenetrate rather than underlie the outward meaning (pp. 9–10).

It is then explained that 'two poor brothers of the spirit [Waite and Machen] conceived between them the ambition to get on in the world by a right ordering of the mind in respect of the real interests and true objects of life. They excogitated these schemes in such taverns by the way as were to them open, and it was given them in due time to see that the path of their advancement towards such success as would include them among the men who have risen, lay chiefly in seeing the Dawn; which duty became henceforth a matter of daily practice . . .' (p. 11).

'After such fashion then began the *Annus Mirabilis* or great year of sorcery, full of rites and questings'.

And then there were the ladies.

At this time also there were given unto them two sisters, daughters of the House of Life, for high priestesses and ministers . . . These were children of the elements, queens of fire and water, full of inward magic and of outward witchery, full of music and song, radiant with the illusions of Light. By them the two brothers were served and refected so long as they were proselytes of the gate, postulants at the door of the temple, dwellers on the threshold, waiting to be passed, raised, exalted, installed and enthroned. And the two brothers proceeded through many sub-grades of the Secret Order of the Dawn, the purgations and perlustrations of magic, till the *Annus Mirabilis* ended (pp. 12–13).

But what followed was the removal of the sisters and the two 'poor brothers' were obliged to fall back upon their own company and to console themselves with drink, 'the mysteries and symbols of the Secret Order'.

Not that any of it is put so plainly. Only the authors' closest friends knew that 'Soror Benedicta in Aqua' was Dora Stuart-Menteath, and that 'Soror Ignis Ardens' (or 'Ignis ex Igne')—'whom we have called Lilith because she is a "soft, sweet woman"'—was Vivienne Pierpont. And even those close friends would not have recognized the ambiguity of Waite's reverie in Letter XIII:

Old are those legends of the soul, gone is that early minister, received into the great silence and reserved therein until the day when the *Sponsus* and *Sponsa* shall meet in the King's chamber, in the secret palace of the King, when I also shall kiss the one mouth which I have desired since the days of my baptism in the cool waters of the kingdom, even the kingdom of love (p. 82).

Nonetheless, it is Dora who is the central character in the letters—Machen's as well as Waite's. The first letter of the series, written by Machen, is from 'A Tarrying Place of the Fraternity' (in fact, Gambino's in Rupert Street), and it sets the tone of all those that follow: 'I announce to you that on Monday next I shall solemnly perform and exhibit the Veritable, Ancient, and Rectified Rite of [Lilith] which is called [lamed] in the Great Book of Avalon. Be, therefore, present without fail between nones and vespers, that then we may partake together of these singular mysteries' (p. 33). Machen ends the letter by urging Waite to bring Dora with him: 'I look forward to this coming *Dies Dominica*, and trust that you will command the Lady of the Waters to attend, that she may put on with us new vestments' (p. 36).

Much of the text is repetitious and tedious for the outsider, but it provides insights into Waite's state of mind at the time. This 'Secret Order' was evidently more important than the Golden Dawn: 'Let us confess that there was nothing in the grades and rituals of the old order, by which we were exalted during that *Annus Mirabilis*, that could be called a greater rite than our *Soror Ignis Ardens* has but now administered' (p. 75). Elsewhere he reflects gloomily that 'There is also some letting and hindering which forbids us to visit the Waste House amidst the waters, where dwells the Lady of the Water' (p. 55), while Machen hopes 'that to you the *Benedicta* of years past may return, but crowned with a most heavenly sweetness' (p. 110). But Waite knows that the adventures with Dora and the Shepherdess cannot last and must come to an inevitable end:

Meanwhile, this is the passing of Lilith and of the Lady of the Water. The *Soror Gloriosa in Igne* has taken her way into the South under a golden canopy . . . The *Soror Benedicta in Aqua* has gone into the West, far over fords and marshes, and the great mists conceal her. She has heard the voices of the sea. It has come to pass, even as I foretold, for we are called above the region of the elements, where these children cannot follow us (pp. 166–7).

At the end of this letter, number XXXIII, is an illuminating footnote: 'At this point it must be understood that certain records were destroyed.' Evidently caution was required.

Waite was not always so discreet about his relations with Dora. In a letter of 1936 Machen reminded him of one embarrassing occasion:

'All so good together'—I remember your comment on that text, 'Does she mean that time when we sat up all night drinking port, with Menteth locked in his bedroom, till at 8 o'clock in the morning, the housemaid came into the room, just as she fell on my neck and I said 'You drunken little cat!' [4]

And Philip Wellby talked too freely when, as was too often the case, he was in his cups: 'The sister Melusine is quarrelling with me because of the scandals and fooling and gabbling of my unfortunate Philip. Philip drunk or Philip sober—it is difficult to say which of these is the greater calamity' (Diary, 29 November 1902). Waite also suspected that Wellby knew altogether too much, and noted some weeks later: 'My Philip has been drawing a suspect trail over some of my secret ways' (Diary, 21 December 1902). But his secret ways were already in the past, for whatever took place between Waite and Dora it came to an end in August that year.

In 1928 a young friend of Machen's, Colin Summerford, sent him an account of a visit he had made to the Stuart-Menteaths at East Molesey; in his reply Machen explained that, for Waite, 'the Rite of Molesey was voided, the sanctuary stripped and bare, the lamps extinguished, and the Relics taken away into a deep concealment'. All of which had happened on 9 August 1902, when,

> it is related, with due veils and concealments, that on the morning of the Coronation of our Sovereign Lord, King Edward of happy memory, seventh of that name since the Conquest, Mrs Menteith came out of Gray's Inn at about eight of the morning, and was seen to get into a four wheeler. And, indeed, (και δα και) it is declared by Waite *that she never got out of it*; that a mere simulacrum and appearance arrived at Molesey; that the word was lost; and that a mere substituted word took its place.[5]

'But', he added, 'these are sacred matters.' There was no more to be said.

Waite and Dora still met and there were regular family Christmases at Polruan, but both the *Annus Mirabilis* (which ended in 1901) and its aftermath were over. Their relationship, while always affectionate, was now more practical, for Waite was a trustee of the Leamington Trust—which provided the Stuart-Menteath income—and he dealt with the financial affairs that neither Dora nor the hopelessly impractical Granville could manage. After Waite moved to Ramsgate in 1920 there were fewer visits to East Molesey; in October 1925 he spent a day at Toftrees for the first time in five years: 'Dora is withered', he noted in his diary, 'but she is still Dora.'

The letters that built up into *The House of the Hidden Light* were written in 1902 but referred to events of the previous year, with occasional references to more recent episodes. Waite began to edit them in January 1903, Machen having 'surrendered to me all the editing with power to cancel all passages in his own letters which are too intimate in character' (Diary, 5 January 1903). It was not an easy task, for at least one letter was missing and had to be 'invented'. To Waite's surprise Machen made no objection, indeed 'it may seem impossible, but he proposed that I should forge it, the power having passed away from him; and to have it at all, it may well be that I shall be brought to this pass' (Diary, 30 January 1903). The letter was duly forged and with the work 'now ready for the press' Waite took it to Wellby, who was anxious to see the book before it was taken elsewhere ('but', wrote Waite, 'I doubt if there *is* an elsewhere'), and once he had seen the manuscript he was eager 'to publish it with the full consciousness that it would be a signal commercial failure' (Diary, 18 March 1903).

It was, of course, commercially impossible and there was the added complication that Wellby recognized Dora—much to her distress and Waite's annoyance—in the character of 'Soror Benedicta in Aqua'. Eventually in 1904 the book was printed in an edition limited to three copies; an expensive conceit, but fully justified as far as Waite and Machen were concerned because of the glorious nature of the *Annus Mirabilis*—and because Philip Wellby was footing the bill.

After Dora, Waite contented himself with more respectable revels among Machen's 'Tosspots' and other Bohemians. In November 1902 David Gow, whom he had known for twenty years both as a poet and as an ardent spiritualist, introduced him to the Pen and Pencil Club, which met at the Napier Tavern in Holborn. Waite was struck by its similarity to the Rabelaisian Order of Tosspots: both had elaborate mock-serious rules and regulations, and both existed primarily to enable their members to drink in congenial company. At the Pen and Pencil Club, however, each member was required to write, draw, or compose something relevant to a chosen theme. Waite produced indifferent verses which were applauded, but he found the meeting far from convivial: 'For a long time we strained and smoked and looked one at another amidst aching spells of long silence broken by monosyllabic utterances and some freezing attempts at jocularity'. It was, at best, 'a dull evening with hot drinks which served to galvanise corpses' (Diary, 20 November 1902) but not to encourage frequent visits, and Waite's attendance at the Club was irregular. On one occasion he was surprised to find that a group of the members had all been asked—by different editors—to review his translation of *Obermann*; they discussed the book and in due course the reviews appeared. All were favourable. 'And these', remarked Waite, 'are the mysteries of reviewing.'[6]

Bored with the Pen and Pencil Club he joined Machen in creating 'The Sodality of the Shadows', which St John Adcock described as 'another unorthodox little club—a club of a dozen or so young writers who met periodically in a wine cellar in Queen Street, Cheapside, the vintner himself being a poet of no mean quality; an exclusive little club to which a new member was only admitted after he had subscribed to an elaborate, grotesquely solemn ritual which was prepared by Arthur Edward Waite' (*The Glory that was Grub Street*, p. 218). When it was formed he does not say (nor does Waite), but it was still flourishing in 1910.

In addition to the ritual, Waite was also responsible for 'The Laws of the Sodality', from which it is quite clear that it was not a club for the sober: 'The object of the Order is the Quest after the Drink which never was on land or sea', but 'It pursues this Quest by means of casual substitutes' (Laws XVIII and XIX). To ensure inebriety Law XXX stated that 'At ordinary meetings of the Sodality a General confession of Thirst shall be recited, and this invariably', while Law XXIX informed members that 'The Falling Sign is the lapse of any Member under the table, as to which: *Absit omen*.' Nor was the Sodality confined to men, for 'The Brothers of the Sodality are known generally as the People of the Shadow and their Sisters who are latent in the secret bosom of the Order are the Daughters of Night.'

The ritual was in twenty-two stages, following the letters of the Hebrew alphabet, and involved the ceremonial filling of a wine glass which was then 'sent round' the members while the 'Secret Maxims of the Order' were recited:

1. *Scriptum est*: The spirit indeed is willing, but the flesh is weak: hence inebriety.
2. *Traditum est*: Man in all ages has recognized by a keen instinct that his relations with the external universe are not of sufficient importance to encourage that total abstinence which maintains them in their natural order.
3. *Recordatus*: Sobriety is the least interesting of the virtues, but it is excellent as an antecedent of drinking.
4. *Memento, Fratres*: As regards the foundation of drink, which is said to be laid in alcohol, it is not so much the potation which is fatal as the vulgarity which surrounds it.
5. *Audivimus*: The black list is local and temporal, but inebriety is eternal.
6. *Et nos quoque*: He who confesses to true thirst asks for the waters of life.
7. *Tu autem*: The highest maxim of all is to drink freely, but the wise man avoids the Waters of Marah.

St John Adcock had presumably listened to these awesome maxims, but who were the other 'People of the Shadow' remains unknown.

Machen also had settled down, for after the *Annus Mirabilis* he had met and, in June 1903, married Dorothy Purefoy Hudleston. He told Waite about her, in a somewhat guarded manner, shortly before Christmas of 1902, but they did not meet until the following March. Waite found Purefoy to be 'Pleasant and nice. She drinks absinthe, smokes when she dares, has no conventions and requires none, takes no exception to the qualifications of Bohemian language, is something of an actress, and wishes [to be] a gentlewoman.' He added that 'I have great hopes for her, although she loves not the Latin tongue' (Diary, 14 March 1903).

Waite did not attend the wedding but was a frequent visitor to the Machens' home at 5 Cosway Street, St Marylebone. He and Machen argued as fiercely as ever over the Holy Grail and all the other subjects that delighted them; but the Grail was important enough to both of them for willing co-operation, not only over Waite's critical study, *The Hidden Church of the Holy Graal* (for which Machen supplied the material on the Celtic Church), but also over a Grail Romance.

The verse drama 'The Hidden Sacrament of the Holy Graal' was printed in Waite's *Strange Houses of Sleep* (1906) with a cryptic prefatory note:

> The initial design of this Mystery Play is referable to a friend and fellow-worker in the mysteries, who, for the present, remains anonymous. The collaboration also embraces a portion of the text, but outside the archaic touch which is occasionally common to each, it is thought that the respective shares will be readily allocated to their proper writers in the virtue of a certain distinction of style (p. 140).

The 'friend and fellow-worker' was, of course, Machen who, in addition to the interpolated drinking-songs, provided the detailed stage directions that would have defeated Waite. He also tried to persuade Frank Benson to produce the play, as he told Waite in a letter:

> Also find herewith a brief acknowledgment from Benson. I shall be curious to learn what he proposes to make of our masterpiece. You see he calls it *my* play: of course I told him that it was our joint labour. In any case, I feel certain that he will not give an order to his wardrobe master for the making of seven dalmatics of red silk—to say nothing of a set of red episcopal vestments. It would be *possible* of course to dress the seven as Eastern Deacons—albs and red stoles—but I should prefer dalmatics (20 September 1904).

It would have been a startling departure for a Shakespearean company.

Their lives, by 1908, were beginning to separate. Machen took up journalism and Fleet Street just as Waite was leaving the City and settling down again to the precarious life of an author. He was also increasingly preoccupied with his 'Independent and Rectified Rite' of the Golden Dawn (of which both Machen and Purefoy, albeit briefly, had been members) and was suffering from the gradual onset of a staid middle age. But they were friends always and could still find time to argue by post and to drink together when they met, even if it was not always for the best—as Machen reminded Waite in 1941:

> Many long years ago, as you sat at your board in Ealing, I remember your filling a small glass—a 'pony' glass I think they called it—with whiskey in its purity, which you thereupon drank. You considered the matter judicially for a short while, and then gave sentence: 'This does me no good, Machen' (letter, 17 September 1941).

When mixed with argument it was even worse, as on the 'glorious occasion' described by Machen's son, Hilary, when 'overcome by some knotty point in the Kabbalah, he [Waite] sat in the fireplace—fortunately it was summer—and Purefoy my mother said "Get up, you old fool: you're drunk"'[7] Joyous for quite different reasons, it was like that 'Grande Trouvaille' in Pentonville: 'an occasion'.

But it would be quite wrong to see Waite as a libertine and carouser; he enjoyed the company of Machen and his Bohemian friends, but he never allowed his indulgences to control him. It would have been singularly inappropriate if he had, for as the *Annus Mirabilis* opened he was settling in to the post of manager for James Horlick, the manufacturer of that most innocuous of drinks, malted milk.

9

'NOT VERSE NOW, ONLY PROSE'

'DO *anything* rather than attempt to live by literature', Browning had urged Waite in 1876, but it was not easy for an eager young poet to follow such sober advice, and it became doubly difficult after 1878 when he reached the age of twenty-one and was admitted to the Reading Room of the British Museum Library. There, for five years—except for interludes by the sea—Waite busied himself with alchemy, theology, magic (in the guise of Eliphas Lévi), mythology, astronomy, and poetry; reading, annotating, and dreaming. But while the Reading Room gave him the appearance of a polymath it did not give him an income. He could not live for ever on dwindling legacies and on the goodwill of his mother, and as there *was* no 'anything' to which he could turn his hand, writing for pleasure must needs become writing for profit.

Waite's first foray into commercial journalism was a short piece on *Some Sacred Trees*, published in *Chambers' Journal* for August 1884, but that was anonymous and his first signed article did not appear until the following December when *The Gentleman's Magazine* printed his highly professional essay on Richard Lovelace, the cavalier poet (an essay, it may be noted, that was utilized in 1930 by C. H. Wilkinson for his Introduction to the standard Oxford edition of Lovelace's poems). There were other essays for *Young Folks' Paper*, but writing for the journals produced little by way of income. Something more substantial was needed—there must be books, but not poetry, for they must also be books for which the author would be paid, rather than be obliged to pay the publisher himself.

One book was already in progress by 1884: an anthology, in English, of Eliphas Lévi, the French occultist whose works had fascinated Waite since he first discovered them some three years before. Lévi had also been a source of inspiration for Madame Blavatsky, and there was thus a potential market for such an anthology among the growing number of English Theosophists, with whom Waite was already at home. He was by this time a regular, if uncommitted, visitor to the London Lodge of the Theosophical Society where he became friendly with the vice-president, A. P. Sinnett,[1] the former editor of the Allahabad *Pioneer*.

Sinnett had returned from India in 1883 after losing his post because of his intemperate promotion of the Theosophical cause in the columns of his newspaper. By 1885, however, disenchantment with the Theosophical Society, arising from the extremely hostile Hodgson Report of the Society for Psychical Research,[2] had led to a decline in both numbers and frequency of meetings in the London Lodge, and the venue was changed from Queen Anne's Mansions to a room at No. 15, York Street, Covent Garden. This was above the shop and offices of George Redway, 'a publisher in a small way of business whom I [Sinnett]—at that time in possession of means—subsidised with a view of stimulating his attention to publications of a theosophical character' (Sinnett, *The Early Days of Theosophy in Europe*, p. 82). Redway had commenced publishing in 1883, having previously worked for the old firm of Rivingtons and the newer house of Vizetelly, and maintained a miscellaneous list before Sinnett's money encouraged him to specialize in books dealing with the occult. These he also sold through his parallel occupation of secondhand bookseller, and when the young Arthur Machen came to work for him in 1885 his first task was to compile a 48-page catalogue of *The Literature of Archaeology and the Occult* (Machen worked at the catalogue in a garret over Vizetelly's premises in Catherine Street).

As the translation of Lévi—a 'digest' rather than an anthology—took shape Waite discussed it with Sinnett, who suggested Redway as a publisher and encouraged Waite to approach him:

> I must have prepared a synopsis after some manner and interviewed my publisher to come, with such results that I carried away from a second visit a very formal Agreement—signed, sealed and delivered. It was taken forthwith to Somerset House and there was duly stamped. I can remember to this day the satisfaction with which it was borne through the Strand and Fleet Street. I had been admitted in authentic wise among the Company of Letters—a child at heart, a child also in experience, but with hopes that knew no bounds (*SLT*, p. 97).

Waite remembered this as happening in 1885, but in this he was mistaken, for *The Mysteries of Magic* was not published until December 1886 and the introductory 'critical and biographical essay' could not have been written more than a few months earlier, for as an unkind reviewer noted, '*The Theosophist* for January 1886 seems to have furnished most of the material for the biographical part'.[3]

Nonetheless, the book was a modest success and was followed first by *A Soul's Comedy* and then by Waite's first full-length book on the occult, *The Real History of the Rosicrucians*. This had been inspired by Hargrave Jennings's *The Rosicrucians, their Rites and Mysteries*, a worthless book that Waite had already attacked, in *Walford's Antiquarian Magazine*, in an article and in a savage review of a newly issued 'third edition'. His own study was historical, objective, and generally sound, although occultists resented it because 'Mr Waite's new book will be welcomed by that large class of readers who regard occultism, alchemy, and all like studies with antagonism and suspicion'. (In this assumption they were quite correct; the reviewer in *Nature* praised it precisely because it was 'free from all attempts at the distortion of facts to dovetail with a preconceived theory'.[4])

The principal fault of the book lies in the clear signs of hasty writing. Waite was well aware of this: 'Later on I wished often enough that it could have been held back for a period; but Redway was in a great hurry, and it was sent bit by bit to the printer and set as I wrote it, without a rough copy and with only my old notes to guide me on the path that I was travelling. "The artist might have taken more pains", said the clement *Saturday Review*, alluding to an unfortunate confusion between Eirenaeus and Eugenius Philalethes. Assuredly he might have done it throughout, had he stood a reasonable chance' (*SLT*, p. 102).

Hurried Redway might have been, but he knew what the public wanted and it was he who, at the last minute, altered the title: 'on the eve almost of publication my simply and soberly entitled *History of the Rosicrucians*—as the left headlines make evident—was changed on the title-page to the *Real History*, too late for any protest on my own part' (*SLT*, p. 101). But not too late for protest by others. Both the title and the cover design (a deliberate copy of that used on earlier editions of Jennings's work) were intended to set the book against *The Rosicrucians their Rites and Mysteries*—devices that enraged Hargrave Jennings, who had expected better from the publisher of his own book on *Phallicism*. When he next met Redway, in Pall Mall, he shrieked at him, '*Et tu, Bruté*!' Perhaps he gained some belated satisfaction from a note in *Light* (16 February 1889) which recorded that in fifteen months only 720 copies of the *Real History* had been sold.

Other books followed. In 1888 Redway issued Waite's expanded edition of the *Lives of Alchemystical Philosophers* (it had first appeared in 1815), and his collection of *The Magical Writings of Thomas Vaughan*, following these in 1889 with the pseudonymous (and worthless) *Handbook of Cartomancy* by 'Grand Orient'. This was a reworking of an American fortune-telling manual of 1865—*Future Fate foretold by the Stars*—supplemented by material from other popular books on divination that Waite found among Redway's secondhand stock. Later editions of the *Handbook*—renamed *The Manual of Cartomancy*—are greatly enlarged and far more portentous; but in every edition Waite wisely refrained from placing his name on the title-page.

During 1889 he also took up what he called 'my first excursion in journalism properly so called': a four-month stint at writing *The Course of Events*, a regular social and political gossip-column of home news for *The Civil and Military Gazette* of Lahore. This was usually undertaken by A. P. Sinnett as part of his duties as manager of the joint London office of the *Gazette* and the *Pioneer*, but for that summer he was absent from London and Waite volunteered to write the column on his behalf. 'I have', he later remarked, 'dark recollections of its burden.' The burden, moreover, was about to be increased.

Sinnett was always willing to put money into new publishing ventures, and in 1884 he had helped Horatio Bottomley[5]—then at a very early stage of his career as a financial adventurer—to establish *The Debator*, a journal which recorded the proceedings of 'local parliaments' (debating societies modelled on the procedures of the House of Commons). This was followed in 1885 by the 'Catherine Street Publishing Association', an amalgamation of Bottomley's publishing concern with a number of printers in Catherine Street. Sinnett became a director, brought in the publisher Kegan Paul, and in 1889 took the first step towards Bottomley's grandiose design of a vast printing and publishing empire by absorbing Redway. Bottomley succeeded in outbidding William Heinemann for the firm of Trübner & Co., whose oriental list was highly lucrative, and the enlarged Association tendered for—and secured—the contract for printing *Hansard's Parliamentary Debates*.

The immediate outcome of all this was the formation of the Hansard Publishing Union Ltd., a vast consortium that aimed to combine under one head every operation of the publishing world from paper-making and printing to publishing and distribution. The initial share capital of £500,000 was over-subscribed and for a time the company flourished, but when a second share issue of half a million pounds was launched within a year, rumours of Bottomley's financial deviousness were already circulating and little of it was taken up. Worse problems were to follow. A Debenture Corporation received none of the interest on the £250,000 of capital it had underwritten and promptly put in a Receiver; Bottomley himself filed a petition for bankruptcy in May 1891, and soon afterwards he was indicted, with his fellow directors, on charges of fraud. But all of this was in the undreamed future when Redway ceased to be Redway and Waite found himself at a loose end. And just as Sinnett had taken away his publisher, so Sinnett now hauled him out of the pit of enforced idleness.

Among the journals published by the Catherine Street Publishing Association was *The British Mail*, a monthly that professed to be a 'Journal of the Chambers of Commerce of the United Kingdom' but was also, in February 1889, without an editor. To Waite's great astonishment, Sinnett offered him the post. That Waite knew nothing of journalism seemed not to matter, for when he pointed this out Sinnett told him that: 'the responsibilities were light enough as the periodical appropriated without acknowledgement anything that came its way. The issues were simply made up by borrowing from current printed sources'—something that would not be expected to bother the putative author of *The Handbook of Cartomancy*, and as it turned out, 'the practice was evidently condoned on all sides, for during the two and a half years that I produced the honourable organ no word of reproach or accusation ever reached me, though a baker's dozen of copyright actions might have arisen every month. The Offices of the *British Mail* were in Catherine Street, Strand, and so far as journalism was concerned my days went quietly enough, with no particular hours attached thereto. The columns were relieved of their robberies by original notices of new inventions and reports of exhibitions, the Grocers', the Brewers', and so forth, at the Agricultural Hall, and the Photographic at the Crystal Palace' (*SLT*, p. 121).

Waite's position was further improved by the friendship he struck up with James Elliott, the husband of Mrs Bottomley's sister. Elliott, impressed by Waite's ability, praised him extravagantly to Bottomley and further editorial work—at a 'liberal salary'—was heaped upon Waite in the form of regular reviews of 'The Magazines' for *The Galignani Messenger* and the effective editorship, in 1891, of *The Municipal Review*. This last was much after the manner of *The British Mail* but concerned almost exclusively with the affairs of local government. It also published biographies of assorted worthies, which included, under Waite's editorship, a flattering 'Municipal Portrait' of Frederick Horniman, with especial praise heaped upon his museum. It is tempting to think that this eulogy of her father encouraged Annie Horniman to look on Waite with favour when he entered the Golden Dawn later that year, but she is unlikely to have recognized Waite's hand, for contributors and editors alike of Bottomley journals remained anonymous.

Indeed, Waite cultivated anonymity to such an extent in *The British Mail* that in one issue, April 1890, he devoted four columns to an unsigned, mocking review of his own anonymous prospectus for *Azoth: or the Star in the East*—a book he had yet to write (it was eventually published in 1893). Similar oddities were a regular feature of *The British Mail*; when there was insufficient secondhand commercial and industrial news to fill an issue, Waite supplied essays of his own on such uncommercial topics as hypnotism, Freemasonry, philosophical idealism, the Rosicrucians, and astronomy (in which he maintained his early interest). In one issue he reviewed a privately printed volume of bad verse by a young man using the name 'Austin Blake': if the theft of his own pseudonym was irritating, it must also have been satisfying to realize that *A Soul's Comedy* had found at least one approving reader.

But in 1891 Bottomley fell and the Hansard Union collapsed, taking with it all the Bottomley journals (and Sinnett—the failure of the Union ruined him). Waite had only his fees for *The Occult Sciences* which was published in November 1891, and such royalties as still came in respect of earlier works; for the first time in his career he was *sans* publisher. The hiatus was not, however, long lasting. Waite amused himself by writing *The Parable of the Receiver and the Thief*, a partisan account of Bottomley's misfortunes, and early in 1892 commenced the correspondence with Lord Stafford that would lead to three years of editing and translating alchemical texts. There remained the problem of a publisher, but this too was solved in the person of James Elliott. Waite told him of Lord Stafford's wish to have the first translation, of Ruland's *Lexicon of Alchemy*, put into print:

> There began forthwith to be open vision and prophecies on his part of radiant days to come. The Hansard Union had crashed terribly, Elliott had nothing on hand, and if things were narrow with me they must have approached desperation in his case. He resolved at once to become an occult publisher, beginning with the already famous *Lexicon*. By hook or by crook he would see Lord Stafford; and my part in the business was (1) to raise a mortgage on Eastlake Lodge, for there must be money to start with and an office to give him a local habitation, from which letters could be written and expected business transacted; (2) to be prepared and to provide whatever was needed, for translating, editing and producing alchemical texts (*SLT*, p. 130).

The mortgage—of £250—was raised, an office was found at Temple Chambers, in Falcon Court, Fleet Street, and in March 1893 the firm of James Elliott & Co. published its first book, *The Hermetic Museum Restored and Enlarged*,[6] followed in rapid succession by five other alchemical translations, all commercially impossible and all underwritten by Lord Stafford. The *magnum opus* of the alchemical series, *The Hermetic and Alchemical World of Paracelsus*, appeared early in the following year, preceded by *Belle and the Dragon* and closely followed by *Avalon*. In effect, James Elliott & Co. existed for the sole purpose of disseminating the wit and wisdom of Arthur Edward Waite, as, apart from those already mentioned and three titles definitely not by Waite, its only publications were reissues of his earlier works and his ambitious 'High-class monthly magazine', *The Unknown World*.

The production of a non-sectarian occult journal (i.e. one that was not devoted solely to the glories of either Spiritualism or Theosophy) had long been one of Waite's dreams. In August 1894, after many delays not unconnected with the search for a printer who did not demand payment in advance for his work, the first issue appeared—embellished with a singularly hideous cover design, drawn under Waite's guidance by Evelyn Stuart-Menteath. (Waite, without conscious irony, later described it as 'amazing' and 'ever memorable'.) *The Unknown World* was intended to embrace all aspects of esoteric thought—'the whole circle of the occult sciences'—and in his first editorial Waite promised that the magazine

> will give the most clear information upon all these subjects in general, and as space and opportunity may allow, upon all their species and variations, while it will provide for the first time such information as can be reasonably and prudently given upon the extent to which they are followed, whether in speculation or practice, by individual investigators, or corporate occult bodies, at the present day.

And while it was to be eclectic—the editor recognized that the various occult movements of the day 'are not rival schools; they are developments in various directions, but they are not in contradiction to each other and they do not exclude each other'—it would lean especially towards 'the exposition of the profound philosophy of Western Mysticism' (*The Unknown World*, vol. i, pp. 2–3).

Among the contributors were Edward Maitland, busily promoting Anna

Kingsford's 'New Gospel of Interpretation'; the Revd G. W. Allen, urging with equal fervour the merits of his Christo-Theosophical Society; Dr E. W. Berridge, eulogizing Thomas Lake Harris and his 'Brotherhood of the New Life' (and hinting darkly, under other pseudonyms, at the awesome power of the Hermetic Order of the Golden Dawn); and Arthur Machen, whose story 'The Shining Pyramid' first appeared in *The Unknown World*. The magazine survived for eleven issues, but came to an abrupt halt when the money ran out. 'Was it forgotten', wondered Waite, 'that only the first instalment of the printer's bill had been paid as yet? So far as I am aware, Elliott kept no accounts, and I was guided only by the general trend of things. The fact remains that the magazine did not stop because itself a complete failure but because there was no money for Elliott to carry it on' (*SLT*, p. 141).

The end of *The Unknown World* coincided with the general collapse of James Elliott & Co., but at least one major debt was avoided. When he reprinted *The Shining Pyramid* in 1925, Machen told an entertaining story about the failure of the publishing house:

> There was, I believe, some difficulty in paying the rent due for the premises which they occupied. It was necessary to ask for a trifle of indulgence in this matter, and the firm wrote to this effect to their landlords, who occupied the lower part of the building.
>
> Now at this point two odd circumstances met together. The landlords were, in fact, an Evangelical society of the strictest Protestant principles. That was one circumstance. The other was this: the firm wrote their letter begging for a slight delay on 'Unknown World' letter paper, which displayed the magazine cover in miniature: a Pentacle of light, a strong Spirit proceeding from it, and, for all I remember, other apparatus of magic. And happy magic, indeed, resulted from this letter. The Evangelical society wrote in horror: they had never imagined that anything so dreadful was being done on their premises; they begged the publishers of 'The Unknown World' not to speak of a trifle of rent owing, but to go forthwith in God's name. And the publishers went with happy hearts (*The Shining Pyramid*, p. 8).

Waite's experiment in publishing had been eventful in other ways, too. In January 1893 the Hansard Union case had finally come to court and lasted until the end of April (with a two-months intermission, owing to the illness of a juryman). Bottomley and his fellow defendents were all acquitted, but while the case was in progress the offices of James Elliott & Co. acted as a kind of headquarters for the defence. It was a celebrated trial, but for this Waite cared nothing; all the coming and going meant only that his office 'was a place no longer in which I personally could edit and produce texts or correct the proofs which printers were pouring in'. The only consolation was the Spanish cigarettes he received from Joseph Isaacs, who, with his brother Sir Henry Isaacs (Rufus, the third brother, later Lord Reading, was not involved), was a co-defendent with Bottomley.

James Elliott & Co. had failed, but as always with Waite, 'another publisher rose up'. He was not financially pressed; his mother's small estate had passed to him after her death in 1893,[7] the mortgage on Eastlake Lodge had been redeemed, and the remaining stock of alchemical texts had been purchased by the bookseller Bernard Quaritch.[8] Even so, writing was Waite's only real source of income and he was greatly relieved when George Redway wrote to tell him that he had left Kegan Paul and set up in business once more, at Hart Street in Bloomsbury. Redway was as eager to publish Waite as Waite was to write for him, and they collaborated happily for four years from 1896 to 1899. During the first year Waite wrote *Devil-Worship in France*,[9] a topical exposé of the spurious anti-masonic rubbish then appearing in France, translated Lévi's *Transcendental Magic*, and persuaded Redway to issue the last of the alchemical translations, *The Turba Philosophorum*. In the succeeding years he issued a collection of James Braid's works on hypnosis, edited bad books into readable form, wrote *The Book of Black Magic and of Pacts* (Redway chose the title: he knew exactly how to appeal to the lowest instincts of the reading public), and saw his most ambitious book disappear in smoke and fire.

There had been, before Waite wrote his study, no reliable or substantial work in English on the Hebrew Kabbalah. But when *The Doctrine and Literature of the Kabalah* was written for Redway it proceded no further than the printer. The book had passed the proof stage and was in process of being printed when, on 9 December 1899, a disastrous fire at the premises of the Ballantyne Press destroyed the sheets and dissolved both the formes and the type; the same fire also destroyed *Green Alps*, a collection of erotic poetry by Aleister Crowley, but although each author still retained a set of proofs, Crowley let his lie in limbo, while Waite surrendered his to the Theosophical Publishing Society and saw the book printed afresh in 1902.

This, however, he did not do willingly, but as with Elliott, so with Redway. The publishing house had got into difficulties, Waite declined to put up money and Redway took himself off to South Africa to fight the Boers, leaving his firm in the hands of a Receiver. Shortly before this, and because of the non-appearance of both his Kabbalistic book and his study of Louis Claude de Saint-Martin, Waite had sold Eastlake Lodge to raise money and now had neither a publisher nor a home. But he did have a job.

From February 1898, for a period of some five years, both London and provincial newspapers were bombarded with a constant stream of brief 'paragraph announcements'—advertisements extolling the virtues of Horlick's Malted Milk. They recommended the drink as a cure for dyspepsia, malnutrition, and influenza, as a means of preventing tubercolosis, and as a specific to 'restore balance to deranged constitutions'. Malted Milk would give stamina to cyclists, restore overworked clergymen, business-men, and 'brain workers', and 'spread health instead of typhoid—which cannot always be said of cow's milk'. It was presented as a significant factor in winning the South African War, while those who did not drink it appeared to be in imminent danger of serious illness or death. One of the second series of 'paragraphs' is typical:

THE CHILD LOOKS LIKE A CHANGELING. It is quite shrunk and shrivelled; its eyes seem dim; its skin is clammy; it wails rather than cries. And it was such a bonny baby a few weeks back. What can have come over it? In a case like this you may be quite sure that the mischief lies in its food. Give it Horlick's Malted Milk, and you will soon find that it is not a changeling, but your own bonny baby once more. Horlick's Malted Milk is the best food for children in health and sickness. It has saved many little lives when they seemed past all medical aid. All like it, all thrive on it. Your chemist will supply it . . .

These advertisements had one thing in common: they were all written by A. E. Waite.

The choice of Waite as a copywriter was due to James Elliott, who had set up as an advertising agent after the collapse of the publishing house and had somehow acquired the Horlick's account. So impressed was James Horlick, the English partner of the firm, that he invited Waite to take the post of Manager of the London Office. Waite was offered the appointment in December 1898 but was not able to take it up until the following February, by which time he was suffering from influenza, and on the day he was due to begin work 'reached Victoria more dead than alive and providentially met Elliott by a mere chance. He saw my condition and could think of but one nostrum, being a half tumbler of neat Scotch whisky, adding a splash of water. It was a bad day at the close of February, 1899; and I believe to this moment that the said nostrum saved my life' (*SLT*, p. 152)

Waite was evidently a man of little faith when it came to the curative value of the product that was about to provide him with his income. The appointment itself was a most casual affair:

The entire charge of premises in Farringdon Road, of a certain acrid book-keeper and a small collection of girl typists and shorthand writers were left in my sole hands, one explanation being that Mr Horlick was starting on a visit to Palestine and would be absent some four or six months. The existing Manager was not in evidence, but I learned that he was about to join the Stock Exchange, so that he might maintain and promote the financial interests of the English partner. This is how I became a business man. Nothing passed in writing, and assuredly I was the only person who came away from the interview with a keen sense of the comedy which was about to open. I concluded that the arrangement would last through the first month and no further before I was found out. Unquestionably the retiring Manager would discover my complete incapacity in less than a single hour (*SLT*, p. 152).

But Waite's initial qualms over his own ability were unfounded; he managed the London Office efficiently and energetically for ten years. Other aspects of James Horlick's affairs, however, were to prove much less straightforward.

In his autobiography Waite made light of his time with Horlick's: 'I saw to the few advertisements which were tolerated at that time and wrote careful pamphlets'. He added that 'all the correspondence passed of course through my hands' and noted that his position 'approached a sinecure during Horlick's absence'. But this was to be unduly modest. The advertisements were many and there were also some two hundred circular letters sent out in a carefully orchestrated campaign to doctors, dentists, nurses, and chemists (and to members of most other professions, from schoolteachers to Members of Parliament), as well as to Temperance Societies, to regular stockists, and to those proud parents who must announce the birth of their children in the newspapers. The 'careful pamphlets' were eight in number[10] and included *Ordered to the Front*, a collection of bold illustrations and stirring doggerel verse. It ended like this:

> Crown'd Heads of Europe, we wish you peace,
> And trust that shortly all wars will cease,
> But when a battle is bound to be fought,
> Let MALTED MILK to the Front be brought,
> And when the struggle is over and done,
> 'Tis still the best thing under the sun.
> On Malted Milk the babies thrive,
> By Malted Milk the sick survive,
> The weak folk take it to make them strong,
> The old because they will then live long;
> The strong ones take it to keep them well,
> And many more people than I can tell—
> Soldiers, Sailors, and doctors too—
> And when you have tried it so will you!
> Send for a sample, don't delay;
> There's much to gain and nothing to pay.
> Drop us a line to our abode,
> Simply; HORLICK, Farringdon Road,
> But if you'd like to add any more,
> Note that the Number is 34.

The correspondence was by no means concerned solely with Malted Milk. James Horlick had extensive property and business interests unconnected with the Food Company and Waite's predecessor, Richard Preston, had for some time looked after these on Horlick's behalf. But although Waite found Preston 'an extremely likeable fellow', James Horlick did not entirely trust him, and in August 1900 he asked Waite to take over the private work previously done by Preston—ostensibly because of the latter's 'increasing engagements'. Waite acted as private

Business Manager—officially he was his Private Secretary—to James Horlick until 1909, for the last two years in an exclusive capacity, having left the Malted Milk company when it moved to Slough in 1907. He became involved with property management, dealt with brokers and solicitors on Horlick's behalf, and attempted to steer him safely through the minefield of Horatio Bottomley's Joint Stock Institute, in which Horlick had invested heavily.

Waite considered the deals with Bottomley to be 'foolish transactions'—and said as much to Horlick. From the beginning he had warned Horlick of the risks inherent in any Bottomley enterprise, and, as the dealings with Bottomley became inevitably and increasingly unsatisfactory, found himself obliged to listen to Horlick's constant and unjust damnings of James Elliott—who had always arranged the purchases of Joint Stock shares. And as the embroilments with Bottomley increased they led to all manner of odd City fish eagerly seeking out James Horlick—who was equally eager to avoid them, so that Waite spent much of his time 'communicating with people and denying Mr Horlick's presence in town while he is listening at the other end of the instrument'. Most embarrassing of all was Horlick's insistence that his son and nephew—both of whom were constantly hanging around the office—be kept in complete ignorance of his private affairs. If he achieved nothing else during his years with Horlick, Waite at least brought the act of dissembling to a fine art.

There was, however, one solid achievement. On 17 March 1903 Waite wrote to Horlick describing a visit he had received from a Colonel Wallace, who brought with him the proposals of two unnamed ladies for establishing a magazine to be funded by James Horlick. The idea of a magazine was evidently already in the air, for Waite related how 'I pointed out to Colonel Wallace that our scheme is simply one of an advertising kind designed to replace certain newspaper advertisements in Australia and that it would be beyond the scope of a business house to run a ladies paper with a view of making it profitable on its own merits independently of the advertisement standpoint'. But a literary magazine was another matter, and when the first issue of *Horlick's Magazine and Home Journal for Australia, India and the Colonies* appeared in January 1904, it was clearly more than 'one of an advertising kind'—although it carried sixteen pages of advertisements, almost half of which were for Malted Milk. It was published by a revived James Elliott & Co. and the editor, of course, was A. E. Waite.

Newspaper reviews of the first and succeeding issues were without exception favourable—as well they might be, for *Horlick's Magazine* contained fiction by Arthur Machen, Robert Lynd, Edgar Jepson, and Evelyn Underhill, and enough 'Colonial Articles and Stories' to satisfy the most chauvinist colonial.[11] Each issue was also heavy laden with essays by Waite himself on one or other obscure aspect of the occult, usually under a pseudonym, and with a multitude of poems—again largely by Waite and again pseudonymous.

The magazine ran for fifteen issues and was then, according to Waite, 'abandoned, not because sales were on the downward grade but because the periodical was not selling as it should'. He claimed that he had 'edited it with the utmost care and had secured a few contributions which belong to literature at its highest' (*SLT*, p. 167). But these—Waite meant Arthur Machen and Evelyn Underhill—he had secured within the confines of the Golden Dawn, and other genuine contributions came in no small part from his friends at the Pen and Pencil Club. Even had sales been better, the magazine would not have survived for much longer: the occult contributions were becoming increasingly rarefied and the literary contents increasingly dull. It was a brave experiment, but it could not last.

The Malted Milk period came to an end in 1907, but Waite still made occasional forays into copywriting. He wrote one promotional brochure for Vivigene—a 'concentrated nutrient animal extract'—in 1909, and another for a similar product, Brainine, as late as 1916. Most improbable of all was a ten-verse rhymed advertisement for 'Sewell's Rival Corset'. It included such gems as these:

> And were anything wanting to prove to the hilt
> The consummate perfection with which they are built,
> We have only to pause in the midst of our lays
> And consult C.A. SEWELL concerning their stays.
>
> The VENUS DE MILO they take for their mark,
> And why they won't leave you to grope in the dark;
> 'Tis by right of the verdict of feminine praise
> Which so long C.A. SEWELL have earn'd for their stays.
>
> The name of these Corsets, so easy and fair,
> Is rightly the RIVAL, since none can compare,
> And ladies all stand in delighted amaze
> And confess C.A. SEWELL unrivall'd in stays.

But these were aberrations. With City life behind him, Waite's whole career would be devoted to writing and to promoting, in theory and in practice, his doctrine of Divine Union.

10

'HE THAT ASPIRED TO *KNOW*' —A NEW LIGHT OF MYSTICISM

THE origins of Waite's esoteric enthusiasms lay in his childhood; in particular in the *Arabian Tales* that had so delighted him with its stories of the 'Hidden City of Ad' and of that 'other and greater city which is called Irem'. This was the city, raised on pillars, that contained the great secret of earthly riches and had as its chief treasure 'a chest of gold filled with a red powder'. Waite could not know then that 'this is the powder of Alchemy and the Philosopher's Stone. It is encircled by a river of Mercury'; for 'what should I know in my childhood concerning the Stone at the Red, or that *est in Mercurio quicquid quaerunt sapientes*? But the talismanic seed of this Romance of Alchemy fell unawares in receptive soil and became a plant which I was destined to tend long after in my own Garden of the Mind' (*SLT*, p. 28).

Before this alchemical plant flowered Waite had discovered both Spiritualism and Theosophy—and found both of them wanting. Spiritualism had been a necessary personal quest, but Theosophy was an intellectual pursuit to which he had been introduced by H. P. Blavatsky's *Isis Unveiled* (1877). He found this curious book 'helpful as an *omnium gatherum* of esoteric claims and pretences, a miscellany of magic and its connections, with the sole exception of Alchemy, in which I cannot recall that H.P.B. ever evinced any personal interest' (*SLT*, p. 68). Nonetheless, although he 'hated its anti-Christian bias', *Isis Unveiled* did bring him to Eliphas Lévi, the most extraordinary magician of the nineteenth century.

Eliphas Lévi, otherwise Alphonse Louis Constant (1810–75), was among the most charismatic figures in the modern history of occultism. As a young man he had been ordained as a deacon in the Roman Catholic Church but never proceeded to the priesthood—he had no true vocation, being quite unable to come to terms with the need for celibacy—and maintained an ambivalent attitude to the Church throughout a life in which he oscillated perpetually between occultism and seeming orthodoxy. After a brief period as a revolutionary Christian Socialist he fell under the influence of the Polish mystic Hoené Wronski and later produced remarkable books on the history, theory, and practice of magic.

His three principal works, *Dogme et Rituel de la Haute Magie* (1856), *Histoire de la Magie* (1860), and *La Clef des Grands Mystères* (1861), were inaccurate, idiosyncratic, and utterly enchanting. They also exercised an enormous influence on occultists and ideas that were born of Lévi's imagination became enshrined as occult dogmas: he reiterated in new forms the Doctrine of Correspondences ('As above, so below'); postulated an all-pervading universal medium, the Astral Light; argued for the supremacy in magic of the Will; and proclaimed the parallel between the letters of the Hebrew alphabet and the Tarot Trumps. All of these ideas were regurgitated, with embellishments, by his successors—not the least of whom was Madame Blavatsky.

Waite came upon Lévi in 1881, read him sketchily in the British Museum, and began his 'serious study' at Deal, where he acquired his own copy of *Dogme et Rituel*. None of Lévi's works was available in English, so Waite determined to provide his own translation—beginning with his 'Digest' of 1886, *The Mysteries of Magic*. Ten years later he translated *Dogme et Rituel* (as *Transcendental Magic*), and eventually, in 1913, issued his English translation of Lévi's *Histoire*, though both of these appeared after he had parted with any vestige of belief that Lévi might be a road to enlightenment. In 1886 he had thought otherwise: Lévi's true greatness lay, he believed, in his attempt to 'establish a harmony between religion and science', in his 'revelation for the first time to the modern world of the great Arcanum of will-power, which comprises in one word the whole history and mystery of magical art', and above all in 'the supreme elevation of his beautiful moral philosophy'. In this, Lévi 'taught us to conciliate those opposing forces, physical and spiritual, whose equilibrium is life and immortality; to harmonise the "liberty of individuals with the necessity of things", and the divine privileges of self-devotion' (*Mysteries of Magic* pp. xli–xlii).

For all his enthusiasm, however, Waite was not uncritical. He disputed the antiquity of the Tarot and condemned Lévi's historical inaccuracies, especially his distorted translations from Trithemius—not that *his* translation of Lévi was impeccable: 'I have not confined myself', he said, 'within the barren limits of a slavish literalism', and was duly taken to task for his liberties, in a hostile review by Edward Macbean of the S.R.I.A.[1] By 1896 Waite had become thoroughly disillusioned with occultism in general and recognized the inadequacy of Lévi's ideas—'there is no way from man to God in his system'—and his personal limitations: 'he was a transcendentalist but not a mystic'. But he still found Lévi to be 'the most brilliant, the most original, the most fascinating interpreter of occult philosophy in the West' (*Mysteries of Magic*, revised edn., p. xiii). Lévi represented the summit of occultism, but Waite was seeking for something more.

Nor was there anything to be found in Theosophy—not, at least, as presented by H. P. Blavatsky. The Theosophical Society had been founded in 1875, by Madame Blavatsky and Colonel H. S. Olcott, for 'The Study of Occult Science;

the formation of a nucleus of Universal Brotherhood; and the revival of Oriental Literature and Philosophy'; but by the time Waite came to know the Society, in 1883, the apparent harmony between East and West suggested by *Isis Unveiled* had given way to an increased emphasis on 'Esoteric Buddhism' and its supposed superiority over all western forms of occultism. Waite had no interest in eastern philosophy, was unconcerned by the furore that followed the Hodgson Report—'I cared nothing whether H.P.B. had manufactured either cups or saucers with the help of alleged Masters in Tibet, or had bought them at a bazaar and buried them' (*SLT*, p. 88)—and was generally unimpressed by 'the strange crew that filled Sinnett's drawing-room at Theosophical gatherings, the astrologers, the mesmerists, the readers of hands and a few, very few only, of the motley Spiritist groups' (*SLT*, p. 87).

None of their concerns had any appeal for Waite, but the Theosophical Society did introduce him to Sinnett, to Edward Maitland, and to C. C. Massey, a real scholar (he translated Du Prel's *Philosophy of Mysticism*) and a theosophist in the mystical sense of Jacob Boehme, who took him to call on H. P. Blavatsky. Waite, regrettably, recorded nothing of this interview, just as he said nothing of his meeting with Colonel Olcott in 1890, save only that it took place. Neither the philosophy nor phenomena of the Theosophical Society satisifed Waite, and he determined that what he sought lay within rather than without.

To such an introspective nature as Waite's, seeking an inward way came without effort. Among his earliest literary efforts in prose had been tales of faërie—not in any sense the robust, traditional fairy-tales of folklore, but strange allegories of the soul's quest for realization—and as he turned away from occultism he used these stories as a means of expressing his concept of the spiritual quest. It was an unhappy choice, for Waite never had a sure touch when writing fiction, least of all allegorical fiction, and his stories are at best affected and uninspiring, and they never succeed in conveying the nature of mystical experience. Two collections of his stories were published: *Prince Starbeam*, written in 1879 and issued, after revision, in 1889; and *The Golden Stairs*, published in 1893 by the Theosophical Publishing Society, who claimed that these 'Tales from the Wonder-World' 'will at once fascinate and instruct the youthful mind'. It is to be hoped that most Theosophical children—who already suffered from 'Lotus Circles' in which they were systematically exposed to simplified Theosophy—were spared these stories, which even sympathetic reviewers saw as 'hardly likely to be much appreciated by many juveniles, not natives of Thibet, for some centuries to come' (*Eastern & Western Review*).

Waite was more successful with fairy poetry. While he was contributing regularly to *Young Folks' Paper* he met William Sharp (better known as his Celtic *alter ego*, 'Fiona Macleod'), who had taken over the 'Literary Olympic' feature in 1887 and had commented favourably on *A Soul's Comedy*, especially on its fairytale 'Dream Tower' sequence. Sharp was also general editor of *The Canterbury Poets*, a series of re-issues of the works of both major and minor poets that also included thematic anthologies. One of these was to be of fairy poems, and Sharp asked Waite—who may well have suggested the theme—to be the editor, giving him a completely free hand as to both contents and title. The collection was issued in 1888 in two forms: a pocket edition entitled *Elfin Music*, and a larger, extended version issued as *Songs and Poems of Fairyland*; in both cases the poems were prefaced by a critical Introduction that traced the development of the literary fairy—although, to the annoyance of reviewers, Waite rejected a chronological arrangement of the anthology. Sharp himself was quite happy with the book, praising it extravagantly in *Young Folks' Paper*—perhaps because it included two poems by his wife ('Graham R. Tomson')—and printing the final poem, 'An Invocation' by Philip Dayre, in the body of his review. What he may not have known was that 'Philip Dayre' was A. E. Waite.

In later years Waite returned again to the fairy theme, both in poetry and in prose, but he was wise enough to recognize that, however significant those works might be to himself, they spoke with a very muted voice to others and he looked for other ways to propagate the esoteric doctrines he was slowly developing. During his years of multifarious reading at the British Museum, Waite had acquired an immense fund of knowledge on the history and practice of the occult sciences, and in the late 1880s he began to put it to good use. He realized that if his speculative writing was to be taken seriously he must first establish a reputation among the 'occult' public as a sound scholar; he must do what had not previously been done in the field of occultism—he must write carefully reasoned historical and critical studies. Studies, moreover, that quoted original sources and argued from established facts to rational conclusions—a method of working quite alien to occultists who were (as they still are) in the habit of setting out preconceived opinions and selecting just those facts to support them as required the least amount of distortion.

Waite's early esoteric studies may seem to the latterday reader—as they did in time to Waite himself—to be unsatisfactory and full of errors, but when they were published they marked a new departure in the field and his reputation as a scholar grew rapidly among his 'occult' contemporaries. *Light* and *Lucifer* might variously dispute his conclusions, but they did not challenge his statements of fact; even the secular press, for the most part, praised his efforts—although Mrs Sidgwick sneered at his 'claims to learning' and pointed out his 'somewhat shallow and secondhand acquaintance with at least his Latin authorities' in her scathing review of *The Occult Sciences* (1891) for the Society for Psychical Research. But occultists are rarely psychical researchers, and few read the Society's *Proceedings*. Waite's reputation remained high—buttressed by his long and learned latters published in *Light*,[2] and by the lambasting he gave critics within the occult camp.

In the columns of *The Medium and Daybreak* a Mr Pfoundes had cast doubts on the originality of Waite's ideas (claiming them for himself) and upbraided him for a lack of modesty in proclaiming that 'For the first time in the history of esoteric science, it has become possible to define in open language the pneumatic secret of the ages, and to indicate plainly, without quibbles and without pretence, the true road to adeptship'. Pfoundes also noted that 'Mr Waite and his writings are both unknown to me'. Waite replied promptly and vigorously, questioning Mr Pfoundes's own literary reputation; suggesting that 'his personal ignorance cannot be considered as the measure of general knowledge'; and referring him for further information on the Waite canon to Redway's catalogues and the columns of *Light*. He added, presumably in hope rather than with prescience, 'If he is anxious for more extended information, my biography may perhaps be forthcoming in the 20th century, or at a subsequent period of convenience which shall be prior to the next millenium'.[3] In the enthusiasm of youth Waite was untroubled by false modesty.

The question which so exercised Mr Pfoundes was that of the true nature of alchemy. Waite believed that 'in the writings of the men called Mystics and Alchemists there is concealed a doctrine of physical and spiritual evolution, which was the fundamental principle of their philosophy, and was applied by them both in practice'. He also genuinely believed that he had been the first to recover this doctrine, and he set out his discoveries in tabular form in a letter to *Light* (15 September 1888). Both 'the discoveries which I have made, and the convictions at which I have arrived', he said, 'will be fully developed in a work entitled *Azoth: or the Star in the East*', but in advance of its publication he trusted that those 'who are acquainted with my books on the Rosicrucians, and the Mysteries of Magic will absolve me from the charge of adopting rash and inadequate theories, and from enriching the domain of verified facts with the fabulous creations of romantic hypotheses'.

His conclusions were presented under twenty-two headings—though without any attempt to relate them to either the Hebrew alphabet or the Tarot Trumps—many of which were offered in support of the first statement that 'The alchemists, in common with other mystics, were in possession of a secret theory of universal development, or evolution, which they believed to be capable of application in every kingdom of nature'. Applying this theory to the mineral kingdom, 'they discovered a method of evolving gold and silver from substances which they deemed inferior', and found too that a parallel process could be applied to Man.

The nature of this process, argued Waite, is hinted at in alchemical and magical texts, and if it is understood and carried out, then the regeneration of Man from his fallen state will follow. The existence and effectiveness of such a process is 'abundantly confirmed by the study of certain higher phases of mesmerism, electrical psychology, and trance clairvoyance'—although in what way Waite does not explain. He concludes his statements by advocating a new religion:

Lastly, in this doctrine, and in the principles connected there with, lies the only adequate basis for a new religion which shall be at once scientific and aspirational, positive and mystical; and such a religion is sincerely and honestly believed to be the supreme need of the age by a large and increasing number of devout and earnest persons.

The publication of *Azoth*—which finally took place in February 1893—was only a part of Waite's scheme. Equally important was the setting up of a body that would work towards the goal of putting his theories into practice. As a first step he requested the readers of *Light* to collaborate with him 'in a small scheme which is likely to be practically useful'; 'I am', he told them, 'seeking to found a private association—devoid of all assumption and pretence—for the study of mystical philosophy. No responsibilities, no special views—beyond a sincere sympathy with the main objects of the association—will be incurred by its members, and, at least in the first instance, it will be of a purely literary character.' Associations of a similar nature—more or less—were destined to play a major role in Waite's life, but in 1888 no one, its seems, listened to his plea.

In the absence of recruits to his association, Waite continued to put forward his ideas in his books. The Introductions to both *Lives of Alchemystical Philosophers* and *The Magical Writings of Thomas Vaughan* set out his thesis explicitly, and in the former the immediate source of his ideas is also revealed. The suggestion that Spiritual Regeneration is the true secret of alchemy had been advanced in 1850 in an anonymous work, *A Suggestive Inquiry into the Hermetic Mystery*. Both the author, Miss Mary Anne South (later Mrs Atwood), and her father, Dr Thomas South, had spent many years immersed in alchemical literature, and the *Suggestive Inquiry* was the culmination of their researches; but immediately after its publication Dr South took fright at the prospect of revealing such stupendous truths to the unenlightened public and destroyed every copy of his daughter's book that could be recalled, together with the manuscript of his own alchemical poem. Miss South had concurred, somewhat reluctantly, in the destruction of her book, but retained a number of copies for further annotation and ultimate distribution to intimate friends; other copies—presumably those sent out for review—occasionally surfaced in esoteric circles, but it remained an exceptionally rare book until it was reprinted in 1918.[4]

Waite had somehow obtained a copy (which he eventually offered for sale through *The Unknown World*), had succeeded also in penetrating its extremely opaque language, and began to propagate its thesis anew. As far as that thesis can be expressed in everyday language, it is that the goal of the alchemical process was the attainment of Divine Union as a consequence of Illumination obtained in an exalted form of mesmeric trance. Waite agreed over the end, but disputed the means; he believed that 'the alchemical transfiguration of humanity' depended on parallel physical and psychical processes (although he never made their precise nature clear); that the alchemists had engaged in a physical as well as a spiritual work of transmutation; and that 'the true method of Hermetic interpretation lies in a middle course'—the path of mysticism rather than of mesmerism. As he expressed it:

> The end in view is identical with Hermetists, Theurgists, and with the ancient Greek mysteries alike. It is the conscious and hypostatic union of the intellectual soul with Deity, and its participation in the life of God; but the conception included in this divine name is one infinitely transcendental, and in Hermetic operations, above all, it must ever be remembered that God is within us (*Lives*, p. 16).

By means of his books, and through lectures on alchemy and mysticism,[5] Waite did gain an active following of sorts and by 1891 he had founded the Order of the Spiritual Temple. It was an Order almost, but not quite, stillborn—progressing no further than preliminary meetings at which a prospectus was drafted (see Appendix A), together with 'An Apology for Ritual', which stated that 'The exercises of devotional Mysticism which will be the object of our meetings will involve some revival of ancient Mystic Ritual', and the outlines of 'A Tentative Rite' for the Order. (The full text of the 'Apology' and 'A Tentative Rite' are printed in *Azoth*, pp. 122–128. See also Appendix A for the *Rite*). The 'Rite' was the proposed religious service of the Order, which Waite—who seems not to have been the sole author—described as 'pleasing, but of little practical value'. Had the Order of the Spiritual Temple not existed only on paper, and had its services ever taken place, Waite would undoubtedly have been more enthusiastic, for the overall structure of the 'Rite' conforms closely to the pattern that would appear in later Orders that were entirely of his own making.

Azoth was published in February 1893 by the Theosophical Publishing Society, who had taken it up when Elliott failed to find subscribers—despite a handsome prospectus—for his projected first publication. Waite was quite content for the Theosophists to have it, for he had been told by the Countess Wachtmeister (who managed the T.P.S.), that 'my things seemed to sell among her people, though nothing to do with Theosophy'. In this instance she was proved wrong, for it failed to sell and was soon remaindered. Waite thought that the Theosophists disliked its western emphasis that 'looked to the Christ in all', but the only fault the reviewer in *Lucifer* found with the book was Waite's 'far too great stress on what he imagines will be, in the future, the increased beauty of outward man, and especially of woman, in that new Earthly Paradise which presents itself to his delighted vision as the outcome of this greater knowledge' (issue of May 1893). *Light* was perplexed by the book and concluded that 'To treat of it properly would require the hand of one who had got somewhere near the perfection described in it as being attainable' (issue of 8 July 1893), while the secular press was derisive: the *Manchester Guardian* jeered at its style and content alike, and *The Echo* dismissed it as 'Two hundred and thirty pages of delirious slush'. Elliott was, perhaps, more fortunate than he realized when he gave up Waite's 'largest and most important enterprise in occult literature'.

Waite, too, was relieved, for he 'outgrew the matter' and 'came to distrust its "inspirational" manner'. Alchemy would be approached more dispassionately in the future—beginning with Lord Stafford and his *Lexicon of Alchemy*.

At an unknown date in 1891, Fitzherbert Edward Stafford-Jerningham—Roman Catholic gentleman and, from 1892, 11th Baron Stafford—wrote to Waite for advice that would 'help him to reach the term of his long Hermetic Researches by directing him on the true path leading to the transmutation of metals' (*SLT*, pp. 128–9)—presumably he had read *Lives of Alchemystical Philosophers*. If Waite 'could not, would not, must not tell him how to make gold' he could yet help by arranging for the translation of alchemical texts, beginning with the *Lexicon of Alchemy* of Martin Ruland. Waite duly found a translator ('a friend with time on his hands'), added a Supplement 'containing the terms of the Philosophers and the Veils of the Great Mystery', and arranged for the text to be printed—in an edition of only six copies—at Lord Stafford's expense.

This idiosyncratic production, which was printed in 1892, was followed by a series of others, for each of which Lord Stafford supplied a translation but without revealing the identity of the translator. Waite's task was editorial and proved to be a light one as the translation was extremely sound 'from the Hermetic point of view'. He suspected that the translator was 'the Rev. William Alexander Ayton, a member of the G∴D∴ almost *ab origine*, a sound Latin scholar and one who had been active for years in all the occult movements, that of H.P.B. included' (*SLT*, p. 134); but in this he was wrong, and it is possible—indeed probable—that the translations were the work of Julius Kohn, an *emigré* Austrian occultist who disputed with the Theosophical Society, exchanged alchemical manuscripts with Ayton, and eventually published editions of *The Prophecies of Paracelsus* (1915) and of Trismosin's *Splendor Solis* (1921).

Part of the editor's task was to provide a biographical or critical introduction to each title,[6] and in the course of preparing these Waite began to change his views on alchemy—a change accelerated by his work on the *Hermetic and Alchemical Writings* of the pragmatic Renaissance scientist Paracelsus. This massive two-volume work was 'the *magnum opus* of the whole incredible adventure', but Lord Stafford had provided no translator; instead, 'as it was his special enthusiasm, and as Elliott had a free license to print what number he chose, my responsibility was to work against time, so that the Earl might not wait unduly. There were translators employed under me, the bulk of the text being indeed "put out" in this manner. My task was to edit the whole, furnish annotations at need and see the volumes through the press. As it happened, however, I did translate a few sections, there and here' (*SLT*, p. 136). Waite added that his 'real ambition lay in another direction and this, as explained in the prefatory part, was to meet with sufficient encouragement for a third volume, devoted to interpretation and commentary'. At the time this remained unwritten, but he returned to the project in 1916 and produced *The Spiritual Philosophy of Paracelsus* only to see it languish in manuscript because the paper shortages of the Great War prevented Rider & Co. from publishing it.

The alchemical series drew to a close in 1896, with the *Turba Philosophorum* and Manzolli's *Zodiac of Life*,[7] which was printed in another minute edition (of fifteen copies) because Lord Stafford hoped that he would find in it the 'Secret of the Great Work'. Waite wrote a brief introduction, and with it Lord Stafford passed out of his life; no one has satisfactorily explained how he came into it in the first place—there is no trace among the Stafford papers of his correspondence with Waite, and nothing whatever to explain either how his obsession with alchemy came about or what ultimately became of it. But for Waite the matter was unimportant; he was turning now away from alchemy and towards another strand of esoteric thought.

The Kabbalah is the system of Jewish mysticism and theosophy that developed in the early centuries of this era (its origins lie in the earlier Merkabah (Chariot) mysticism), reached its zenith in the late medieval period with the *Sepher ha Zohar* (Book of Splendour), and fascinated Renaissance figures such as Reuchlin and Pico della Mirandola, who believed, quite erroneously, that kabbalistic texts contained trinitarian doctrine and would provide a means of converting the Jews to Christianity. From the sixteenth century onwards the strange and complex symbolism of the Kabbalah had been utilized frequently by occultists, and by the nineteenth century it had come to be associated largely (but unjustly) with magic. Waite made his acquaintance with the Kabbalah through the fantasies of Eliphas Lévi, but he had sense enough to dismiss Lévi's bizarre misunderstandings of kabbalistic texts, to seek other authorities, and to draw conclusions of his own.

It was through the Kabbalah—specifically through two sections of the *Zohar*: the *Idra Rabba* (Greater Assembly) and the *Idra Zutta* (Lesser Assembly)—that Waite first discovered the concept of the 'Holy Assembly', and having found it he transformed it into a doctrine of his own. Similarly, as he increased his knowledge of the major divisions of esoteric theory and practice—alchemy, magic, Freemasonry, Rosicrucianism, and the Kabbalah (he added the Tarot and the Holy Grail later)—and subsumed them under the general heading of mysticism, he developed his idea of a unifying Secret Tradition that had perpetuated esoteric doctrines through the work of this continuing 'Holy Assembly'. But it was far from being the instituted secret society of occult dreams; indeed it was far from being an institution at all.

1. The young A. E. Waite (*c.* 1880).

2. The original buildings of St Charles's College, Bayswater.

An Ode to Astronomy

AND OTHER POEMS,

BY

ARTHUR E. WAITE,

PRICE SIXPENCE.

LONDON:
Hare & Co., Printers, 6, Desboro' Place, Harrow Road.
1877.

3. *An Ode to Astronomy* (1877), Waite's first published book.

4. Eastlake Lodge, Harvard Road, Gunnersbury.

5. Dora Stuart-Menteath (*c.* 1900).

6. Ada Waite.

7. Toptrees, East Molesey, home of the Stuart-Menteath family.

8. Cover design by Evelyn Stuart-Menteath for *The Unknown World*.

0=0.-91 Waite, Arthur Edward, 99
1=10-Sept. 91. Eastlake Lodge Isis.
2=9. Oct. 91. Harvard Road
3=8. Oct. 91. Gunnersbury W.
4=7. April. 92 in abeyance
Re-admitted by ballot 17. Feb. 1896.
Sacramentum Regis Poverty clause?

100
0=0. Carden, Alexander James Isis.
1=10. July-91. 32 Leinster Square
2=9. Oct. 91. Bayswater

9. Waite's entry in the address book of the Hermetic Order of the Golden Dawn.

We the undersigned
Chiefs of Isis Urania
Temple
hereby recommend
the Hon Frater Sacramentum Regis
4-7
for re-admission to membership,
which he has allowed to be demitted,
and we are prompted to do this
by the fact that
at a ballot held in the Isis Temple
on Feb. 17. 1896,
the votes cast were unanimous in
his favour.

Signed -
Levavi Oculos Imperator Praem Canc
Sapere Aude — Sub Imperator, pro tem -
Fortiter et Recte — Sub Praem
Anima Pura Sit. Sub Canc

10. The official record of Waite's re-admission to the G∴D∴

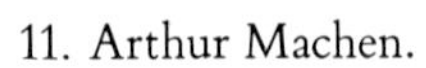

11. Arthur Machen.

12. A. E. Waite (*c*. 1920).

13. A. E. Waite (1922).

14. A. E. Waite in his robes as Imperator of the Fellowship of the Rosy Cross (photograph by Coburn, 1922).

15. A. E. Waite and his daughter, Sybil (*c.* 1930).

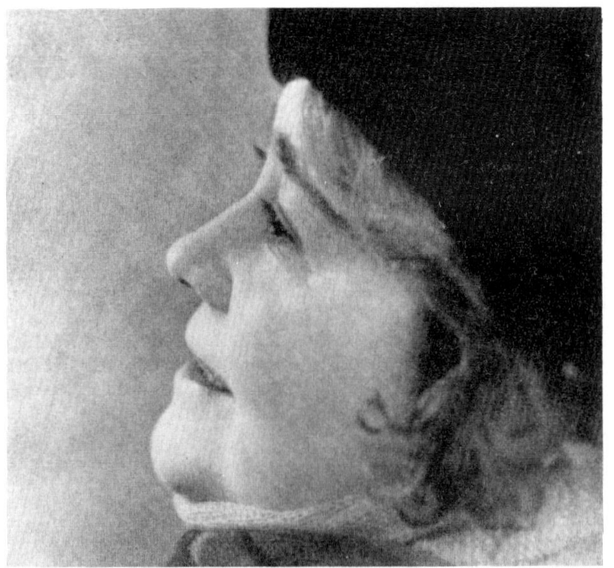

16. Mary Broadbent Schofield, Waite's second wife (*c.* 1930).

11

THE HIDDEN CHURCH AND A SECRET TRADITION

WAITE'S early study of the Kabbalah led him to argue that 'The points of contact between occult science and the Kabalah are very numerous, but between Mysticism and the Kabalah they are, comparatively speaking, few'; in general the Kabbalah was 'more especially a rationalized system of mystic thought'. He concluded that 'The existence of a concealed doctrine of religion perpetuated from antiquity cannot be proved by recourse to Kabalistic literature' although, 'the question itself does not stand or fall by the Kabalah', because, 'it is in Christian channels that this doctrine must be sought by those who assume it, by which I mean that the transcendental succession has passed into the Church of Christ' (*Doctrine and Literature of the Kabalah*, pp. 484, 486, 490).

At this time (1899) Waite did not use the term 'Secret Tradition', although the concept of such a tradition was already implicit in the majority of his published works. His definition of the term was first set out in clear and precise terms—as clear and precise, that is, as was possible given the peculiarities of Waite's literary style—in *The Secret Tradition in Freemasonry* (1911). There he says that 'The Secret Tradition is the immemorial knowledge concerning man's way of return whence he came by a method of the inward life' (vol. ii, p. 379). Within that tradition are, 'firstly, the memorials of a loss which has befallen humanity; and, secondly, the records of a restitution in respect of that which was lost', and these are maintained by 'the keepers of the tradition', who 'perpetuated it in secret by means of Instituted Mysteries and cryptic literature' (vol. i, p. ix). And whatever form these 'instituted Mysteries' take, they invariably testify to '(a) the aeonian nature of the loss; (b) the certitude of an ultimate restoration; (c) in respect of that which was lost, the perpetuity of its existence somewhere in time and the world although interned deeply; (d) and more rarely its substantial presence under veils close to the hands of all' (vol. i, p. xi).

His specific concern was with the 'Traces of a Secret Tradition in Christian Times', and it was for this reason that he turned from the Kabbalah to the problem of the Holy Grail and its symbolism. Waite had also been drawn to the legend of the Holy Grail by the enthusiasm of Arthur Machen, and their subsequent long and furious debates over the interpretation of the Grail Romances had stimulated both a stream of articles and Waite's first truly significant book, *The Hidden Church of the Holy Graal* (1909).[1]

In outline, the story of the Grail—which is a part of the Arthurian Romance cycle—is this: before the burial of the crucified Christ, Joseph of Arimathea collects blood from His body in a cup (the Grail) that had been used at the Last Supper. After the Ascension, Joseph travels to Britain, founds a monastery where the Grail is housed, and appoints a Keeper of the Grail, who is known as the Fisher King (as are his successors), because he has caught a great fish with which his companions are miraculously fed. The Fisher King takes the Grail to the castle of Corbenic, where it is hidden from view, together with the lance, sword, and dish that are also associated with the Passion of Christ; these four objects together constituting the Grail Hallows. In due course, the knights of King Arthur's court set out in search of the Holy Grail, but only the purest of them (Galahad, Perceval, and Bors) succeed in their quest—becoming themselves the guardians of the Grail, which is eventually withdrawn from this world into the heavenly Kingdom.

The mythological origins of the Grail story did not concern Waite; nor did mere historical study of the Grail literature. His concern was with the theological implications of its symbolism:

> After accepting every explanation of modern erudition as to the origin of the Graal elements, there remain various features of the romances as things outside the general horizon of research, and they are those which, from my standpoint, are of the last and most real importance. A scheme of criticism which fails to account for the claim to a super-valid formula of Eucharistic consecration and to a super-apostolical succession accounts for very little that matters finally. I have therefore taken up the subject at the point where it has been left by the students of folklore and all that which might term itself authorized scholarship (*Hidden Church*, p. viii).

His purpose was to show 'that its elements were taken over in the interest of a particular form of Christian religious symbolism' (ibid., p. xi).

That symbolism was found within a 'Secret Church', which, so Waite argued, had perpetuated the mystical doctrines implicit in the Grail story. By this 'Secret Church' he did not mean any instituted body, but 'the manifest Church glorified and installed in the spiritual kingdom, as this was first set over the kingdom of the visible world. It is therefore the withdrawn spirit of the outward Holy Assembly, and it would be unreasonable for those who acknowledge the visible body to deny that which transcends it' (ibid., p. 641). Of the 'Secret Church' he further says, 'In the outer courts are those who are prepared for regeneration, and in the *adyta* are those who have attained it: these are the Holy Assembly' (ibid., p. 640). And those who make up that Assembly are not the product of any esoteric school, for 'There are no admissions—at least of the ceremonial kind—

to the Holy Assembly, but in the last instance the candidate inducts himself' (p. 641). Finally, the 'Secret Church' may be summarized as 'the integration of believers in the higher consciousness'. All of which seems to leave little place for the esoteric Orders with which Waite was so closely involved and which he so assiduously promoted. *Their* role would seem to be that of a preparatory school, because, 'for those secret fraternities at the present day which confess to two incorporated orders and to have recipients in both, it corresponds to that third Order from which they claim to hold—though how they do not know' (p. 636). Waite, on the other hand, clearly *did* know.

Waite differed from the occultists of his day in that he wished to disseminate his ideas rather than to confine them within a closed circle of initiates, and—fortunately for both posterity and the immediate well-being of his family—his publishers were equally eager for that dissemination. By 1900 Redway's publishing firm had failed, but before the end he had taken on an 'articled pupil' in the person of Philip Sinclair Wellby, a young Cambridge graduate whose people had 'paid something for a seat in Redway's Office and an opportunity to get an insight into publishing affairs'—although 'what he could have learned at Hart Street may be left an open question' (*SLT*, p. 153). Apparently he learned enough to feel confident in setting up as a publisher on his own account, and from 1901 to 1908, when his business was amalgamated with that of William Rider & Co., Philip Wellby published a miscellaneous selection of books that included fiction, finely printed gift books, expositions of Spiritualism, and 'The New Thought Library'—a series designed to promote the popular metaphysics that derived from New England Transcendentalism. The most successful 'New Thought' titles were two collections of essays, edited by Waite: *The Gift of the Spirit* (1903) and *The Gift of Understanding* (1907), the work of Prentice Mulford: 'a fresh and suggestive writer, with quaint turns of thought amidst much fantasia', although 'his English was impossible, except only in America. It would be impossible there outside New Thought circles' (*SLT*, p. 154).

The Gift of the Spirit had first been edited for Redway, and Waite later returned to Mulford in 1913 when he edited *Prentice Mulford's Story*; but neither Waite nor Wellby was especially interested in New Thought, the Mulford titles being purely commercial undertakings. Waite had other wares for Wellby to distribute, the first of which was *The Life of Louis Claude de Saint -Martin*, which Redway had printed, but failed to issue, in 1900. Wellby, who had acquired the sheets, published the book in May 1901, but his first independent publication of Waite took place twelve months later, when he issued the new collection of poems, *A Book of Mystery and Vision*. By this time Wellby had become a personal friend of Waite and of Waite's circle; he was captivated by Dora and *A Book of Mystery and Vision* was designed with great care (the cover design is by Mary Tourtel, who was destined to fame as the creator of Rupert Bear) in order to please her.

When Waite died, *The Occult Review* carried an obituary in the form of 'A Personal Tribute' by Wellby (issue of July 1942). Among his reminiscences Wellby describes his own participation in the junketings with Machen—he recalled Waite's 'rendering of "There were three sailors of Bristol City" *in recitativo* [which] was more forceful than melodious', the 'all-night conferences' on esoteric matters at Waite's home in Ealing, and days spent at Polruan with Waite, Dora, and Granville. But he says nothing of the books he published for Waite, although he could have been justly proud of any of them.

After *A Book of Mystery and Vision* came a translation of De Senancour's *Obermann* (1903); a reissue of Eckartshausen's *Cloud upon the Sanctuary* (1903), with a new introduction by Waite; *Strange Houses of Sleep* (1906); and a little collection of aphorisms entitled *Steps to the Crown* (1907). Among these aphorisms—often splendidly cynical, as with: 'Conventional morality is like elementary education—all that is needed by the bourgeois'—are some which refer to his relationship with Dora—either defensively ('There are certain conditions under which it is more sinful to keep the law than to break it') or ironically ('Many of us escape from happiness only by the skin of our teeth').

But Wellby was not his only publisher. As a result of corresponding, in 1905, with the Revd W. Robertson Nicoll, Waite was asked to produce a collection of essays on mysticism for Hodder & Stoughton (for whom Nicoll was a consultant). He promply pillaged the columns of *Horlick's Magazine* for both his acknowledged and pseudonymous articles and compiled *Studies in Mysticism*—which misleading title his publishers urged upon him as they could not understand what he meant by *Studies in the Secret Tradition*. Failing to understand the title they necessarily failed to comprehend the text and Waite's first book for Hodder & Stoughton was also his last.

The Holy Grail was a different matter. *The Hidden Church of the Holy Graal* was completed in 1908 and ought to have gone with all the other Wellby publications to Rider & Co.—the more so in that many of the chapters had first appeared in *The Occult Review*, a journal founded in 1905 by the Hon. Ralph Shirley, who not only owned Rider & Co. but was also a friend of Waite. It was taken, however, to Rebman & Co., an unlikely choice given that the firm specialized in medical books; but there were esoteric rather than commercial reasons. One of the partners in the firm of Rebman was Hugh Elliott, a masonic colleague of Waite's and an active member of the Golden Dawn—more precisely of the Stella Matutina, the Chief of which was Dr Robert W. Felkin, who was also involved with Rebman & Co. At the time Waite was involved (as we shall see) in arranging a Concordat between the Stella Matutina and his own branch of the Order; Felkin was anxious to have the *Hidden Church* published by Rebman, and as it suited Waite to accommodate Felkin, to Rebman it went.

The firm also published *The Secret Tradition in Freemasonry* for Waite, presumably because of its perceived importance from an esoteric point of view: commercially it was a hopeless proposition, as there could never be adequate sales to recoup the cost of printing two large and profusely illustrated volumes on such a specialized subject. Shortly afterwards, 'a day came when the publishing business of Rebman shut up its doors'. It was not an uncommon fate for Waite's assorted publishers.

Rider & Co. was, however, made of sterner stuff. The firm was well established on the basis of its profitable *Timber Trades' Journal* and Ralph Shirley (1865–1946), a younger brother of the Eleventh Earl Ferrers, was well able to indulge his penchant for occult literature. He began with *The Occult Review*. In the first issue, for January 1905, he published seven articles which outlined and justified various approaches to 'the investigation of super-normal phenomena and the study and discussion of psychological problems'. He urged his readers not to condemn prematurely 'an attempt to deal on scientific lines with subjects which have fallen into disrepute through association with charlatanry, on the one hand, and through the long refusal of scientific minds to investigate the evidence on which they are based, on the other'. The editorial ended with a series of questions and a firm commitment:

> How many of the beliefs condemned or ignored at one time or another by the science of the day are capable of resuscitation in the light of fuller knowledge? Which of them is to be regarded as a *chose jugée*? Which has a claim to a fresh hearing?
>
> This is the field of inquiry which it is proposed to cover in the pages of the OCCULT REVIEW'

Waite supported the journal from the beginning (his article 'The Life of the Mystic' was printed in the first issue), and when Rider & Co. swallowed up Philip Wellby, Waite was well content for he now had a publisher who sympathized with his work and was not in the slightest danger of commercial failure. Over a period of twenty years Ralph Shirley would publish twenty books for Waite and provide him with an even more secure income from his contributions to the *Occult Review*: in the summer of 1907 Waite wrote the editorials during Shirley's absence abroad, and four years later took over the 'Periodical Literature' feature (the regular review of the journal's contemporaries), giving it up only in 1931 when its format was changed. All this in addition to a constant stream of book reviews.

But the *Occult Review* was aimed at a popular market, and for more learned papers Waite was obliged to look elsewhere. Initially he attempted to set up a publishing scheme of his own, a grandiose affair that styled itself 'The Hermetic Text Society'. It progressed as far as a prospectus, printed in 1908, which offered a list of sixty potential titles for translating and editing, arranged under five headings (with a sixth section for 'Miscellaneous and unclassified works'): Great Texts of Christian Mysticism; Lesser Texts of Christian Mysticism; The Literature of the Rosy Cross; the Archaeology of Freemasonry and Templarism; and, The Literature of Alchemy.

According to the prospectus, the 'primary intention' of the Society was 'to place within the reach of its members the great and memorable texts of Christian Mysticism, of all schools and periods, excluding nothing on the ground of difficulties in doctrine, but distinguishing clearly the position of each text in relation to the chief schools of doctrine'. Two 'subsidiary objects', which followed from this, were 'to illustrate the mysteries of sanctity as exhibited in Christian Mysticism by reference to all concurrent sources of esoteric knowledge in Europe, and to test that knowledge in the light of Christian Mysticism'. The Director General of the Hermetic Text Society was to be Waite, the Secretary General was to be Philip Wellby, and Dora Stuart-Menteath was to be Treasurer. There was also to be a ten-man 'Advisory Committee' of experts in various fields of esoteric lore, but as Waite got no further than drawing up a provisional list of likely candidates—almost all of whom were his cronies in the ranks of the Golden Dawn—the list of projected titles (which included *The Hidden Church of the Holy Graal* and others of his future works) was evidently his, and his alone.

The Hermetic Text Society never descended into the World of Action, but other societies did. One member of Waite's proposed 'Advisory Committee' who was not a member of the Golden Dawn was the former editor of the *Theosophical Review*, G. R. S. Mead;[2] he would have advised on 'Neoplatonism and Gnosticism', on which subjects he was an acknowledged authority (in Theosophical circles at least; his association with the Theosophical Society had condemned him—quite unjustly—in the eyes of the academic world). He was also, in 1908, the leader of the 'soberer, saner and more decent members' of the British Section of the Theosophical Society which was then embroiled in the 'Leadbeater Scandal'.

Mead had joined the Theosophical Society in 1884, becoming, in 1889, the private secretary of Madame Blavatsky and sub-editor of *Lucifer*. After her death he became editor of the journal, which he renamed *The Theosophical Review*; edited the third volume of *The Secret Doctrine*; and achieved such prominence in the society that he was appointed General Secretary for Europe. He did not, however, follow Annie Besant—Madame Blavatsky's effective successor in the society—in her admiration for the seership of C. W. Leadbeater, which Mead felt was an 'insidious influence' in the society. In 1906 Leadbeater was accused of teaching boys who had been placed in his care the practice of mutual masturbation, but when the parents of these boys complained privately to Annie Besant she refused to condemn her pederastic ally and upbraided the parents for making their accusations. They then made their complaints public, Leadbeater was condemned by a judicial committee of the society and forced to resign, and all seemed to be well.

But in 1907 Colonel Olcott, the president of the Theosophical Society, died and Annie Besant was elected to succeed him. Shortly after this an American theosophist, Dr Weller Van Hook, openly advocated the desirability of Leadbeater's sexual teachings and Annie Besant invited Leadbeater to renew his membership. Mead, and some seven hundred other members of the British Section, immediately expressed their outrage at Leadbeater's restoration to grace by resigning *en masse*. Not all of them supported Mead in his desire to promote a scholarly approach to the 'Comparative study of Religion and Philosophy', but those who did helped him to found a new journal, *The Quest*, and a new society named after it.

Mead's intention was 'to found a clean society, an association that should be genuinely undogmatic, unpretentious, claiming no pseudo-revelations, and truly honest inside and out,—to gather together a group of seekers who desired greatly and earnestly to be instructed by any who had competent knowledge of the many subjects which could enter into the wide programme of our Spiritual Quest. "Esotericism" and "occultism" were to be eschewed as corrupting rather than helpful' ('The Quest—Old and New', in *The Quest* April 1926, p. 297). He was also insistent that the society should have a quarterly Journal, and having settled on a name for it, *The Quest*, he decided to give the society the same name.

Towards the end of 1908 Mead drew in a number of his non-Theosophical friends, Waite among them; a provisional constitution was drawn up, and the officers and committee of the society were elected. Mead, of course, was president but it was Waite rather than any of the escapees from the Theosophical Society who became vice-president, and it was Waite who was responsible for the final form of words in the Society's published 'Objects'. These were.

(i) To promote investigation and comparative study of religion, philosophy and science, on the basis of experience.
(ii) To encourage the expression of the ideal in beautiful forms.

A preliminary meeting, to finalize the 'Constitution, Rules and Regulations', was held on 29 January 1909, to be followed by the inaugural public meeting at Kensington Town Hall on 11 March.

At the first meeting both Mead and Waite addressed the audience; Mead spoke on 'The Nature of the Quest' but there is no record of what was said by Waite. He spoke again at the Society's third meeting in April, and that lecture was printed in the first issue of *The Quest* (October 1909) under the title 'The Romance of the Holy Graal'. Initially, the Society 'was practically ancillary to the Review, designed to support it; for outside the Quarterly its activities consisted solely in giving some half-a-dozen public lectures a term at Kensington Town Hall' ('The Quest—Old and New', p. 299). Gradually, however, both public and private lectures increased in number, the society grew, and in 1919 it obtained a home of its own at 27 Clareville Gardens, South Kensington ('Two large Studios, one for a Lecture Room and the other for a Library and Reading Room'). Here it remained, as energetic as ever, until pressing financial problems brought it to an end in 1930.

The Quest Society was unique. It had been the first—and indeed, the only—scholarly body devoted to the sympathetic study of subjects that are generally classed as 'metaphysical', or, somewhat less kindly and rather unfairly, as 'esoteric'. The quarterly had been a forum for sound academic debate and had published the work of scholars of the stature of Bultmann, Martin Buber, and Coomaraswamy, together with literary contributions from such figures as Ezra Pound, Gustav Meyrink, Arthur Machen, and W. B. Yeats. Somewhat surprisingly, but possibly because he depended on his writing for his income and contributions to *The Quest* were 'all for love. We could not afford to pay our contributors a penny', Waite wrote little for the quarterly, although he remained a staunch supporter of the society—and a friend of Mead—to the end of its days.

But while the Quest Society flourished another esoteric body, and one much dearer to Waite's heart, floundered—its troubles due, in no small part, to the actions of Marcus Worsley Blackden, who was the first 'ordinary member' of the Quest Society's council. He was also a founder member of another body, the Independent and Rectified Rite: Waite's version of the Hermetic Order of the Golden Dawn.

12

'GOLDEN DEMONS THAT NONE CAN STAY'— AN HERMETIC ORDER OF THE GOLDEN DAWN

EARLY in 1867, at a time when the young A. E. Waite was preparing for his first communion, the prehistory of the Golden Dawn was being acted out. Two English Freemasons, R. W. Little and W. J. Hughan, were advanced through a series of Grades in the Rosicrucian Society in Scotia (they had been admitted to the first, or Zelator Grade on 31 December 1866), so that they would be qualified to form a similar society in England. On 1 June 1867, at Aldermanbury in the City of London, the *Societas Rosicruciana in Anglia* held its first meeting, although it was looked upon as a reconstitution rather than an inauguration, for the members maintained that they were reviving a dormant society that had been active during the 1850s. This society, in turn, was thought to have preserved the ethos, if not the historical continuity, of the original Rosicrucian Brotherhood of the early seventeenth century; that such a Brotherhood may never have existed did not trouble the members of the S.R.I.A.: what mattered was that they should preserve its principles.

The three pamphlets (known as the Rosicrucian Manifestos) on which the Rosicrucian myth was founded, were published in Germany between 1614 and 1616. They were the *Fama Fraternitatis*, *Confessio Fraternitatis*, and *Chymische Hochzeit* (The Chemical Wedding); all thought to have been the work of a prominent Lutheran scholar, Johann Valentin Andreae, and were possibly issued with a political intent. Whether or not this was so, they caught the popular imagination and stimulated theologians, occultists, and satirists to write innumerable attacks upon, and defences of, the putative Rosicrucians.

As for the myth itself, it concerned the life and work of one Christian Rosencreutz, a mystic and adept of the fifteenth century who founded, it was claimed, a secret Fraternity with the aim of propagating the esoteric wisdom he had acquired during his travels in the Holy Land, Egypt, and North Africa. In addition to their esoteric studies, the members of his Fraternity sought for spiritual development and 'practised acts of benevolence'—especially the healing of the sick. After the death of Christian Rosencreutz, in 1484, his body was embalmed and sealed within a seven-sided vault, the location of which remained secret for 120 years until 1604, when it was discovered by chance, opened, and found to contain not only the perfectly preserved body, but also secret manuscripts, an ever-burning lamp, and other marvels. The vault was resealed and the Fraternity, revitalized by the discovery, continued to flourish—albeit in secret—down through the centuries.

At various times during the seventeenth and eighteenth centuries self-styled Rosicrucian bodies arose, briefly flowered, and invariably faded away, leaving nothing behind them save greater or lesser additions to the accumulated store of esoteric wisdom. The S.R.I.A., however, was significantly different from its predecessors: firstly, it arose in a country where it would not be persecuted by either Church or State; secondly, it displayed remarkable staying power (it is still active today); and thirdly, it confined its membership to freemasons who were also professed Christians. By 1880 it was well established as a thoroughly respectable body whose members engaged in nothing more nefarious than the intellectual pursuit of the occult sciences; and in that year the Society gained a new member whose inventive genius in the field of occultism was second to none: Dr William Wynn Westcott.[1]

Westcott was, as befitted a Rosicrucian, a medical practitioner as well as being an active freemason and an enthusiastic believer in the reality of the Rosicrucian myth. He was also a kabbalist, a keen theosophist, and a supporter from its inception, in 1884, of Anna Kingsford and Edward Maitland's 'Hermetic Society', which laid great emphasis on the Western as opposed to the Eastern tradition of occultism. All these activities led him to recognize the contribution that ladies could—and did—make to the advancement of occult knowledge, and he developed the notion of creating a secret society of men and women 'for the purpose of the study of Occult Science, and the further investigation of the Mysteries of Life and Death, and our Environment'. There was also, so Westcott argued, every justification for not including a masonic qualification and for including members of both sexes: 'on the Continent many groups of Rosicrucian initiates and adepts had admitted men who were not Freemasons, and even learned women, to their grades and assemblies. This may have been a departure from the original rules of the Society, as first designed by C.R. our Founder; it is a point left undecided by the early Rosicrucian *published* literature, but there are extant documents to show that women were admitted in the 17th and 18th centuries' (*The Rosicrucian Society of England*, 1915, p. 3). But Westcott was unwilling that the onus of creation should be placed on his shoulders alone; an additional, more esoteric creator was also needed.

Being a competent occultist, Westcott accordingly created the creator. At some time during 1887 Westcott had obtained, from what source he never made clear, a series of manuscripts in cipher, which proved, upon decoding, to be outlines of the initiatory rituals of an occult order. Also among the manuscripts was the name of a German adept—Fraulein Anna Sprengel, or Soror Sapiens Dominabitur Astris—together with her address at Stuttgart. Westcott promptly wrote to her and, in November 1887, received an effusive reply appointing him to the Grade of Adeptus Exemptus and authorizing him to found a new English Society of the Golden Dawn. He was further empowered to 'choose two learned persons in order to make up the first three Masters', and these he duly selected from within the ranks of the S.R.I.A.

He was by now Secretary-General of the Society, and chose as his companions two equally prominent members: Dr W. R. Woodman (1828–91), the Supreme Magus (i.e. Head) of the Society and a learned kabbalist, and S.L.M. Mathers,[2] a member of the Society's High Council who had already expanded the rituals on Westcott's behalf and converted them into workable form. On 1 March 1888 the three Chiefs issued themselves with a charter to found 'Isis-Urania Temple No. 3', and gave themselves roles that mirrored their positions in the S.R.I.A.: Woodman was Imperator; Westcott was Cancellarius (Secretary); and Mathers Praemonstrator (effectively Director of Ceremonies—in the S.R.I.A. he was at that time Conductor of Novices). Now that the Order had been founded, Anna Sprengel had become a liability and Westcott disposed of her—although not before she had 'sent' him a variety of occult manuscripts and five further letters. In August 1890 a final letter arrived, from an unknown Brother of the Order, announcing the sudden death of 'our learned friend S.D.A.'. Careful examination of the letters has indicated the virtual certainty of their having been forged on Westcott's behalf;[3] and it is almost as certain that he forged the original cipher manuscripts (certainly they were of very recent origin); but however reprehensible his actions may have been, they were not carried out for personal gain.

The Hermetic Order of the Golden Dawn was created in order to further the systematic study of the occult sciences and was immediately welcomed by the occult establishment of its day (although Madame Blavatsky had reservations until she was reassured that membership of the Order would not deplete the ranks of the Theosophical Society). It offered its members a sequence of initiatory rituals of a very eclectic nature that combined Egyptian, kabbalistic, and Rosicrucian symbolism, together with prescribed courses of study appropriate to each step in the five Grades of the Outer order—the Grades being those of Neophyte, Zelator, Theoricus, Practicus, and Philosophus. Each Grade above that of Neophyte was related to one of the ten Sephiroth of the kabbalistic Tree of Life, and these continued beyond the Outer Order into a yet more secret Second Order, whose rituals were distinctly magical.

The Second Order, the *Rosae Rubeae et Aureae Crucis*, had existed from the beginning but had worked no rituals, and members who advanced to become adepti of the Second Order did so by means of passing examinations. In 1892 this changed, for Mathers had developed his own highly impressive initiatory rituals, based upon the myth of Christian Rosencreutz, for the 5=6 (each Grade was numbered) Grade of Adeptus Minor. And whereas the Outer Order represented theoretical occultism, the Second Order existed for the working of specifically magical rituals, although not of the debased kind associated with medieval grimoires.

By the time that a working Second Order had been developed, the Golden Dawn had some 150 members in three temples: Isis-Urania in London, Osiris in Weston-super-Mare, and Horus in Bradford. Two years later, two further temples had been founded—Amen-Ra in Edinburgh, and Ahathoor in Paris—and the membership had risen to two hundred. By 1900 there were, in theory, over 300 members, but many of these were members in name only and the active membership was little more than half that number. Women formed some one-third of the total, but in the Second Order—to which all active members aspired and which most of them attained—they comprised almost one half of the total. But for all its growth, the Golden Dawn was not a healthy body.

Dr Woodman died in 1891 and was succeeded as Imperator by Mathers, whose autocratic manner soon provoked dissension. In the early days of the Order's existence awkward or recalcitrant members could be overawed by either Westcott or Mathers, but as the Second Order grew so did the numbers of independent and self-assertive members, who were quite capable of standing up to their Chiefs when they believed themselves to be in the right. The first serious dissent came in 1896 when Mathers issued a Manifesto to justify his authority and subsequently expelled Annie Horniman, refusing to reinstate her even though the majority of Second Order members petitioned him on her behalf. Further trouble became inevitable after 1897, for in March of that year Westcott resigned from all offices in both the Outer and Second Orders as a consequence of Home Office pressure (he was a Coroner, and the State did not approve of his magical activities; as Aleister Crowley put it, he 'was paid to sit on corpses, not to raise them'). Without Westcott's moderating influence, Mathers's autocratic manner became unbearable and open rebellion was inevitable; but it did not come until 1900.

Long before this, A. E. Waite had joined the Golden Dawn, having heard of it in 'Theosophical and kindred circles' where, 'the rumours of an Occult Order making great pretences were abroad in those days . . . Obscure persons were placing cryptic sigils after their names in unexpected communications, as if to test whether I was already a member. Dark hints were conveyed in breathless murmurs.' His descriptions of the 'obscure persons'—and of those, less obscure, whom he names—are picturesque, if somewhat unkind:

'A Disciple of Thomas Lake Harris [Dr Berridge] was disposed to be confidential, if he could obtain licence. People from the North, one of whom made spectacles [T. H. Pattinson; in fact, a watchmaker], went so far as to say that those who knew could speak and mysteriously referred to one. Rough customers from the Lowlands of Scotland [J. W. Brodie-Innes; an urbane and cultured lawyer] talked about strange things abroad in the modern world. It transpired presently that Macgregor Mathers—who had assumed the additional patronymic presumably to sustain the cause—was something to do with the darkly glittering business. The name of Wynn Westcott also loomed remotely. Mathers was like a comic Blackstone of occult lore and Westcott like a dull owl, hooting dolefully among cypresses over tombs of false adepts' (*SLT*, p. 124).

This jaundiced picture was painted almost fifty years after the event, and long after disenchantment with the Golden Dawn had set in. At the time, Waite was not unfriendly towards either Westcott or Mathers—and he was eager to join the Order.

He had met Mathers in 1883, when they were both 'haunting the British Museum, trying many paths of search', and having been introduced, 'I suppose that we must have spoken of occult books or subjects in one of the corridors, for he said to me in a hushed voice and with a somewhat awful accent: "I am a Rosicrucian and a Freemason; therefore I can speak of some things, but of others I cannot speak."' Waite was unimpressed—real Rosicrucians would not 'parade the fact', he thought—and looked on Mathers as an eccentric. He recalled another occasion, when he encountered Mathers 'staggering as usual under a load of books, and he said: "I have clothed myself with hieroglyphics as with a garment", so I inferred that he was then deep in Egyptology. He had a natural faculty for suggesting in his mystery-language that he had a most profound acquaintance with any subject he took up, and it went a long way with the unversed'—as on those other occasions when they met 'at various occult gatherings of an informal kind—gatherings of people "interested" and mostly of people agape' (obituary of MacGregor Mathers, *Occult Review*, April 1919, pp. 197–8).

It is possible that Westcott, too, was at these gatherings—especially if, as seems most likely, Waite was referring to meetings of the Hermetic Society—and he may have seen Waite as a likely candidate for the S.R.I.A., for a letter of 1884, in which Westcott outlined the actitivities of the Society, was found among papers that had belonged to Waite. But any initial enthusiasm for Waite was destined to be dampened at the publication of *The Real History of the Rosicrucians*. In a final chapter, Waite had written about 'Modern Rosicrucian Societies' and had printed in full the *Rules and Ordinances* of the S.R.I.A. The members were at first outraged and then chagrined when they discovered that none of their publications was protected by copyright. Denied any legal redress, Westcott appealed to Waite for an apology, which he duly received. Waite assured Westcott 'that the citations in question will be withdrawn in the next edition, and in the meantime I shall be pleased to make public any statement concerning the mistake which has unfortunately occurred in the occult periodicals which I am connected with' (letter of 13 October 1887; printed in the *High Council S.R.I.A. Minutes*, October 1887, p. 6). This was the last thing that Westcott wanted, for it would have only further publicized the *Rules* and emphasized Waite's satirical comments upon the Society. Honour was satisfied and Westcott's ruffled feathers were smoothed.

But not yet Waite's path into the Golden Dawn. He was urged to join by Dr Berridge and finally agreed, only to meet with 'the not unexpected and not regrettable result of being refused promptly'. This was not to be taken, however, as a final refusal: 'my application must be repeated a second time, after a certain space. I was to learn later on that those of whom nothing was known were admitted readily, others with preliminary rejections which were cancelled afterwards' (*SLT*, p. 125).

On being admitted, every member took a motto, usually in Latin, that became his or her name in the Order, the motto being inscribed on the parchment Roll of the Order, in chronological sequence, below the solemn Obligation that was repeated by the Neophyte at the beginning of the Ceremony of Admission. For some unknown reason Waite signed the Roll twice. The first occasion was in January 1891, when he was admitted as a Neophyte and became the 99th member of the Hermetic Order of the Golden Dawn. The second was in the following December, after he had attained the 3=8 Grade of Practicus, and this time he entered his motto of 'Sacramentum Regis' ('The Sacrament of the King', from the Vulgate of Tobit, 12:7). He would not have repeated the Obligation a second time—nor would he have wanted to, for once is quite enough to accept willingly the 'awful penalty' for betraying the Order's secrets, 'of voluntarily submitting myself to a deadly and hostile current of will set in motion by the Chiefs of the Order, by which I should fall slain or paralysed without visible weapon, as if blasted by the Lightning-Flash!'

Waite's admission took place at Mathers's home near the Horniman Museum (of which he was then the curator), and he recalled that he told his wife, 'in appropriately sardonic terms', that 'I was engaged on a dark errand, of which nothing could be declared or hinted, so if I failed to return she must communicate with Scotland Yard and offer certain leading lights on place and time'. As he had expected, nothing untoward happened and the occasion turned out to be rather dull: 'I met, however, with nothing worse than a confounding medley of Symbols, and was handed a brief tabulation of elementary points drawn at haphazard from familiar occult sources: on these I was supposed to answer given questions, did I wish to proceed further. They were subjects about which it turned out that the G∴D∴ had nothing to communicate that was other than public knowledge.'

Nonetheless, he stayed the course. 'My dues were paid, my status thus secured, my membership straggled on; and I took some further steps with a vague idea of seeing the business through.' He also arranged for Ada to join—which she duly did on 2 December 1891, but 'she attended one Meeting only, if I remember rightly, and at that was tempted to hold up the whole galanty-show, in order to win her retreat. This kind of thing was not done in such Temples, and I recommended that she should reserve her speech' (*SLT*, pp.125–6). Neither Ada Waite's name nor her motto appear on the Roll and it is possible that she so reserved her speech that her husband signed on her behalf.

In April 1892 Waite advanced to the 4=7 Grade of Philosophus, but although he 'stood on the threshold of the Second Order' he proceeded no further. At this time, he states, 'I began to hear things which, in my several positions at the moment [he was embarking on the James Elliott venture], told me that I should be well out of the whole concern. It was not on the score of morality, seeing that there were *Fratres et Sorores*; for on this ground it is just to say that no breath of scandal ever arose in the G∴D∴ during all that period. It was a question of things which had an equivocal legal aspect and in which leading Members of the Order should not have been concerned, had I been informed accurately, as there seems no doubt that I was.'

It is not at all clear what this dubious affair was, and Waite evidently did not make his reasons for withdrawing from the Order clear to the officers: in the address book of the Order his entry is variously annotated 'in abeyance'; 'Demitted 1893'; and 'Poverty clause?' (the Chiefs could waive fees at their discretion). Waite himself says only, 'I retired or rather demitted without explanation; and if I thanked my stars that in so doing I missed but little, it is more than probable that the Hermetic Order of the G∴D∴ missed even less. I had no grist in my granaries for a mill of that kind' (*SLT*, p. 126).

But Waite had no intention of going without news of the Order's doings. He remained friendly with Dr Berridge, who contributed regularly to *The Unknown World*, heaped extravagant praise on *The Hermetic Museum Restored*, and warned readers of the magazine of the perils of betraying the secrets of Rosicrucian societies. Gossip he undoubtedly relayed to Waite. Eventually Waite applied to rejoin the Order, although in expectation, and 'perhaps mischievously hoping to hear', that his application would be rejected. It was not; and on 17 February 1896 he was 'Re-admitted by ballot', which Waite felt to be due to 'a comparative stranger working in my favour—otherwise Soror Fortiter et Recte [Annie Horniman]—and I returned to the dubious fold by the unanimous voice of the Fellowship' (*SLT*, p. 160). Perhaps she had discovered, after all, Waite's eulogy of her father in *The Municipal Review*.

His own account of his re-admission is otherwise inaccurate. He states that it was on account of assurances that 'I was missing things that I should value and of which I could have no notion at the stage of my demission'; which assurances came from Robert Palmer Thomas, a railway official who lived at Horbury Crescent, Notting Hill, and with whom Waite had become friendly. Palmer Thomas was an enthusiast for all things Rosicrucian (he joined the S.R.I.A. in

1895) and Waite enjoyed both his company—'He aimed at Culture, and we drank White Capri at his table'—and his conversation—'he was very fair company along his particular lines and an incessant talker'. But Palmer Thomas did not enter the Golden Dawn until 7 November 1896, nine months after Waite had rejoined. He did, however, proceed rapidly towards the Second Order, and entered it on 21 April 1898; it was the glories of the Adeptus Minor Grade that he urged upon Waite, not the prosaic doings of the Outer Order.

Waite entered the Second Order on 3 March 1899, the 116th member of the Golden Dawn to do so (he is number 123 on the Roll, but the first four names are fictitious and Westcott, Mathers, and Woodman are all entered twice); but once he had passed through the Adeptus Minor ceremony—which required the candidate to be bound symbolically on the 'Cross of Suffering' and to witness the resurrection of the Chief Adept, who represented Christian Rosencreutz, from a tomb within an elaborately painted, seven-sided vault—he took little part in the Second Order activities. Presumably he worked his way through the prescribed rituals for making and consecrating magical implements and for constructing Enochian tablets, as well as studying the detailed symbolism of the Tarot cards, together with the true method of using them for divination. All this, and a great deal more, was required of the Adept who wished to pass the examinations that would take him from the sub-grade of Zelator Adeptus Minor to that of Theoricus Adeptus Minor; but there is no evidence that Waite took his examinations—or that he even considered doing so.

The Order itself had increasing problems, both from Mathers's autocratic manner and from the constant fraying of tempers that followed upon the perpetual squabbling amongst the members; but these were minor irritations compared with the bombshell that burst upon the members in February 1900. Florence Farr,[4] who was then Cancellarius of Isis-Urania and occupied a similar position in the Second Order, had written to Mathers, who was living in Paris, concerning problems within the Order and was horrified by his reply. Mathers evidently thought that she was about to form a schismatic group with Westcott and warned her against him, making the astonishing claim that Westcott, 'has NEVER been *at any time* either in personal or written communication with the Secret Chiefs of the Order, he having *either himself forged or procured to be forged* the professed correspondence between him and them, and my tongue having been tied all these years by a previous Oath of Secrecy to him, demanded by him, from me, before showing me what he had either done or caused to be done or both' (quoted in Ellic Howe, *Magicians of the Golden Dawn*, p. 210). If this was true, then the whole Order was a sham.

A group of the most prominent members discussed the matter and set up a committee to investigate the charges against Westcott, but as Mathers refused to substantiate the charges, and Westcott declined to deny them, there was little that they could do. Mathers, however, fulminated against them for even considering the matter and demanded that they should surrender the Second Order vault to his charge and submit themselves unconditionally to his authority. When they declined to do so, Mathers sent Aleister Crowley—who had supported Mathers because the London Chiefs refused to admit him to the Second Order after he had passed through the outer Grades—to enforce his demands. The subsequent events were farcical. Crowley arrived at the Order's premises in Blythe Road, Hammersmith, attired 'in Highland dress, a black mask over his face, and a plaid thrown over his head and shoulders, an enormous gold or gilt cross on his breast, and a dagger at his side' (Report of E. A. Hunter, quoted in Howe, op. cit., p. 225); he was promptly turfed out, his hired 'chuckers-out' sent packing, Mathers was suspended from his own Order, and the *R.R. et A.C.* declared its independence.

Freed from Mathers's paranoid rule, the Second Order framed a New Constitution on 21 April 1900 and elected a new executive of three Chiefs and seven ordinary members who were 'specialists in the various studies of the Order'. Waite was not among those elected, but he was present at the meeting and he seconded Florence Farr's resolution that both Chiefs and ordinary members of the executive 'shall stand annually for re-election'. Independence, however, did not bring harmony to the Order.

Apart from Mathers, one of the principal causes of dissension was the existence within the Order of 'Secret Groups' dedicated to private and unofficial 'occult working and ceremonial'. Chief among them was Florence Farr's 'Sphere Group', in which twelve members obtained astral visions by means of ritualized meditation upon a sphere on which were projected symbols taken from both the Tree of Life and the Star Maps used in the Order. The Sphere and other groups were bitterly opposed by Annie Horniman and W. B. Yeats, both of whom looked upon them as magically wholly undesirable, but no satisfactory solution of the dispute was arrived at and Miss Horniman eventually resigned. There was also the very different but equally serious problem of Mme Horos and her husband. This pair of criminal adventurers had tricked Mathers out of parting with G.D. rituals and had set up in London a spurious temple of their own that was a cover for sexual debauchery. It could not last, and in September 1901, Mr Horos was charged with rape, found guilty—after a trial at which the Golden Dawn was held up to ridicule—and gaoled for fifteen years; his wife was sentenced to seven years imprisonment for aiding and abetting him. The more timid members immediately flocked out of the Order as eagerly as they had earlier flocked in.

The troubled Order was now in urgent need of reconstruction, but a provisional plan for reform—which would have swept away examinations, Second Order rituals, and the very name of the Order—was rejected, and at a meeting of the Second Order in May 1902, three members (Percy Bullock, Dr R. W.

Felkin, and J. W. Brodie-Innes)[5] were elected as Chiefs to govern the Order for the ensuing year. Brodie-Innes felt that as a Chief he should rule for life, but, as it turned out, he was to be disappointed in his desire to govern the Order.

None of this concerned Waite, for before 1903 he took little part in the affairs of the Order (which he dubbed 'The House of the Hidden Stairs') and showed no interest in its tribulations. 'I did not go yesterday to the House of the Hidden Stairs', he recorded in his diary (7 December 1902). 'I had no wish to hear the final part of the Triad on the "groups question". I cannot dance to these children however much they may pipe and sing.' He had, however, worked during 1901 on the Order's 'Ritual Sub-Committee' until its suspension, and in January 1903 Yeats wrote to him seeking support for his efforts to have the Sub-Committee revived. At this time Waite evidently had little interest in the future of the Order and had not considered what his own role in that future might be. He received Yeats's letter on 10 January:

The Frater Demon est Deus Inversus [Yeats's motto in the Order], otherwise Frater Diabolus and yet otherwise Brother Devil, well known poet, also polytheist, idolater, vision-monger and theurgist, of the Brotherhood of the House of the Hidden Stairs, writes me under the hand of the impossible Soror Fortiter et Recte [Annie Horniman] asking whether I will join him in petitioning the unspeakable triad to reappoint the Ritual Sub-Committee, more especially as regards the 2=9 Ritual on which he and I worked together, but owing to throes, convulsions and revolutions the revision was suspended and our labours threaten to be wasted. They had nearly passed out of my memory. I have written an amicable reply, for until such time as a competent architect gets out the schedule of the House's dilapidations, our very joining in anything for it means & can come to nothing. By all means then let us revise . . . (Diary, 10 January 1903).

He was more interested in the 'great heap of unpublished MSS' that Yeats had acquired from the family of William Stirling, the author of *The Canon*, a curious kabbalistic work that had appeared in 1897. Waite was anxious to see these manuscripts and arranged to dine with Yeats later in the month. The visit is duly recorded in his diary:

This is how it fell out yesterday [19 January] and in its way it was curious. I reached 18 Woburn Buildings through a desponding slough of roadway and an atmosphere which held mud in solution. I rang the bell. Brother Devil descended to receive me looking gaunt in the gaslight and distorted in the mist which came in with me from the street. He escorted me up to the top floor where a fire burnt in a common open range provided with an oven and in this the dinner plates were warming. The cloth was laid upon the table towards the window end of the room. I observed the flagon of Funchal wine partially emptied. A vast female [Yeats's housekeeper, Mrs Old] was preparing the meal in a room which opened towards the back part of the house and is, I believe, on ordinary occasions the poet's bedroom.

He made excuses to avoid long discussions on Lady Gregory and ancient Irish Romances, but discussed the Grail legends, Waite's books and the Golden Dawn:

He told me that the unfortunate Frater —— [Waite omits the name] of the House of the Hidden Stairs had suddenly lost his wife and he evidently found that this was irreparable otherwise than in the conventional way for she had looked after him most faithfully in the periodic fits of drink-craving which came over him. This scandal I had not heard previously.

Yeats promised to send on the 'pile of MSS' (they proved to be disappointing—Waite sent them back and observed that it 'was not a serious loss to the world' if they should not be published), and they ended their evening by agreeing that 'allegory in fiction was a product of the middle classes and was typically bourgeois. Bourgeoisérie is his enemy and is mine.' And yet when Waite scuppered the plans of Brodie-Innes and took over the Golden Dawn himself, it was the most eminently respectable part of the membership that supported him.

13

THE INDEPENDENT AND RECTIFIED RITE: THE MIDDLE WAY

WHEN the idea of gaining control over the Golden Dawn first occurred to Waite he saw it as a means to an end—it did not become an end in itself until it was a *fait accompli*. He intended to create an entirely new Order of his own, and to this end he proposed to his colleagues Palmer Thomas and Marcus Worsley Blackden[1] (another prominent member of the Golden Dawn) the creation of a 'Secret Council of Rites' that would bring together the various lines of what Waite saw as a type of masonic (or quasi-masonic) apostolic succession. They were enthusiastic, and on 2 December 1902 the Secret Council was founded; 'we shall be', Waite noted, 'indeed an occult Order of Unknown Philosophers—a concealed kind'.

Both Waite and Blackden had recently been made freemasons, and for twelve months they had gathered together all the obscure masonic rites they could find. Not that Waite had any intention of falling foul of the masonic authorities; he would not encroach on the jurisdiction of Grand Lodge, Grand Chapter, Great Priory, or Supreme Council, and would seek possession of only those rites that were moribund, quasi-masonic, or unrecognized in England. The rituals of his own Order would utilize suitable elements from those of all the rites that the Secret Council controlled. And by the time that the Constitution of the Secret Council of Rites had been drafted (see Appendix B), in May 1903, he was determined that the faction-ridden Golden Dawn should be one of the rites that it controlled.

In March 1903 Waite got wind of serious dissatisfaction within the Order, when Percy Bullock asked him to a meeting to discuss the Order's future. He immediately sought out Blackden and 'hinted at another *coup d'état*' which Blackden 'seemed disposed to entertain, if by any means we could return the Order to real vitality'. But Waite still wondered 'whether it is worth all the panics and exercisings that will be involved in the attempt', and added 'Moreover, there may be another way' (Diary, 21 March 1903).

This was probably a reference to the Egyptian Rite of Florence Farr, which Waite may have seen as an alternative to the Golden Dawn. On 4 March he learned that he was to be 'received into the nameless rite which I am not betraying by the initials S∴O∴S∴'. 'If my receptions go on at this rate', he observed, 'I look shortly to be the most initiated man in Europe' (Diary, 4 March 1903). Waite did not describe his initiation, which took place on 22 March, beyond saying that 'it was an experience altogether strange and sudden, and it took place as most ceremonies will in an obscure street where faded respectability struggles unsuccessfully enough with bad drains and a thriving trade in harlotry'. He attended further meetings in April, but nothing came of the S∴O∴S∴ and he resumed his plotting of the *coup d'état* within the Golden Dawn.

Also in April Waite travelled to Saffron Walden to visit the Revd W. A. Ayton,[2] an elderly clergyman who was at the same time an alchemist, a senior member of the Golden Dawn (he was admitted in July 1888), and an obsessive believer in Jesuit conspiracies against Church, State, and occult establishment alike (Yeats considered him to be 'the most panic-stricken person I have ever known'). Ayton was convinced that the cipher manuscripts were genuine and that it was of supreme importance to preserve the Order; he was unsure how best to proceed, but did not demur when Waite 'pointed out that what we wanted was the Tomb of C.R. [i.e. the Second Order Vault] and that I did not quite see how we were going to secure it unless I myself was in power, contrived to remain therein, and shaped the brotherhood to our continued purposes' (Diary, 20 April 1903). Waite moved a step closer to this goal at the annual general meeting of the Order on 2 May.

In his autobiography Waite describes the meeting at some length, but gives little detail. He records how 'Brodie-Innes declaimed the successive clauses of his Constitution with histrionic magnificence', adding that, 'It fell upon myself subsequently to take the clauses successively, reciting objections and securing promises of variations or amendments in several cases. It began to look ominously as if the draft might pass, subsequent to alteration there and here, and that Brodie-Innes would be claiming the Headship of the Rite in consequence' (*SLT*, p. 228).

In fact there was not the slightest chance of Brodie-Innes succeeding, and in his diary account of the meeting Waite is both more precise and less inclined to poetic licence:

[The meeting] divided itself speedily into two factions. Sub Spe [Brodie-Innes] with a meagre majority which once failed him completely and myself with a solid determined minority which completely blocked everything. The 'facts' will stand recorded in such hurried letters as I can write tomorrow and this is no occasion to go over ground which I must then tread. But it was almost pitiful to notice the change which came over the poor small pope of Edinburgh and to compare the grandiloquence of his accent when he first spoke with the crestfallen tones of his later utterance when he found the tables of the previous annual meeting turned upon him. When I proposed a separation among the elements of this chaos *magnum et infirmatum* there was complete disarray: even L.O. [i.e. Levavi Oculos = Percy Bullock] who in secret is less or more with us was thunderstruck, and chief as he was at the moment, though he has now retired, when we succeeded in electing M.W.Th. [i.e. Ma Wahanu Thesi = Blackden], my ally to fill his place until the calling of an emergency meeting, he confessed to me that the Sub Spe faction had fallen into a great trap unwittingly (Diary, 3 May 1903).

The autobiography is probably correct, however, in stating that, 'This third Annual Meeting dissolved in chaos, so far as other matters were concerned, with Brodie-Innes in a state of white rage' (*SLT*, p. 228).

During the two months that followed, a series of meetings was held at which the position of both factions was clarified. Waite's group, which was the minority, set out its views as follows:

1. That a return to the *status quo ante* 1890 on the lines proposed by the Draft Constitution of 1903 was impossible or at least undesirable.
2. That the alleged derivation from a Third Order was a matter of opinion and could not be affirmed certainly.
3. That the election of Chiefs whether autocratic or otherwise was not in accordance with the *status quo ante*.
4. That the Chiefs of the Order were originally Masons and that on a return to the status in question they must again be Masons.
5. That the principle of examination within the Second Order was objectionable.
6. That the continued use of the defective rituals and the setting aside of the revised rituals could not be tolerated.
7. That the draft constitution of 1903 was designed to further individual ambitions.
8. That several persons in the minority felt that a Third Order was about to be forced upon them without credentials that could be investigated.

Neither Brodie-Innes, nor Felkin, nor any of their followers could be expected to agree with these views, which were so decidedly opposed to a magical view of the Order, and an agreement that would unite the two factions was clearly impossible.

The minority group, accordingly, opted for a division of the Order, made the following suggestions—with which Dr Felkin initially concurred—and eventually issued a Manifesto demanding independence (see Appendix C). They suggested:

1. That division was necessary.
2. That division should be so effected as to secure absolute recognition of the independence and legitimacy of both bodies who for this purpose should enter into a concordat hereafter to be drawn up.
3. That the V.H. Frater SACRAMENTUM REGIS in his capacity as deputy should lay before the Chiefs certain misconceptions which had originated as to the intentions of the minority.
4. That there should be an equal division of the properties, the followers of SACRAMENTUM REGIS taking those of the Outer order and those of SUB SPE the Inner, the books to be divided equally.

5. That the Lords and Ladies of the Portal [i.e. those who had taken the first steps towards entering the Second Order but had not reached the Grade of Adeptus Minor] should be notified concerning the division and permitted to choose their side.
6. That the Outer Order members should fall to those who introduced them.

Brodie-Innes had returned to Scotland after the annual general meeting but continued his discussions with Waite by way of letters from July to December 1903, when Waite, irritated by what he perceived as Brodie-Innes's nit-picking and general obtuseness over the points at issue, brought it to a close. The letters bring out Brodie-Innes's anxiety to obtain his fair share of the plunder: in his first letter, of 27 July, he told Waite that 'what requires adjustment and, if you will forgive my saying so, patience and tact is so to arrange that you and your followers shall have all your legitimate liberty of action without interfering with the equally legitimate wishes and aspirations of the other and certainly larger section.' In other words, to continue their magical progress with Brodie-Innes as their absolute Chief.

He did not take this position openly, however, and in his next letter, of 5 August, he told Waite: 'I represent no party or section. I have no following, no authorization. I am either a Chief or a humble private member, and since you hold the view that three Chiefs are essential to government and that a third has not yet been duly elected I am obviously towards you only in the latter capacity.' He added that, 'I happen to be the only practising lawyer in the Order and have been technically trained in formulating and criticizing statements and dealing with evidence.' As a consequence, 'I thought I might be able to help in getting the points so far threshed out that we might all know what you and your followers were driving at and what you wanted and also that being all in black and white there might be no mistake from trusting to memory of interviews, the points may thus be clearly laid before the Order'.

This he followed with a long letter on 8 September, raising questions about the Manifesto of 24 July. The questions are phrased in a sarcastic manner and are all unnecessary given that the minority made it quite clear that they wished for a division into two independent factions and would thus not try to foist their views upon the putative majority. In reply to this letter Waite pointed out that the aim of the correspondence was to ascertain the meaning of specific clauses in the Manifesto, whereas the questions Brodie-Innes asked 'are points raised on the issues and I suppose that they might be extended indefinitely'. He also rather tartly observed that 'you assured me that you were writing simply as a member of the Order and not in any official capacity' although 'you are now acting as the interpreter of the remainder of the Order' (letter of 15 September 1903).

The somewhat fussy correspondence dragged on until December, with Brodie-Innes maintaining that the minority were mistaken in their views and Waite advocating a Concordat and recognizing the right of the other faction to use rituals which were a 'combination of spurious archaisms with the worst style of journalistic English' (letter of 18 November 1903). Brodie-Innes seemed unprepared to let the matter go and continued to write to Waite, although the exasperated Waite declined to answer. There was, indeed, nothing to say because the newly formed Independent and Rectified Rite of Waite's faction had officially come into being with its inaugural meeting of 7 November—at which a new constitution was proclaimed (see Appendix C), and Waite, Ayton, and Blackden established as the three Chiefs.

At the time of the Manifesto, which was also a Declaration of Independence, there were only fourteen Second Order members of the minority faction, but by the time of the Second Convocation, held on 16 April 1904, Waite was able to report an increase of eight Second Order members and seven from the Outer Order (including Algernon Blackwood, Arthur Machen, and Pamela Colman Smith). He was also able to tell the members that revised rituals for the Neophyte and Zelator Grades had been completed and were ready for use.

Meetings of the Outer Order of the Independent and Rectified Rite were held at Mark Masons' Hall, Great Queen Street—as had always been the case with the Isis-Urania Temple; but it was not until early in 1905 that a home was found for the Second Order and Waite could report to the members that 'the properties of the Second Order have been removed from the depository and placed at 16 Allison Road, Acton, where they are under the care of C. H. Frater MAWAHANU THESI [Blackden] who has made himself in part responsible for the expenses of the Home, wherein he has himself arranged to live, and thus our interests have passed into the best possible hands' (*Report of the Chiefs* [of the I & R Rite], 1905). But in 1909 the owner of 'the best possible hands' chose to marry a first cousin and retire to Fawley in Hampshire. The Second Order vault was then moved to 36a Penywern Road, Earls Court, and set up in the home of Mrs Helen Rand (Vigilate), where it presumably remained until the demise of the Order in 1914.

Meanwhile Dr Felkin had established his own version of the Golden Dawn, the Stella Matunina, and while he was anxious to promote the Third Order and to retain as much magic as was possible, he was also desirous of entering into the Concordat with Waite. Negotiations were difficult and protracted, and Felkin tended to vacillate; but when Waite suggested that the two factions might merge with Felkin succeeding Ayton as the Third Chief, Felkin took fright at the prospect of losing his autonomy and agreed to draw up the terms of the Concordat.

His followers tended to be suspicious and urged him not to give up anything to the Independent and Rectified Rite. In particular they resented Waite's suggestion that the Rolls of the two Orders 'which are now in the possession of Finem Respice [i.e. Felkin] shall be used in common'. Hugh Elliott (Nobis est Victoria) wrote to Felkin about this: 'Our real claim to the possession of these rolls is our connection with the 3rd Order. This of course we can't bring forward but the fact remains, *L'Ordre c'est nous*. It might be possible to make trustees, but I don't like giving up our control over these rolls' (letter of 26 April 1906). Elliott also objected to the possibility of Waite's members working Stella Matutina ceremonies, for 'we certainly can't confer on them any of our special knowledge'—knowledge, that is, derived from the Secret Chiefs on the Astral Plane; that it had filtered down through Dr Felkin's somewhat eccentric mind seemed not to bother them. The objections, however, were overcome, and eventually—after Felkin had consulted Brodie-Innes and obtained his agreement, 'on the understanding that he [Felkin] is personally responsible for the same'—the Concordat was signed in April 1907. (No copy of the document has survived, but the *Notes* upon it, which quote some of the clauses, are given in Appendix D.)

The two offshoots—the one magical and the other mystical—of the old Golden Dawn continued in uneasy harmony for three years. They co-operated over the printing of a revised Neophyte ritual which had been written by Waite, with alterations on Felkin's part in the smaller number of copies printed for his faction (of 506 copies printed, 350 were for Waite and 150 for Felkin; the remaining six were fine-paper copies, apparently for Felkin's officers). But the cost—£11.2*s*.0*d*—horrified Felkin and he declined to participate in producing rituals for the more advanced Grades. The Independent and Rectified Rite proved less parsimonious and by the end of 1910 all the Outer Order Grade rituals had been printed, together with that of 'The Portal of the Rosy Cross' and the Solemn Festival of the Equinox.

Felkin was more concerned to find the Secret Chiefs, whom he believed were active somewhere in Germany, and to this end he sent, in 1911, one of his members, Neville Meakin (Ex Oriente Lux), to visit Rudolf Steiner and to take part in his Rosicrucian ceremonies. Before his departure Meakin had been elevated to the Grade of Adeptus Minor by Waite, 'acting as Adeptus Exemptus in Felkin's Stella Matutina Temple at Bassett Road'—in order, said Waite, that he should carry with him 'the fullest Ritual advantage that was possible in his case' (*SLT*, p. 221). In fact, Waite was intensely curious as to Steiner's role in the Rosicrucian movement on the continent, and he questioned Meakin closely on his return, only to discover that the ceremonies were not as impressive as those in England and served mainly as a vehicle for propagating Steiner's philosophical teachings. When Felkin himself visited Steiner in the following year he came back with a far more flowery account of his own initiation (he and his wife 'were received together into four grades'), but Waite suspected that many of his experiences had occurred on the Astral Plane rather than in the real world.

Later in 1912 Steiner himself visited London and Waite had a long talk with him (through an interpreter), in the course of which he discovered that the Felkins' initiation had indeed been a prosaic affair. Imagination was proving to be only one of many faults on the part of Felkin—he was also becoming somewhat devious.

According to the terms of the Concordat, 'in the one case there is a triple Headship and in the other the Head is the Most Honoured Frater Finem Respice, 7=4, and him only'; but in July 1910 Waite discovered that Felkin maintained a system of three Chiefs in the Stella Matutina and had thus breached the terms of the agreement. In itself this may have mattered little, but Waite suspected that one of the three Chiefs was Brodie-Innes who had recently revived the Amen-Ra Temple at Edinburgh. When challenged over this Felkin denied that he had any 'co-equal Chiefs', or indeed any 'that were not co-equal', despite statements to the contrary that Felkin's members had made to Waite.

The Concordat survived this episode but was becoming increasingly unworkable. Felkin *was* working with Brodie-Innes, who encouraged him to break with Waite. He told Felkin that Waite had 'behaved very badly, indeed I should say rather dishonestly. He obtained possession of the properties that were ours by means of a dodge, which to say the least was sharp practice. He took the title of ISIS URANIA, to which he had no more right than to call himself Prince of Wales. He changed the constitution of the Order in essentials without the smallest authority, and at his own hand. Indeed in refusing to acknowledge a Third Order, it is questionable whether he is validly a member at all' (undated letter, probably of 1911). Brodie-Innes continued, 'Is there any benfit in maintaining the Concordat? or do we get any good out of it? I understand the Masters take precisely the same view.' This appeal to the Secret Chiefs was enough for Felkin and the Concordat came to an end in 1912.

At the same time the Independent and Rectified Rite was developing problems of its own. In general its members were more educated than those of the Stella Matutina, and while this had its advantages—Waite and D. H. S. Nicholson, who joined the Order in 1910, worked together over the English edition of Lopukhin's *Some Characteristics of the Interior Church*, Waite providing the Introduction to Nicholson's translation—the members tended to challenge anything with which they disagreed. Thus in March 1910 Battiscombe Gunn, who was an artist, an Egyptologist and an oriental linguist, argued at great length over the correct transliteration of Hebrew terms used in the Grade rituals; Waite was wise enough to listen and in the printed rituals Gunn's corrections were made. The other Egyptologist in the ranks of the Independent and Rectified Rite was to prove more difficult to placate.

After his marriage, Blackden had retired from an active role in the Order, but as Waite became increasingly sceptical about the contents of the cipher manuscripts the members—who wished to believe in their antiquity—became restive and called upon Blackden for support. He 'emerged from retirement' and argued that the fact of the manuscripts being allegedly earlier than the date of the discovery of the Rosetta Stone (which first enabled translation from the Egyptian to be made) was of no consequence, because 'the Egyptian fellaheen, long prior to the discovery in question could have been and probably were acquainted with the fact that certain hieroglyphic texts were Funerary Rituals'. Faced with such total opposition to his own views on the part of his co-Chief, Waite was placed in an impossible position and in 1914, after 'an unprofitable debate', he 'withdrew his copyright Rituals and dissolved the Rite as at that time constituted' (Waite, *Historical Notes* on the 'Ordo S.R. et A.C.').

For Waite it was the end of the Isis-Urania Temple and the end of the Golden Dawn, but his dream of a Rosicrucian Order was still very much alive. On 9 July 1915 he and ten former members of the Independent and Rectified Rite consecrated the Salvator Mundi Temple of the Fellowship of the Rosy Cross, in a room at De Keyser's Hotel on Victoria Embankment. Nine others, who were not present, brought the new Order's strength up to twenty.

Within a year Waite had produced new rituals for all the Outer Grades; the structure of the Order was still based upon the kabbalistic Tree of Life but the new rituals were very different from the old: all Egyptian and pagan references were gone, the symbolism was wholly Rosicrucian and Christian, and magic was utterly eschewed. The hierarchy of the Fellowship was also different; there was one head of the Order only: the Imperator, who was Waite; and none of the offices called for a masonic qualification. The days of a 'triple masonic headship' were over. In future Waite's masonic activities would be confined to their proper place.

14

'BROTHERHOOD IS RELIGION' —AN ADEPT AMONG THE MASONS

AT THE time the Independent and Rectified Rite of the Golden Dawn was declaring its independence from the old Order, Waite had been a freemason for barely two years; but his enthusiasm for Freemasonry was boundless, for he saw it, not as did Grand Lodge—as 'a peculiar system of Morality, veiled in Allegory, and illustrated by Symbols'—but as yet another aspect of the Secret Tradition, and thus one more secret path to a direct experience of God. In his earlier years his approach to the Craft had been more prosaic, and it was not until he reached the age of 43 that he was entered, passed, and finally raised as a Master Mason.

His earliest comments on Freemasonry, in *The Real History of the Rosicrucians*, were somewhat disdainful:

Originally an association for the diffusion of natural morality, it is now simply a benefit society. The improvement of mankind and the encouragement of philanthropy were and are its ostensible objects . . . It preaches a natural morality, and has so little interest in mysticism that it daily misinterprets and practically despises its own mystical symbols' (pp. 403–4).

He also described the titles given to the 18th degree of the Ancient and Accepted Rite as 'splendid inanities of occult nomenclature' and compared the degree unfavourably with the true Rosicrucian fraternity. But in the course of a very few years his attitude had changed.

In 1890 he returned to the subject of Freemasonry in an article for *The British Mail*. 'The true object of the Masonic Fraternity', he declared,

differs from the aims which have been ascribed to it precisely in that way in which a universal institution would be expected to differ from the purpose of a fanatical craze. In its vulgar aspect its object is benevolence and providence; in its esoteric significance it is an attempt to achieve the moral regeneration of the human race; by the construction of a pure, unsectarian system of morality, to create the perfect man.

And this secret purpose remains inviolate because 'the vacuous nature of the great arcanum of allegorical architecture is its permanent protection' (issue of March 1890). This conviction, that the true nature of the Craft had become hidden and that Freemasonry had lost its way, was stressed by Waite in the chapter on

'The Freemasons' in *The Occult Sciences* (1891). There he counsels 'the soul-student at the threshold of mystic research' to 'overcome this gravitation of his desires towards Masonry', because 'There is no light there; there is no secret of the soul enshrined in the recesses of its suggestive ceremonial.' But although Masonry 'has been corrupted by worldly wealth and magnificence', its true principles still lie hidden within it, and Waite hopes 'that within the ranks of the brotherhood, but without if not within, it will be possible to inform them with new life' (pp. 213, 215). It is also made quite clear that if the restoration of those principles is done from without, it will be the work of Waite himself.

Waite does not expect his readers to take him on trust: 'At the same time we ask only a tentative faith. In a forthcoming "Esoteric History of Freemasonry", he will find the entire subject exposed, with the necessary proofs, documents and available sources of knowledge. (p. 214). He had completed his *Notes on the Esoteric History of Freemasonry. Its Doctrine, Symbols and Science* by 1893 but the book was never published, perhaps because even the ever-optimistic James Elliott felt that there was no market for it. The text of the book (which survives in a slightly later typescript version) is divided into five parts, commencing with a straight-forward 'Notes and Collections for a Chronology of Masonry', containing information that Waite had obtained from his researches at the British Museum. This is followed by an account of Cagliostro's 'Egyptian Masonry' and similar obscure rites of the eighteenth century, while a third part, on 'Alchemy and Masonry' draws parallels between the two sets of symbolism. The last two parts, however, are quite different: 'Notes on the Historical Connection between Masonry and Mysticism' and 'Masonic Doctrine and Symbolism in the Light of Mysticism', both show considerable insight into the intricacies of masonic symbolism and foreshadow the ideas that Waite was to develop later in *The Secret Tradition in Freemasonry*. But the *Esoteric History* was shelved, and it was by a quite different path from that of mysticism that Waite drew closer to the Craft.

During the early 1890s there had been much fluttering in masonic dovecotes over the publication in Paris of the sensational tales of one 'Dr Bataille', under the title *Le Diable au XIXe Siècle*; as the plot of this luridly illustrated part-work unfolded week by week, it became clear that it was built upon the earlier revelations of 'Leo Taxil', who had proclaimed the existence of the 'New and Reformed Palladium', an allegedly androgynous and satanic rite ultimately derived from Albert Pike, one of the most prominent of American freemasons. To this mass of sensational rubbish was added the *Mémoires d'une Ex-Palladiste*, the supposed confessions of 'Miss Diana Vaughan', a penitent from the satanic fold who had become a convert to Rome. In due course the authors of these ridiculous tales of satanic wonders, Charles Hacks (Dr Bataille) and Gabriel Jogand-Pages (Leo Taxil/Diana Vaughan) revealed themselves as hoaxers who had set out to discomfit the clerical anti-masonic lobby in France, but not before they had outraged freemasons in England.

'Diana Vaughan' had claimed that the 'real head of the English Luciferians' was Dr William Wynn Westcott, whose address she correctly gave and whom she also described, also correctly, as Supreme Magus of the S.R.I.A. In addition she listed all the members of the High Council of the Society whom she claimed were 'Chiefs of the Third Luciferian Order'. The honour of Westcott and his colleagues—who were quite innocent of these startling charges—was defended by Waite, who analysed and demolished the whole story of the Palladium in his book *Devil-Worship in France*(1896) after previously rebutting the charges of Diana Vaughan in the columns of *Light*. Westcott, who had just welcomed Waite back into the fold of the Golden Dawn, was delighted at Waite's exposure of a 'gross libel which is at the same time an abominable and cruel falsehood' (*Devil-Worship*, p. 280). Waite was further praised by John Yarker, who reviewed the book for *The Freemason* and who was especially pleased because he himself had been described not only as head of the Rite of Memphis and Mizraim (which he was) but also as a prominent Satanist (which he was not).

The Diana Vaughan affair was nothing more than a flash in the pan, and Waite's second book on the Palladium, *Diana Vaughan and the Question of Modern Palladism*, remained unpublished. But his role was not forgotten, and when he became interested in Martinism—a rite based loosely on the philosophy of Louis Claude de Saint-Martin, 'The Unknown Philosopher' (1743–1803), and on the teachings of his mentor, Martines de Pasqually (1715–79)—John Yarker, to whom he wrote for advice about the Martinist Order, encouraged him to join:

> I found an objection in the *Masonic* branch of the Order of St Martin to receive a non-mason, and I have no doubt that it would be found inconvenient both to you and to them. However, that need not interfere with my conferring the Order upon you as I had it myself from a non-mason, the Baron Surdi of Prague. The Ritual is properly in 4 books—I enclose you the first, and you need only send me a short note that you conform yourself entirely to carry out the Ob[ligation]. You can then proceed on your own account to form a nonmasonic branch, and when you have done something I daresay you might get a Charter from 'Papus', for a London body (letter of 30 January 1897).

Waite was delighted, and sent his obligation by return, at the same time expressing a wish to promote the Order: 'I thank you most cordially for the honour which you have done me in conferring upon me the Order of St Martin. The fact that I am not a Mason makes that honour somewhat exceptional, and I can but value it the more highly in consequence.' He returned the rituals to Yarker and added the hope that 'I shall prove useful, as I shall certainly endeavour to be active, in the diffusion of the Order among occult students who are not Masons' (letter of 5 February 1897). There is no evidence that Waite applied for a Charter, but Papus (Dr Gérard Encausse, 1865–1916), the founder in 1884 of the Martinist Order, referred to the setting-up of two new 'Formations' in England when he addressed the International Congress of Spiritualists in 1898; one of these may have involved Waite.

He did, however, send Papus a copy of his book *Louis Claude de Saint-Martin* when it was published in 1901, and expressed his satisfaction on hearing that Papus liked it: 'I learned with very sincere satisfaction that you had formed a good opinion of the book. There is no opinion that I could hold in such high estimation as you have every means of knowing and have done such admirable work yourself in the same direction' (letter of 25 May 1901). It *is* an extremely thorough study of Saint-Martin and Waite succeeded in the difficult task of presenting Saint-Martin's ideas clearly and systematically; but Papus could not have read the book carefully, or he would have taken undoubted exception to Waite's statement that Martinism is 'a body of mystic doctrine, and not a Masonic Rite devised by Saint-Martin to replace the Elect Cohens [i.e. Pasqually's Rite]' and to his advice to his readers 'to bear in mind that upon historical questions the criterion of evidence is not invariably so rigorous in France as it is in England (pp. 73, 459).

Papus was, in fact, so impressed that he awarded Waite the degree of 'Docteur en Hermétisme' from his 'Ecole supérieure libre des Sciences Hermétiques'. The degree was academically worthless but Waite eventually put it to good use when it provided him with a pseudonym for his anthology of the writings of Andrew Jackson Davis. Once he had entered Freemasonry Waite broke with Papus when he learned of the bad odour in which Papus was held by orthodox masonic bodies; but the man who advised him to make the break, Edouard Blitz, the head of the Martinist Order in America, would in turn provide him with something far more significant than Martinism.

In 1901 Waite was firmly established within the Golden Dawn, but he realized that it was effectively a moribund body and both he and Marcus Worsley Blackden began to look for some means to revive it—or at least to provide a substitute. Waite's own account of his entry into Freemasonry makes this clear:

> A day came when Blackden and I began to think seriously of Freemasonry and to wonder whether a deeper insight into the meaning and symbolism of Ritual would be gained by joining the most predominant and world-wide combination of Rites . . . There is no question that an important side of the tentative consideration was whether, were such a course adopted, the Order of the Golden Dawn might profit thereby (*SLT*, p. 161).

This was not exactly the whole truth, for Waite already knew enough of masonic ceremonial and its symbolism to satisfy the needs of any reconstituted rituals within the Golden Dawn, and his further statement 'that I did not fail to anticipate an extreme probability of meeting in the High Grade circles, if not in Craft and

Arch, with at least a few others of our own dedications, to whom symbolism spoke a language and Ritual opened a realm of grace' (*SLT*, p. 161) gives a wrong emphasis, for those few freemasons who were 'of our own dedications' were to be found already within the confines of the Golden Dawn.

The most probable reason for Waite's seeking admission to Freemasonry at this time was his growing awareness that only by passing through the Craft degrees and the Holy Royal Arch would he be able to enter those Higher Degrees whose rites he so eagerly desired. To this end he sought the help of Palmer Thomas, who 'offered high encouragement' and persuaded W. F. Kirby, the entomologist who was also a member of the Golden Dawn, to propose both Waite and Blackden for initiation in his lodge. Thus on 19 September 1901 Waite was made a mason in Runymede Lodge, No. 2430, at Wraysbury in Buckinghamshire. For reasons that were never explained, Waite and Blackden were not raised to the degree of Master Mason in Runymede Lodge but, 'as a courtesy', in St Marylebone Lodge, No. 1305, on 10 February 1902.

Initiation into Craft Masonry brought no spiritual enlightenment to Waite; perhaps because, at his initiation, 'It was so patent throughout that I could have told the Worhsipful Master all that he was communicating to me'—he 'awaited the Grades beyond' (*SLT*, p. 162). He was, however, a conscientious mason and attended his lodge regularly until he was installed as Worshipful Master in 1910; after that his attendance declined, ceasing altogether when he moved permanently to Ramsgate in 1920. It was, as he had intended, a means to an end, and as soon as he had been raised, Waite began his quest for the 'Higher Degrees' (which are now termed 'Additional Degrees') in earnest.

During the seven years that followed, Waite became a member of ten distinct rites and degrees; beginning with the Holy Royal Arch, Knights Templar, Knights of Malta, and the Swedenborgian Rite in 1902, and proceeding to the Mark Degree, the Red Cross of Constantine, Secret Monitor and Ancient and Accepted Rite. There were also others that he considered even more important. The first of these, the Early Grand Scottish Rite, was also something of a means to an end.

As a result of corresponding with Edouard Blitz, Waite had come to see the *Régime Écossais et Rectifié* as maintaining more than any other rite the essence of the Secret Tradition; it was, he believed, 'the head and Crown of Masonry', while its Grade of *Chevalier Bienfaisant de la Cité Sainte* was a 'great and holy Grade of Christian Knighthood spiritualized'. But to attain it he must first be installed as a Knight Templar (which was duly done on 8 May 1902 in King Edward VII Preceptory, No. 173), and he felt that it would also be advisable to receive the Early Grand Rite of 47°; for, as he noted in his diary, 'Obscure or not, 47° means at least 44 rituals which cannot fail of material for my paper against the time when I shall unsay all that has till now been said as to the symbolic builders' (13 October 1902).

To obtain his 44 degrees, however, he must first travel to Scotland, which he did early in February 1903. His visit did not begin well: 'My projected journey to Scotland . . . took place by the midnight train on Friday and I reached Kilmarnock in the early morning, as might well have been expected, in drenching rain.' It was afternoon before he met his host, Colonel Spence, 'coming from the station through a sea of mud'. Spence did not impress him 'as being of any particular attainments or of more than average education', nor did the other Kilmarnock masons meet his expectations: 'A considerable proportion of them belonged to the mechanic order while one or two looked as if they were shepherds'. Waite was also disappointed with the ceremony, which he recorded as 'an almost indescribable initiation', in which 'There was no attempt at reciting the ritual from memory, books being used for the purpose and the ceremony was simply muddled through'. Worse was to follow:

> After the meeting I was introduced to my brethren and a good deal to my dismay Colonel Spence then engineered the assembly, still through the pouring rain, back to my hotel where in a small smoking room he ordered drinks for all, they then proceeded to make speeches on the subject of my visit to Scotland, on my literary labours etc. and to these I had to reply. The whole experience was incredibly squalid and yet more curious than I can give an account of in a hasty description (Diary, 8 February 1903).

But he had obtained the rites he sought.

All was now ready for his journey to Switzerland to be received into the *Régime Écossais et Rectifié*. His path had been smoothed by Blitz, who was Great Prior of the rite for America, and after returning his completed pledge and forms of admission (in which he awarded himself appropriate armorial bearings: 'argent, a cross sable, between four roses gules, which is, of course, purely Rosicrucian and is assigned to me by myself for that reason'), he prepared to set out for Geneva on 27 February.

The journey was uncomfortable and depressing. Waite dreaded the prospect of attempting to speak in French and was delighted to find an English fellow-traveller who accompanied him from Calais to Paris. Beyond Paris he was happier because he was left alone: 'I had but one fellow traveller for a moment, a Frenchman who finding that I could not pass muster in his language, mercifully relieved me in search of more congenial company & I was therefore alone to my utter thankfulness the whole way from Paris to my destination.'

He arrived in Geneva as he had in Kilmarnock, in pouring rain, but the company proved far more congenial. Waite was taken to his reception by Joseph Leclerc (1835–1927), the Great Prior of the masonic body governing the Rite, the Independent Great Priory of Helvetia, and on the evening of 28 February he received the two grades of Squire Novice and Knight Beneficent of the Holy City. In his account of the evening Waite unwittingly emphasizes his innate snobbery:

> The gathering from an English point of view was exceedingly mixed, consisting (a) of respectable tradesmen, as e.g. booksellers; (b) members of the French parliament; (c) persons who had the appearance of Genevan gentleman of good position; (d) an Englishman holding some official appointment under this government; (e) a few who might have belonged to a class inferior to the tradesmen so far as their appearance goes; (f) various representatives of the Genevan government. I had throughout especial marks of kindness & consideration from all those who were evidently the better placed of the gathering (Diary, 3 March 1903).

The ceremonies themselves impressed him greatly, and he returned to England well pleased.

Early in May, Waite learned that he was to be granted jurisdiction over the rite in 'England & the Colonies', and in May 1907 he was received (by correspondence—he never again visited Geneva) into the additional degrees of *Profès* and *Grand Profès*; but he made no attempt to disseminate the rite and never worked the grades which had been conferred upon him. He may have discovered too few suitable candidates, but as he was most likely to find them within the ranks of the S.R.I.A., a more probable reason for his leaving the rite to lie dormant was his dispute with that society.

Waite and Blackden had been admitted to the Metropolitan College of the S.R.I.A. on 10 April 1902 and immediately began to play an active role. Within a year Waite had been appointed chairman of the Study Group and had 'kindly consented to act as Editor' of its proceedings. These proceedings were never published and many of the papers were subsequently destroyed—by a unanimous decision of the members of the group, who felt that their debates had been of little consequence. But other members of the S.R.I.A. were annoyed at this action and the *Report of the Study Group* condemned the action and implied, quite unjustly, that Waite alone had been responsible. Waite himself chose to ignore this and continued his progress through the society, confident in a general support for his views—his paper of 1906, 'The Place of Masonry in the Rites of Initiation', had been well received—unaware that those in authority were becoming uneasy about him. Westcott, in particular was unhappy. He had asked Waite for help in 1910 when he became involved in the legal dispute between Mathers and Crowley (over the publication of Golden Dawn rituals in *The Equinox*), but Waite had done little or nothing and merely persisted in demanding from Westcott a sight of the original cipher manuscripts. The row in the Independent and Rectified Rite made matters worse, and at the time it came to a head Waite was due for election to the office of Celebrant (i.e. Master) of the Metropolitan College. Westcott approached Waite, told him of strong objections to his candidature and advised him to withdraw. Waite was furious and promptly resigned—taking with him years of bitterness at what he saw as shabby treatment by the society. He took his revenge by sprinkling acid comments—on both Westcott and the Society as a whole—throughout his masterly study of Rosicrucianism, *The*

Brotherhood of the Rosy Cross (1924).

He remained active in most of the additional degrees whose ranks he had joined, acting as secretary for both his Rose-Croix Chapter and Knights Templar Preceptory for periods of twenty and thirty years respectively. But his principal concern in masonry now became the dissemination of his ideas through his writing.

His first major 'contribution to masonic literature' was *The Secret Tradition in Freemasonry* (1911), which received wide praise from the masonic and non-masonic press alike. The masonic writer W. J. Wilmshurst (who was a member of the Independent and Rectified Rite) claimed that the book 'unquestionably exceeds in importance any that has yet appeared in regard to what may be called the problem of Freemasonry' (*The Freemason*, 25 May 1912); but John Yarker criticized the book—albeit in the columns of the *Co-Mason*, the organ of an unrecognized, androgynous body—because Waite 'does not seek to hide his contempt, often expressed in uncourteous language, against all who differ from him': which 'all' included Yarker (issue of January 1912).

By the time that the Fellowship of the Rosy Cross came into being, Waite's activities in the 'Higher Degrees' had led him to see 'more than ever the unexpressed things that lie behind the Rites' and he felt that another masonic work was called for. He decided upon an encyclopaedia, for although there were several already in existence, 'it seemed to me that here was the most convenient form in which to introduce a multitude of personal views and standpoints' (*SLT*, pp. 203–4). In May 1917 he suggested the book to Ralph Shirley of Rider & Co., who took it up, and within eighteen months he had completed almost the whole of the work. There was however, much argument over illustrations and over money (he never received satisfactory royalties and disputes over payment of these dragged on for many years), which delayed the book for another year. Finally, in March 1921, *A New Encyclopaedia of Freemasonry* was published. Waite's delight at its appearance was tempered by his expectation that 'The vested authorities and the diehards of dead Masonry might rise up of course to curse me' (*SLT*, p. 208). And so they did.

The reviewers in the scholarly masonic periodicals attacked it with a will. Writing in *Ars Quatuor Coronatorum* (Vol. 33, 1920), W. J. Songhurst condemned the arbitrary and bizarre arrangement of the subject matter: 'to find any particular subject one has to resort to a system of guess-work, the Index affording scarcely any help'; and he listed with glee Waite's errors of fact, examples of his ignorance, and his abusive and unjust comments on earlier writers. It is a damning review, but, alas, wholly justified, for the book is both badly constructed and unreliable. Nonetheless, it was well received by the non-masonic press and sold extremely well, if not to the extent that Waite himself claimed in 1938: 'No less than nineteen thousand sets of the costly volumes have been sold'[1] (*SLT*, p. 208). But for all that it has remained Waite's best-known work, it served him ill: a projected 'revised edition' never appeared and his total reward in royalties amounted to little over £300. His business career had not succeeded in teaching him how to draw up contracts with publishers as wily as Ralph Shirley.

Waite's ideas on Freemasonry were never widely accepted in England, but in America—largely as a result of fulsome praise in Dr Joseph Fort Newton's *The Builders: a Story and Study of Freemasonry* (1914), a book with an enormous circulation—his reputation grew and his theories were respected. Enthusiastic American freemasons wrote to him, visited him, and encouraged him to give lectures in the United States; but Waite wished for nothing more than the peace to continue his writing. His last masonic work, a revision of *The Secret Tradition in Freemasonry* (1937), he considered to be the most important. 'It is', he said, 'so altered, extended and transformed that it may claim to be a new undertaking and to supersede in fact that which it preserves in name' (p. x).

In his prospectus for this revised edition Waite had stated: 'In English Freemasonry the seal of a certain distinction attaches to the name of Arthur Edward Waite'; but it was a small and unobserved seal, for when he died, in 1942, the masonic establishment virtually ignored the event—he was accorded only a brief, three-paragraph obituary in *The Freemasons' Chronicle*, and their was no mention of his speculative work. His success as a mystic lay elsewhere.

15

THE WAY OF DIVINE UNION

WAITE was always at pains to present himself as 'the exponent in poetical and prose writings of sacramental religion and the higher mysticism, understood in its absolute separation from psychic and occult phenomena', and his friends and colleagues saw him in that light; but it was not how his public perceived him. 'Occultism' has invariably proven a more saleable commodity than 'mysticism' and to Waite's publishers he was an 'occultist'; indeed, it is difficult to see how else they were supposed to approach the author of *The Book of Ceremonial Magic* and the translator of Lévi's *Transcendental Magic*. Even his major works on the Secret Tradition were rarely seen as Waite wished; they might reveal the spirituality to be found behind the symbolism of alchemy, of the kabbalah, and of Freemasonry; or offer a true understanding of what lay at the heart of the Holy Grail; they might indeed concern the way to attain the Presence of God—but they fell into that ill-defined borderland between magic and religion, and were not seen as mysticism in the sense that either readers or reviewers understood the word.

And when Waite *did* write on mysticism proper (or, rather when he translated and annotated the works of those mystics who appealed to him), the Roman Catholic Church—which saw itself as the arbiter of good taste in such matters—assailed him. 'A dreamer of dreams, of a neo-Gnostic type', is how *The Tablet* typified Saint-Martin in its review of *The Life of Louis Claude de Saint-Martin*, adding for good measure that 'A re-hash of his transcendental vagaries may perhaps do some mischief, but so far as we can see it can be of real use to no one, and is of the smallest possible interest' (20 July 1901). Waite's translation of De Senancour's *Obermann* (1903) was generally treated more kindly, but it was, after all, seen in terms of Matthew Arnold's admiration for the book and treated as a work of literature rather than a mystical text.

But not all churchmen were hostile to Waite. Both *Obermann* and *Saint-Martin* had been read and appreciated by the Revd W. Robertson Nicoll, an eminent Free Church minister and editor of *The British Weekly*. In June 1905 he was due to lecture on 'The Practical Uses of Mysticism' at the Summer School of Theology to be held in Glasgow, the aim of the lectures being 'to point out how Christian mysticism helps Christians (1) in the conduct of life; (2) in the shaping of theology'. Nicoll was unsure of his ground and wrote to Waite for advice. He wished Waite to explain the mystical doctrine of prayer, to answer the question 'Has mysticism any real place for the atonement?', and to rebut Wesley's objection against mysticism 'that it was not practical, that the mystics did not work' (letter of 29 April 1905, quoted in Darlow, *William Robertson Nicoll: Life and Letters*, 1925, pp. 396, 399, 400).

Waite wrote a 'long and carefully considered answer' to this letter, in which he set out his own feelings on mysticism, and argued that the mystic is most certainly practical,

> because he is doing the one thing worth doing—getting back whence he came. It seems to me that the historical basis on which mysticism rests is the primordial fact that we came out of the great centre and that our destiny and our rest are in the centre; There can be only one business in life, which is the interior understanding of the hidden meaning of that voluntary poverty, perpetual chastity and entire obedience by which we ultimately return.

As to prayer, 'I do not see', he wrote, 'that it can be otherwise in his [the mystic's] case than that the answers to prayer are standing continually around him and this much more closely than the hills around Jerusalem'; while the attitude of the mystics to the atonement, 'outside all doctrinal questions', was best expressed by Eckartshausen, who saw it as 'the great event of the Grand and Holy Assemblies which are leading the Churches'. In more prosaic vein he added that, 'it is certainly a great truth that the divine has made itself abased so that none at last shall be left out of the union' (letter of May 1905).

Nicoll utilized all that Waite had written, and his lectures (which were later printed in his book *The Garden of Nuts*) put forward many of Waite's own ideas—in particular the doctrine of the Holy Assembly, which, Nicoll told his audience, 'is a testimony catholic to all mysticism. It is concerned with a withdrawn brotherhood in whose hands the experimental knowledge of God has remained and has increased. It is the doctrine of the esoteric Church of the Illuminated' (p. 69). What his audience made of all this is not recorded, but the vision of rows of earnest young ministers, sternly Calvinist in outlook, busily noting down the heterodox doctrines of A. E. Waite is delightful.

Nor was Nicoll alone in his appreciation of Waite. Evelyn Underhill, who had known Waite in the early days of her own spiritual quest (she had joined the Independent and Rectified Rite in July 1904 and had progressed at least to the 3=8 Grade of Practicus before quitting the Order), accepted that his 'dicta upon mysticism are often brilliant and profound' while criticizing him, in her essay on 'Magic and Mysticism of Today' (*Hibbert Journal*, January 1908), for his 'curious inability to separate himself from the false lights of a merely occult philosophy'. She also found Waite to be 'a deeply interested and sympathetic observer of certain aspects of the mystical experiment, and, in his most recent books, he shows a growing inclination to approach the boundaries of true mysticism'. And yet 'the reader may detect in his work a strain of intense desire and gathering sadness: of all the material having been ordered and investigated, yet something—and that the veritable object of the quest—ever eluding the pursuer'. Insofar as this was written about *Studies in Mysticism*, there was some truth in the statement, for the essays that comprise the book had been written in 1904—at which time there was no hint of other than a purely intellectual understanding of mysticism on Waite's part. But within a year a change had taken place and Waite began to know by experience what he had previously done no more than guess at.

On 27 March 1905 Waite noted, in the business diary that he kept while working for James Horlick, that 'I returned to the office . . . having been absent through severe illness since February 22nd'. The 'severe illness' was due to an accident, as he records in his autobiography:

It was in 1905 that I paid one of my periodical visits to a certain building estate of James Horlick which had been placed in my charge some few years previously [these were at Barnes, in South-West London]. It was late Autumn [see above for the correct date] and as the day closed in I missed my way on some stairs without banisters and fell heavily. The result was concussion of the brain, during which I was practically unconscious for an entire month . . . I was very, very ill, with nameless sensations in the head, as if all were dead therein and yet could ache numbly. I was haunted even by vague fears for reason itself. Another month must have passed in this manner and then I returned to town, *laesus* indeed assuredly but also *non victus*, as shewn fully thereafter. My business occupations were resumed, much as if nothing had occurred to disturb their outward and normal course; but I was made conscious slowly of a substantial change within, as if some new door had opened in the mind. A great and dangerous illness began to assume the aspect of a hidden providence, as if it were a thing decreed (*SLT*, p. 168).

By whatever obscure neurological process, a change had indeed taken place and his conception of the final end of the mystic way had altered.

It is shown most clearly in the gradual change that came over Waite's poetry. *A Book of Mystery and Vision* was, he says, 'like a song of the Sacramental World through all its pages', but the succeeding collections—*Strange Houses of Sleep*—'is a book on the verge of things, of veridic dreams and of quickenings towards the awakened state. It is less of mystical experience than of visions thereof. The preceding volume of verse stood for earlier stages.' Neither book, however, seemed adequate: 'The Soul in both is encompassed by a great splendour of images which testify to their wealth of meaning but do not part their curtains to shew the light behind. There is above all no suggestion of liberation from the world of images into the still being of pure unmixed intelligence' (*SLT*, p. 17). *That* would not be conveyed until he began to construct, in poetic form, the rituals for his Fellowship of the Rosy Cross.

But there is no question that Waite had experienced this state himself. 'It has been given to me', he continues, 'to know of this state under the influence of ether in a way that I may never look to experience until the end of all travellings; it has been given to me to find its threshold in a still state of mind.' 'Under the influence of ether' is a reference to experiences during the course of two dental operations. Waite described them fully while commenting on a similar happening recorded by Sir Arthur Conan Doyle:

In this connection it may be pardonable to mention a personal experience of the present writer, also under gas at a dentist's. During the normal course of intellectual work, prior to the dental operation, he had been dealing with certain mind-problems arising out of our mode of self-realization by the reflex act, and had not reached their solution; but during the higher state of awareness produced by sense-isolation these problems were solved, and this not by any ratiocinative process but by a direct inward seeing of which no adequate indication can be given in words. A short time after there was another operation, again under gas, and on this occasion the writer, who does not remember having been dealing previously with specific problems, experienced an inward state of being in pure mind, to which nothing in normal life offers any analogy, at least for him. It was a state of beatitude in realization within the self, if one likes to approximate without reaching a true description (Periodical Literature, in *The Occult Review*, April 1916).[1]

The title of the second collection of poems also came to Waite in an odd way. He could not remember when, but, 'it shall be remembered to my dying day how I woke up once—as it might be, at morning-tide—and a bell-like voice of clearness, apart from all stress and all touch of the personal, pronounced these words: STRANGE HOUSES OF SLEEP. They came, as it seemed to me, with a note of warning. Beyond all question and beyond all doubt, I knew at once that a book must be written under that title by me and no other' (*SLT*, p.p. 169–170). This knowledge had come to him early in 1902, for on 11 October of that year he noted in his diary: 'I laid down the schema of "Strange Houses of Sleep", containing nine schemes of romance concerning the loss and miscarriage of aspirations. It would seem as if it must be a mournful and pessimistic book, but it is one side only of the great research, and a side that has to be faced.'

Although the book was thus begun in 1902, 'it was only after the catastrophe of 1905 that I went to work upon it and wrote in all kinds of places, in Trains and Trams and Buses, as well as in my own Sanctum'; But the most important part of the book was neither the many brief poems drawn from the pages of *Horlick's Magazine*, nor *The Hidden Sacrament of the Holy Graal* (the 'Mystery Play' he had written with Arthur Machen), but a second verse drama, *The Book of the King's Dole*. It is, said Waite, 'a pregnant illustration of truth in the spiritual world; that there is a Church behind the Church on a more inward plane of being; and that it is formed of those who have opened the iridescent shell of external doctrine and have found that which abides within it. It is a Church of more worlds than one, for some of the Community are among us here and now and some are in a stage beyond the threshold of the physical senses' (*SLT*, pp. 170–1). It is also more than this; it is—in intent wholly and in structure partly—a recension of the initiation ceremony for an Adeptus Minor in the Independent and Rectified Rite.

Before the Second Order established its vault at Acton early in 1905, it was not possible to work the 5=6 Adeptus Minor ritual; nor are there any records to indicate when the first working of the ritual took place, but it was unlikely to have been before the end of 1906 (earlier Reports to the Convocations of the Second Order lament the difficulties of advancing candidates). The work of revising the 5=6 ritual was also incomplete and Waite would not have wished to use that of the old R.R. et A.C. without removing those elements he considered to be non-Christian; thus, while no manuscript of Waite's 5=6 ritual has survived, the text of *The Book of the King's Dole* may be considered to give a relatively accurate illustration of the experience undergone by candidates for the Second Order. The Temple is arranged correctly; the officers are present; the symbolism is accurate; and, above all, there is the central theme of death and resurrection.

Nor was his poetry the only medium through which Waite gave public expression to the symbolism and ideals of his Order. They were also given out—for those with eyes to see—in the designs of the cards that illustrate his *Pictorial Key to the Tarot* (1911). In its essence the Tarot is a pack of seventy-eight cards used variously for gaming or for divination; as with ordinary playing cards, the pack is divided into four suits, with the addition of a fourth court card to each suit and a series of twenty-two pictorial cards known as the Major Trumps. There is no conclusive evidence—whatever occultists believe—that the Trump cards predate the Italian Renaissance, and their basic symbolism probably dates from that time.[2] For members of the Golden Dawn, however, the Tarot epitomized Egyptian wisdom, and the numbered sequence of the Major Trumps, which paralleled the order of the letters in the Hebrew alphabet, enabled them to be associated with paths on the kabbalistic Tree of Life. Thus, as members of the Order progressed from Grade to Grade, so they learned the symbolism of the Tarot Trumps appropriate to that Grade. Waite, however, was dissatisfied with both the traditional Tarot cards and the designs devised for the Order by Westcott and Mathers; with the founding of the Independent and Rectified Rite the Tarot designs were jettisoned in company with the old rituals and he determined to create a wholly new pack.

At some time subsequent to Mathers's expulsion from the Order, a young American artist, Pamela Colman Smith, joined the Golden Dawn and took the motto 'Quod tibi id aliis'; but she seems to have had little interest in the Order, for when the schism came in 1903 she had attained only the Grade of Zelator.[3] She sided then with Waite's faction, presumably because, as Waite says, she 'loved its Ceremonies—as transformed by myself—without pretending or indeed attempting to understand their sub-surface consequence'. But he recognized that she was 'a most imaginative and abnormally psychic artist' who, it seemed, 'under proper guidance, could produce a Tarot with an appeal in the world of art and a suggestion of significance behind the Symbols which would put on them another construction than had ever been dreamed by those who, through many generations, had produced and used them for mere divinatory purposes' (*SLT*, p. 184).

Waite guided her over the designs to ensure that they 'kept that in the hiddenness which belonged to certain Greater Mysteries, in the Paths of which I was travelling', for although the Golden Dawn did not have at that time 'any deep understanding by inheritance of Tarot Cards', it was at least 'getting to know under my auspices that their Symbols—or some at least among them—were gates which opened on realms of vision beyond occult dreams' (*SLT*, p. 185). Most important were the High Priestess, the Hanged Man, and the Fool, over which 'she had to be spoon-fed carefully'. The symbolism in question was, however, unique to Waite's Order—'For the variations in the symbolism by which the designs have been affected, I alone am responsible' (*Pictorial Key*, p. 68)—for he felt quite at liberty to alter the cards as he saw fit, because 'there is no public canon of authority in the interpretation of Tarot symbolism' (*SLT*, p. 194)

The specific interpretation he placed upon the cards is given, in varying degrees of intelligibility, in *The Pictorial Key to the Tarot*, in 'The Book of the Secret Word' (in the pseudonymous *Manual of Cartomancy*, 1909), and in a private lecture given to members of his order, 'The Tarot and the Rosy Cross'.[4] The cards were also published separately, and there are further hints as to their meaning in an article, 'The Tarot: a Wheel of Fortune', which Waite wrote for *The Occult Review* (December 1909) to coincide with their publication. In the article the Fool is described as 'a card of the joy of life before it has been embittered by experience on the material plane. On the spiritual plane it is the soul, also at the beginning of its experience, aspiring towards the higher things before it has attained thereto'; while the Magician is 'he on whom "the spark from heaven" has fallen, who draws from above and derives thence to below'; it is also 'the card of illumination, and so looks the Fool when he has seen God'. Even more significant for Waite is the High Priestess, who is called 'the House of God, the Sanctuary and even the Kabalah, or secret tradition. She is really the Great Mother and the Secret Church.' The Tarot was thus also a channel for perpetuating the Secret Tradition, and it was necessarily a sympathizer with that tradition who was, as Waite states in the same article, that 'one who is deeply versed in the subject' who helped Waite and Pamela Colman Smith to complete the pack. Waite does not identify the helper, but there seems little doubt that it was W. B. Yeats, who had remained friendly with him even though he had sided with Felkin at the time of the schism.[5]

But while the varied channels of the Secret Tradition were presented to the public as separate entities—with occasional leading hints: Waite did point out that the four Tarot suits of Cups, Wands, Swords, and Pentacles correspond to the Grail Hallows, but he left his readers to draw from this what conclusions they could—they were drawn together for the members of his Order. At first the synthesis was tentative, but as the last vestiges of magic dropped away with the passing of the Independent and Rectified Rite, and as the rituals of that rite were transformed into the religious ceremonies of the Fellowship of the Rosy Cross, it became more sure. And in the true understanding of the Secret Tradition lay the essential difference between the old Order and the new; by its very nature the Independent and Rectified Rite could not entirely rid itself of the magical practices of the original *R.R. et A.C.*—nor did its members wish it to do so. For all that Waite urged mysticism upon them, the members of the rite would not willingly give up astral travelling, visions, and phenomena; faced with a demand to reject the cipher manuscripts, they could not bring themselves to accept the inevitable consequence: the rejection of the glamour of magic. Instead they rejected Waite.

It would not be correct, however, to see the demise of Isis-Urania and the whole Independent and Rectified Rite as wholly due to the clash between magic and mysticism. Some of the members desired to follow a mystical path—but as their own masters, and that, under Waite, they could never be: the Fellowship of the Rosy Cross, however benign, was a thoroughly autocratic Order. According to its 'Constitution and Laws' (See Appendix E for the full text), 'The Constitution of the Fellowship is hierarchic and not elective, its government being vested in the Imperator of the Rite, who has power to appoint his successor, subject to confirmation by the body general of Adepti Exempti, and also to appoint substitutes for the government of the Temple.' From the time of its founding to the time of his death, the Fellowship of the Rosy Cross had no other Imperator beside Waite.

Not that his rule was either malign or capricious; Waite had no desire to emulate the paranoid MacGregor Mathers, and his government of the Order was both sane and sensible. There was no seeking out of Secret Chiefs or 'Sun Masters' in the manner of Felkin or Brodie-Innes; the Fellowship saw itself purely as 'the guardian of a path of symbolism communicated in Ritual after the manner of the chief Instituted Mysteries, past and present', and that symbolism 'is concerned only with the quest and attainment of the human soul on its return to the Divine Centre: it is sought thereby to recall its members to the true object of research and the living method of its attainment'. At the very outset of his career in the Order, the would-be Neophyte was told 'The fulfilment of earthly life is in the life which is eternal, and the sole purpose of man's sojourn in the material world is that he may attain union with the Divine.' It was also no accident that in 1915, the year the Fellowship was founded to provide a path of mystical experience for those who sought it, Waite published a literary exposition of that path, in the form of his most important work on mysticism, *The Way of Divine Union*.

It is a most extraordinary work. It attempts, as must all mystical works to express the inexpressible, but Waite emphasized the role of the mind in translating the mystical experience—even within our own consciousness—so that the reader should fully recognize the inadequacy of language and not suffer the temptation of treating the aesthetic satisfaction to be gained from absorbing lyrical prose as in any way comparable with the overwhelming transformation of self that comes with the mystical experience itself. The mystic, for Waite, is an intensely practical person and the mystical life is 'an exploration of self', but it is yet 'the most difficult enterprise which can be undertaken by the human mind'. The final state of Divine Union cannot be attained in this life, but there are other states that can, and it is towards these that Waite urges his readers:

> God knows, and all His mystics, that such absorption is not attainable now; but there is a deep and undistracted preoccupation in God which is not beyond some of us, and therein are moments, brief periods, certain halves of hours, when that preoccupation is 'lifted higher', when the love becomes so transcendent that the knower and the known, subject and object, are wrapped up together in an indescribable unity, and this is that attainment of which we possess the precious records in Mysticism. Its barriers are burned away and all the barbed wires of intellectualism are melted (p. 318).

It was towards the attainment of this state that the ceremonies of his Fellowship of the Rosy Cross were directed.

The Way of Divine Union is also intensely Christ-centred, without being sectarian, and was praised by Catholics and Protestants alike. Mgr William Barry, in the course of his review for *The Bookman* (January 1916), gently upbraided Waite for his lack of Catholic orthodoxy but praised both the book and its author. Mrs Herman, a Protestant scholar of mysticism, described the book as: 'A profound and illuminating study by one who writes out of an unparalleled knowledge of mystical literature, and who is not only a master of the interpretation of mystical doctrine and experience, but himself a mystic of the first order' (*The Meaning and Value of Mysticism*, 1916, p. 387). She yet pointed out that 'he does scant justice to the mystical element in Protestantism'.

All the reviewers pointed out the book's principal fault: it is not written in language that can be understood by the man in the street, although Divine Union is for all men. This difficulty—that he wrote as a specialist for specialists—Waite was never able to overcome in his writing. But when his words were accompanied by the ritual of his Order there was a change. Within the Fellowship of the Rosy Cross even the most simple member could experience directly what Waite's words could only inadequately describe to the outside world. The mystical state is not attained by reading about 'Love in the Transcendence' but by the act of that love.

16

FRATER SACRAMENTUM REGIS AND HIS FELLOWSHIP OF THE ROSY CROSS

REFERRING to the Fellowship of the Rosy Cross in his autobiography, Waite said of it, 'there is no story to tell, either by myself or another. May that most sacred centre give up no outward form' (*SLT*, p. 229). But he made the public aware of its existence by cryptic references to a 'Hidden Rite' (in *Emblematic Freemasonry*, p. 151), as well as to a rite which 'claims to contain the Mysteries of Ancient and Primitive Masonry' and which 'communicates in secret instructions a certain Doctrine of the Soul' (*Secret Tradition in Freemasonry*, 1937, p. 461). He also carefully preserved the rituals, the Minutes, and lists of members of the Fellowship, and from these it is possible to present a picture of the form of his Order, if not of the content of its workings.[1]

The Independent and Rectified Rite of the Golden Dawn had been instituted for the benefit of those who saw the Order as 'capable of a mystical instead of an occult construction', and in similar manner the Fellowship of the Rosy Cross was mystical, but unlike its predecessor in that it was *wholly* mystical; and, although based upon the kabbalah, it was also wholly Christian, as laid down in its constitution: 'The mode of interpretation in respect of Kabalistic Tradition is a Christian Mode.'

The Fellowship was divided into four Orders that corresponded to the four Worlds of kabbalistic symbolism, and as the members progressed from Grade to Grade so they also passed from World to World. The progression was as follows: The 0=0 Grade of Neophyte, and 1=10 Grade of Zelator (corresponding to the sephirah of Malkuth on the Tree of Life) were in the World of Action (Assiah) and comprised the First Order. The next three Grades, of 2=9 Theoreticus; 3=8 Practicus; and 4=7 Philosophus; corresponding respectively to Yesod, Hod, and Netzach, comprised the Second Order and were held to be in the World of Formation (Yetzirah); while the Third Order, in the World of Creation (Briah), comprised the Portal of the Third Order, and the Grades of 5=6 Adeptus Minor; 6=5 Adeptus Major; and 7=4 Adeptus Exemptus, corresponding to the sephiroth Tiphereth, Geburah, and Chesed. There was a Portal Grade for the Fourth Order, in the World of the Supernals (Atziluth), but no rituals for Grades corresponding to the first three sephiroth were ever worked, although Waite began to construct them towards the end of his life. There were also a number of additional ceremonies for the Consecration of a Temple, the Festival of the Equinox, the Solstices, and the Installation of a Celebrant.

As the Order grew it was felt desirable to separate the first two Orders from the Third and Fourth, and in 1922 the higher Grades were gathered under the *Ordo Sanctissimus Roseae et Aureae Crucis*. Between 1926 and 1928 Waite produced a series of rituals specifically for the *O.S.R. et A.C.* which he termed collectively 'The Book of Life in the Rose'; this he revised continually, creating the final form of the rituals under the titles of 'Mysterium Briah' and 'Mysterium Atziluth', in the late 1930s. These were printed between 1937 and 1943 and constitute the summation of Waite's mystical philosophy in dramatic form. Their correct performance requires such an exalted state of consciousness on the part of each of the participants that their working was—and is—virtually impossible. Below this level, however, the Order thrived.

Waite saw his Order as a religious organization, and stressed this to potential recruits in an account of the requirements of a candidate for the 'Hidden Rite': 'A truly prepared Candidate must be able to realize that all true Ritual is sacramental, the outward sign of a meaning and grace within . . . that the sacramentalism of such Ritual is not arbitrary but essential; that all means of instruction available to man are of a sacramental order; that God communicates with His creatures through a sacramental universe' (*Emblematic Freemasonry*, p. 281). And as religious ritual was, for Waite, that of the Latin Mass, so the vestments, regalia, and fittings utilized in the rituals of his Order were reminiscent of those used in the Mass; in appearance, however, they were quite different (see Appendix E).

Such elaborate ceremonial could not for long be expected to manifest in the hired rooms of a public hotel, however grand. (Early in 1917 the Order had moved to the Imperial Hotel in Russell Square, following the commandeering of De Keyser's Hotel in 1916 by the Government; during the brief intervening period meetings were held at Sidmouth Lodge, Waite's home in South Ealing). Eventually a permanent home was found in a flat at No. 14 Earl's Court Square; or so the members hoped.

The Temple, which was consecrated on 24 March 1919, took up only a part of the flat, the remainder being occupied by one of the members, George Barrett Dobb—Frater Paratum cor meum in the Order. For five years the Order worked its ceremonies contentedly, until the perilous state of the building became increasingly evident: on 20 July 1924, 'about 6.15 p.m. the porch ceiling fell with a heavy crash'. Alarmed by this, Waite made sure that the Order would not be held responsible, by bringing in 'the large framework from the Temple balcony to the Temple itself, lest it should be pretended that this caused the porch to collapse, which is impossible' (Diary, 20, 21 July 1924).

At the same time other—and worse—trouble befell the Order: in October Frater E tenebris in lucem vocatus (H. M. Duncan)—in the profane world an employee of the Lanston Monotype Corporation, and a man of chronic ill-health—committed suicide by shooting himself. It was a terrible blow for Waite, coming less than a month after the death of his wife and depriving him of both a friend and one of the principal financial supports of the Order. Waite also became aware at this time of the presence in the Order of 'a traitor' who was assiduously filching sections of the rituals for the benefit of a rival organization. He was soon identified (see p. 148 below), but the uncertainty engendered by his activities disturbed the harmony of the Order, and Earl's Court Square became an increasingly unhappy home for the Salvator Mundi Temple.

Leaving it was not as straightforward as the members might have wished. Frater Paratum had no desire to give up his flat: 'I have a letter from Paratum', wrote Waite in his diary, 'who is in one of his paroxysms, and on this occasion it may lead to trouble' (Diary, 30 August 1926). Fortunately, it did not, and he was finally persuaded to leave soon afterwards when Waite had mollified him. The second home of the Order was at 10 Scarsdale Villas, South Kensington, where the Temple shared the house with Soror Sub Sole Amoris Serviens (Miss A. M. Collett), who was a temperamental tenant—on one occasion 'she fell into a livid rage' because Waite preferred to stay with friends at Kew rather than remain overnight at Scarsdale Villas—but less awkward than Frater Paratum had been when the time came for the Order to move on. ('The place', recalled Waite in 1936, 'was damp and destructive to the properties, so we removed . . .')

Lack of money was invariably the principal reason for the Order's periodic ramblings round London, and finding suitable premises at a reasonable rent was never an easy task. The members refused to consider a house outside the city, but they were unable to find an alternative to Scarsdale Villas in spite of spending the early months of 1929 scouring the western suburbs in search of suitable premises. Eventually a three-year lease was taken on No. 30 Lansdown Crescent, Notting Hill—at £125 per annum—but as Soror Sub Sole did not move into the new home she gave up the post of Cancellarius (i.e. Secretary; she seems previously to have paid only a nominal rent on account of these duties), and Waite was reluctantly obliged to take it upon himself.

After the expiration of the lease there was a hiatus in Order affairs for some nine months until March 1934, when rooms were obtained for the Temple at 104 Maida Vale, the headquarters of an androgynous masonic body, the Order of Ancient, Free and Accepted Masonry for Men and Women, several of whose members were also active in the Fellowship of the Rosy Cross. Here the Order remained for five years, finally leaving London in August 1939 for Broadstairs, where a second Temple had been established in Waite's home. The move out of the city had been forced upon Waite because, as he told his friend William Semken, 'It is quite impossible in my existing state of health to go searching about in London, and there is no-one else to do so'; he hoped, however, 'that people who want the Grades of the Order will get here in quest of them' (letter of 16 July 1939). But war dashed that hope and, for all practical purposes, the Order fell into abeyance.

But what had kept it alive throughout its twenty-five years? Waite did not conform to the popular image of a hierophant; he was neither lean, tall, nor ascetic, but short, stocky, happy to indulge in the more inoffensive pleasures of the flesh, and possessed of ordinary human weaknesses—as recalled after his death by G. E. Bridge, a masonic friend: 'Until one "stood up to him" [Waite] was inclined to be pontifical—when he found that other folk sometimes had views of their own he became quite human, and would either discuss them with all the powers of his very keen intellect, or boil over in vitriolic attack on the person, ancestors, and posterity of his imagined opponent. In that latter respect I think he just missed real greatness' (letter to an unidentified correspondent, 15 October 1943).

Within his Order, however, he attained that greatness. His rituals carried conviction, for they were the work of a true mystic, and he was a magnificent ritualist. In his obituary for *The Occult Review*, Philip Wellby said of Waite:

> There are three things in which Arthur Waite surpassed any of my acquaintance. First of these was the possession of a phenomenal memory, a memory that was both encyclopaedic and accurate. Owing to this he excelled in the conduct of rites and rituals, whether in Temple, Chapter, Preceptory or Conclave. Added to this was his masterly rendering of the prescribed form of language in every rite, which imparted a living force to the phrase or peroration, and conveyed an inspiration so often lacking in a perfunctory recital. Whether officiating in Masonic or extra-Masonic orders he made each occasion memorable to his hearers by the infusion of this vitality of spirit into the spoken word. I can recall certain times when he appeared to be a veritable channel of force, dispensing power that was beyond his own disposal in his ordinary daily avocations (July 1942).

And it was this power that drew into the Fellowship of the Rosy Cross earnest but unremarkable people, and having drawn them in, transformed their inner lives.

The Order was never large. By 1929 there were 171 members—99 women and 72 men—and rather less than fifty more joined over the next ten years; but the number of active members at any one time was never more than sixty, and often less (in 1929 Waite sent out 56 Summonses for the Festival of the Equinox—which all members of the Fellowship were entitled, and expected, to attend; in 1930, 62 Summonses were issued for a meeting in February, and in July 45 'demands for Order subscriptions' at two guineas each).

Before admission to the Grade of Neophyte, each member signed a 'Form of Profession for Postulants', by which he or she 'solemnly and sincerely' affirmed:

I. That, exceeding all definition, there is one Eternal Source and Principle, called God.
II. That, from this Principle, the soul of man derives everlasting life.
III. That I desire the knowledge of my Source and union with God in consciousness.
IV. The being on the Quest of God I ask of my own free will to be admitted into the Fellowship of the R∴C∴, which communicates the knowledge of the Quest and its terms in symbolism.
V. That I accept the obligations imposed by the bonds of the Fellowship, subject to my civil, moral and religious duties.
VI. That I will at no time and under no circumstances admit any one into the Fellowship, save only under the Warrant of the Imperator.
VII. That I will not on my own authority found any Temple or Chapter of the Fellowship, nor make any use of its Rituals for the initiation or advancement of any one, except by the Warrant of the Imperator.

During the ceremony the Neophyte also accepted 'The Solemn Obligation of a Novice', which was analogous to that of the old Golden Dawn but without any mention of penalties, bloodcurdling or otherwise, to follow a breach of the Obligation.

None of this was exceptional and was familiar to most new members who were drawn largely from masonic or esoteric circles. The members were also almost entirely unknown outside such circles, only a few of them having achieved fame in the outside world. Of those few, Dr Helen Worthington (Soror Lumen Sapientiae) had entered the Independent and Rectified Rite in 1913 and followed Waite into the F∴R∴C∴. She had been a student of Elizabeth Severn, a prominent 'alternative' medical practitioner, and set up as a psycho-therapist. In time she developed a Harley Street practice and treated Waite for his various real and imagined complaints. She remained one of his most faithful supporters. John Brahms Trinick (Frater Donec Attingam), a stained glass artist whose work was often exhibited at the Royal Academy, joined the Order as a young man when he arrived in England with the Australian Army during the First World War. He painted the 'Symbols of the Paths' (substitutes for traditional Tarot designs) used by the Order and drew the portrait of Waite, in his robes as Imperator of the order, that appears as the frontispiece to Volume I of *A New Encyclopaedia of Freemasonry.* Later in life he took up Jungian psychology and wrote on the psychological interpretation of alchemy, his book *The Fire-Tried Stone* being published in 1967.

More eccentric than either of these was John Sebastian Marlow Ward (Frater Custos Custodiens), who entered the Order on 22 March 1921. He was the leading exponent of what is known s the 'symbolist' school of masonic research—seeking the origins of Freemasonry through a comparative study of analogous initiatory rituals; he was instrumental, with Sir John Cockburn, in founding, also in 1921, the Masonic Study Society, of which he became Secretary-General (the Deputy

Vice-President was Waite) and to which he delivered lectures that were incorporated in his best-known work, *Freemasonry and the Ancient Gods* (1921, 1926). Another of his brain-children was the Order of Indian Wisdom which Waite was invited to join—perhaps to reciprocate Ward's membership of the F∴R∴C∴—but although he attended several of its meetings in 1921 and 1922 he thought that the ceremonies 'seemed rather frivolous' and took no further part in them. By the end of 1923 Ward had left the Fellowship and concerned himself increasingly with esoteric activities, culminating in 1928 with a vision (perceived jointly with his wife) 'in which they were ordered to found a mixed community of men and women to prepare for the Second Coming of Christ' (Peter Anson, *Bishops at Large*, 1964, p. 283). This resulted in the founding of the Confraternity of the Kingdom of Christ, which, after initial support, was frowned upon by the authorities in the Church of England, causing Ward to turn to the Orthodox Catholic Church in England (an unorthodox and microscopic body), in which he was consecrated as a Bishop in 1935. Ward died in 1949 after a distinguished career in the ecclesiastical underworld.

Two members of the Fellowship of the Rosy Cross stood out from all the others: one was to attain international standing as a novelist, critic, and poet, while the other had already achieved fame before his entry into the Order. On 1 February 1921, Alvin Langdon Coburn (1882–1966) and his wife were initiated into the F∴R∴C∴ as Frater Deus Portarum Lucis and Soror Deus Principium Meus; his reputation as a photographer had been established over the previous decade by his delicate topographical work and remarkable portrait studies,[2] and Waite was delighted to admit such a distinguished candidate. Coburn had long been interested in Waite's works (in 1922 he wrote that 'On the shelves of my little library are nearly fifty volumes of the writings of Arthur Edward Waite') and wished to meet him; at last,

> one fortunate day I met him. We seemed friends almost at once. Perhaps it was that I knew his mind so very well from friendship with his printed pages—even perhaps there may have been some link out the past—[3] be all this as it may, I am one of many who have much to thank him for. In an age of outward turmoil and unrest he has told us of the things within: of how the base metal of material desires may be transmuted into spiritual gold. In 'The Way of Divine Union' and 'The Book of the Holy Grail' he has given to the world priceless treasures. Hidden within them are deep mysteries (*More Men of Mark*, 1922, p. 22).

They were not destined to remain friends for long.

Initially all went well; Coburn took a series of photographs of Waite as Imperator of the Order, at Earl's Court Square, and three portrait studies for publication; one of these appears in *More Men of Mark* and a second was exhibited by Coburn at the Royal Photographic Society in February 1924. Within the Order Frater Deus Portarum Lucis attained the Grade of Adeptus Minor on 6 February 1922 (his wife following him two days later), and advanced to the Grade of Adeptus

Major one year later. But in 1923 he was following other esoteric interests. He had developed an interest in 'The Shrine of Wisdom', a body founded in 1911 to propagate Universal Wisdom, more specifically as presented in Neoplatonism; when Coburn took it up he altered the name to 'The Universal Order' and incorporated a certain degree of ritual practice. Unknown to Waite—who had been a guest in Coburn's home at Harlech, in North Wales, for three weeks in July of that year—Coburn was developing the rituals of the Universal Order from materials extracted from the F.·.R.·.C.·.. By the end of 1924 it became clear that a 'traitor' was at work and he was rapidly identified as Coburn (no other members seem to have joined the Universal Order); there was a final, embarrassing meeting with Waite on 6 February 1925. Whether Coburn admitted to adding rituals to the list of things that he had 'to thank him for' is unclear; but they parted finally and without friendship.

When a Neophyte was initated into the Order, the 'Step, Sign, Token and Words of the Portal' were entrusted to him by the Auxiliary Frater Zelator, acting as 'Proclamator et Lucifer'; on the occasion of Coburn's initiation, this office was performed by Frater Qui Sitit Veniat, who at that time had himself been a member of the Order for more than three years. On his Form of Profession he gave his address as 18 Parkhill Road, Hampstead, NW3; and his occupation as 'Proof-reader & editorial work'; his name he gave in full—Charles Walter Stansby Williams.

Among students of Charles Williams and his work it has been fashionable—indeed, it still is—to play down both the influence of Waite and the role of the F.·.R.·.C.·. in Williams's life. Such an attitude stems partly from a feeling that membership of the Golden Dawn—with which critics invariably confuse the F.·.R.·.C.·.—somehow brings discredit upon Williams, and partly from a belief that Waite's writings, not being the work of an academic in the strict sense of the word, are of little worth and ought not to have exercised any significant influence upon the literary figure they seek to lionize. In maintaining such an attitude they perpetuate not only their own prejudices but also errors of fact in the biography of Charles Williams.

On his own admission,[4] Williams sent Waite a copy of his first book, *The Silver Stair* (1912), after reading *The Hidden Church of the Holy Graal.* He gives no date, but the book was sent during the summer of 1915, for Waite replied on 24 August and Williams visited him at South Ealing on 4 September, signing his name in Sybil Waite's autograph book. Whether they discussed poetry or the Grail is not clear, but Waite retained *The Silver Stair* until the following April when Williams visited him again: 'He came and I returned his poems. We had a long talk' (Diary, 22 April 1916). By this time Williams was certainly aware of Waite's poetry, for he was proof-reading *The Oxford Book of English Mystical Verse*, which contained six poems by Waite—included because the editors, the

Revd A. H. E. Lee and D. H. Nicholson, not only admired Waite's work but had also been active members of the Independent and Rectified Rite (neither of them, however, continued in the new Order). It is possible that they told Williams something of the nature of the Order and they may, consciously or not, have encouraged him to seek admission to the Fellowship of the Rosy Cross.

In 1917 Williams asked Waite for a Form of Profession, signed it on 18 July, and was 'received into the Portal Grade of the Rosy Cross under the Sacramental Name of Qui Sitit Veniat' on Friday 21 September. After the ceremony, 'The Celebration of the Autumnal Equinox was celebrated in solemn form', which Williams as a Neophyte, would have witnessed while wearing the black habit of the Order together with 'a collar of white silk, emblematic of purification in progress, from which depends a crimson Calvary Cross'; all of which he had obtained, on Waite's advice, from Spencer & Co., the masonic outfitters.

Frater Qui Sitit Veniat progressed rapidly through the lower Grades, and on 26 August 1919 he was 'Raised upon the Cross of Tiphereth' and entered the Grade of Adeptus Minor. Beyond this he moved more slowly, attaining the Grade of 7=4 Adeptus Exemptus on 10 July 1924 and reaching the Portal of the Fourth Order on 27 July of the following year, when he was 'integrated by Dispensation on the part of the Headship into the Blessed Company'. His final advancement, on 29 June 1927, was to be a participant in 'The Ceremony of Consecration on the Threshold of Sacred Mystery', which was the first ritual of Waite's more exalted order, The Hidden Life of the Rosy Cross. It was also William's last ceremony; after taking part in this rarefied ceremony he ceased to attend any of the rituals, although he remained an inactive member of the Order. Waite visited him at Amen House, the home of the Oxford University Press, in September 1928, and wrote to him periodically until 1931, but he never succeeded in persuading him to resume an active role.

Williams had been a valuable member of the Order. Unlike many of the members, who were, so he told Anne Ridler, 'content to read words from a script when it came to their turn', he himself 'took pleasure in memorizing what had to be said, so that he could celebrate with dignity'.[5] This he did during the two six-monthly periods (commencing 23 September 1921 and 30 September 1924) when he acted as Master of the Temple and worked all the grades up to that of 4=7 Philosophus. After Waite, he would undoubtedly have been the most impressive Master.

Although he had been brought to Waite by way of the Holy Grail, Williams was most interested in Waite's kabbalistic doctrines as set out in *The Secret Doctrine in Israel* (1913), and it was probably this book that stimulated his attempts to formulate a theology of marriage and provided a basis for his ideas about the symbolism of the body. Certainly he utilized kabbalistic terminology and symbolism in *Taliessin through Logres*, and there are clear similarities between the

Tarot figures in *The Greater Trumps* and the images in Waite's pack. Like Coburn, Williams had much to thank Waite for, but unlike Coburn, what he took he took honourably.

The loss of Charles Williams to the Order was a disappointment to Waite, but his work continued. As a means of propagating the Order he attempted, in 1922, to resuscitate his old dream of 'The Secret Council of Rites', but after discussion with his closest colleagues he changed its name to 'The College of Sacred Mysteries' and arranged for the printing of a manifesto. But among those involved in drafting the manifesto were both J. S. M. Ward and Alvin Langdon Coburn; when Ward drifted away, plans for the 'College' were postponed, and when Coburn was banished they were altogether abandoned.

Lectures, however, continued to bring in occasional new members. He addressed the Theosophical Society in 1919 on 'Some Mystic Aspects of the Holy Grail' (one member of the audience recalled that he arrived late; but she joined his Order nonetheless);[6] he spoke frequently at Masonic Research Societies,[7] and in 1923 he lectured to the Porchway group on 'The Great Symbols of the Tarot' and to the Students' Research Society on 'The Kabbalah and the Mystic Quest'. Both lectures were for audiences of eager theosophists and on both occasions new recruits duly followed. The last public lecture Waite gave was to the Poetry Lovers' Fellowship; on 7 December 1931 he spoke on 'Some Great Awakenings', but no dormant vocations woke to life and none of the Poetry Lovers passed into the Order. The Fellowship of the Rosy Cross, for all it grew more slowly, remained the centre of Waite's life and much of his later life was devoted to writing and rewriting the Order rituals. There was also, of necessity, other writing—Waite might live for the Order but he had yet to write for the world at large in order to live.

His series of works on the Secret Tradition had continued with *The Book of Ceremonial Magic* (1911), which Waite sub-titled 'The Secret Tradition in Goëtia'. It was little more than an expansion of his earlier *Book of Black Magic* but he had felt it necessary to illustrate the negative side of the Secret Tradition and to warn against the perils of magic once again. The final subjects to be approached were Rosicrucianism and alchemy; the former was treated exhaustively in *The Brotherhood of the Rosy Cross* (1924)—including an account of the origins of the Golden Dawn, complete with a reproduction (upside-down) of one page of the cipher manuscripts—while the latter he dealt with in *The Secret Tradition in Alchemy* (1926), a book that came about in a curious way.

Late in 1922 Waite discovered that Kegan Paul & Co. were planning to reissue *The Occult Sciences*, although they had not told him because Mr Stallybrass, the publisher, 'claims to have thought that I was dead' (Diary, 23 October 1922). They did allow Waite to insert a note to the effect that, the reproduction, though sanctioned, has not been superintended by the author himself, who desires to state that it was written about thirty-three years ago, and does not represent his present views on matters of occult research or on several pretensions of occult arts and processes, while in respect of mesmerism, spiritualism, and modern theosophy the effluxion of time has transformed many of their aspects.

And despite having every right to reprint the book Mr Stallybrass felt guilty and offered to publish the book on which Waite was currently working. He expected something 'occult' but the Prefatory Note should have warned him: what he got was *Lamps of Western Mysticism*. This collection of 'Essays on the Life of the Soul in God' was Waite's last major work on mysticism and contained papers drawn largely from *The Occult Review* and *The Quest*. It is a difficult book that sold slowly and, as with almost all of Waite's works, was ultimately remaindered (Kegan Paul & Co. sold the remaining copies to John Watkins, the occult bookseller, in 1928).

The study of alchemy was begun in November 1924, as a way of escape from the trauma of Ada's death. Waite completed it in under a year and persuaded Stallybrass to publish it on the grounds that it would be a fit companion for *Lamps of Western Mysticism*; it was accepted and in due course appeared. Waite says of it in his Preface, that it: 'completes my examination of the Secret Tradition transmitted through Christian Times, Alchemy being the one branch so far unexplored of that which has claimed to constitute Theosophy in Christ, illustrated in experience rather than by formal doctrine'. He concludes by saying, 'If I am spared for further efforts in these directions, they will belong to the work of revision, when the series at large may come to be drawn together into a collected form' (p. xxii). The revisions were published—as *The Holy Kabbalah* (1929), *The Holy Grail* (1933), and *The Secret Tradition in Freemasonry* (1937)—but his cherished project of a collected edition of his works remained a pipe dream. He had succeeded in publishing his *Collected Poems* in 1914 but he wished to incorporate both *Avalon* and his last poetical work, *The Book of the Holy Graal*—which John Watkins published in 1921 simply because he liked it, and which Katherine Tynan praised in *The Bookman* as 'poetry of great beauty, never uninspired, never crabbed, and difficult'. It was quite impossible from a commercial standpoint and even the selection of poems, *The Open Vision*, which he had helped Phyllis Leuliette, a friend of his daughter, to make in 1931 was not printed until 1951—and then privately.

Alchemy, however, was more saleable, even if the book repudiated views he had put forward with fervour as a young man. His altered viewpoint—away from that of Mrs Atwood's *Suggestive Inquiry*—had been made clear in 1911 (in *The Secret Tradition in Freemasonry*) and had led to Isabelle de Steiger taking him to task for his *volte face* in the pages of *The Occult Review*. Waite replied by pointing out that, 'The eighteen years that have elapsed since the publication of *Azoth* and the twenty-three years since that of my *Lives of Alchemystical Philosophers* represent a continuous life of thought and research; there should be no need for surprise that I have changed some critical opinions expressed so long ago' (*Occult Review*, January 1912).

He yet lost neither his interest in alchemy nor his friendship with Mme de Steiger. When the Alchemical Society, for 'the study of the works and theories of the alchemists in all their aspects, philosophical, historical and scientific, and of all matters relating thereto', was founded in November 1912 the two honorary vice-presidents were A. E. Waite and Isabelle de Steiger; during its brief, two-year existence they both contributed papers and argued for their respective points of view. Many years later, when he was asked to write a preface to her posthumous autobiography, *Memorabilia* (1927), he was less charitably disposed. He noted in his diary, 20 April 1927, how 'I sat in a Waiting Room at Victoria and finished that silly Preface to *Memorabilia*. [I] have found it almost impossible to do these few pages because of their subject.'

The Theosophical Society was also interested in some of his work. In 1918 their Library Committee had commissioned Waite to prepare an edition of *The Works of Thomas Vaughan*, which proved to be a sumptuous production when it was published in the following year and which was not superseded until the appearance of Alan Rudrum's definitive edition of 1984—but that is so poorly printed that Waite still outdoes in form what, perhaps, has outdone him in substance. They took up Waite again in 1927 when S. L. Bensusan, whom he had met at the Authors' Club at Christmas of 1925 and found to be 'sympathetic and excellent company'—adding patronizingly, 'quite distinct from and quite unlike the ordinary sons of Israel' (Diary, 23 December 1925)—offered to publish Waite's revised Fairy Tales. The book appeared, finely printed but utterly incomprehensible to theosophists or to anyone else, and immediately failed; Waite received almost nothing in royalties and gained only the dubious satisfaction of seeing the Theosophical Publishing House itself fail within two years.

Most of his books were still published by Rider & Co., but his relations with the firm were becoming strained. In 1925 Ralph Shirley sold his company, and the occult publications—which the purchasers of *The Timber Trades Journal* did not want—passed to Hutchinson & Co. They proved to be harder taskmasters and eventually overhauled the somewhat antiquated style of *The Occult Review*. Waite's contributions were sharply reduced in number and he was warned that his regular 'Periodical Literature' feature would be taken over by the magazine's sub-editor, Harry Strutton. Although he was told of this impending change in March 1930 it was not until November 1931 that he ceased to write the column; at first he thought that it was petty spite 'because I have made it clear that in remaindering my books without consulting me, Rider & Co. have broken at least two contracts' (Diary, 27 March 1930). In fact, as Strutton later told him, it was to save expense for a journal that never made a profit. Waite was also finding the task of a monthly analysis of dozens of English and foreign journals too heavy to bear and his only regret in parting with his column was the loss of income.

His books never brought enough by way of royalties to provide an adequate income and he relied heavily upon money from writing articles and reviews (Robertson Nicoll had secured for him a steady stream of reviews for *The Bookman*, often on subjects not remotely connected with things esoteric). When 'Periodical Literature' ceased he sought an alternative and acquired the job of producing a quarterly column of a similar nature—'The Land of Psyche and Nous'—for a minor theosophical publication, *The Aryan Path*. In addition to shrinking royalties he had only similarly shrinking returns from unwise investments in War Loans, made on behalf of his wife and daughter. In 1930 he noted that 'my expenses during the last ten months . . . exceed £200—say, £230. My income from investments is £145 before tax is deducted. How I can make up the difference in future is an anxious question with books remaindered and O[ccult] R[eview] work impaired'. (Diary, 29 March 1930). The Order members assisted with a regular season ticket for his travels to London and occasional gifts of cash; there was also a little money from writing reports for publishers. One of these reports was a decisive rejection of a book that, with hindsight, he might have viewed differently.

In June 1935 Waite worked conscientiously on a report on 'Israel Regardie's G.D. revelations, the introductory volume of which has been submitted for my opinion by George Routledge & Sons'. By the end of the month, 'on the authority of my reports', Routledge had declined the book. Waite did not approve of the publication of the G.D. rituals—although he toyed with the idea himself in 1937 and Rider announced on the dust-jacket of *The Secret Tradition in Freemasonry* the imminent publication of the *Secret Rituals of the Rosy Cross*, i.e. the non-Grade ceremonies of the Independent and Rectified Rite—and prided himself on scotching Regardie's plans in England. In December 1936 he wrote to a former Order member, Frater In Aeternum, to advise him that

> There are spurious Temples in existence, and as an illustration of the kind of persons whom they include it may be mentioned that a Jew is attempting to find a publisher in America or here (where he has so far failed) who will risk capital over the publication of all G.D. Rituals, Knowledge Lectures and so forth. I spoilt his chance here with a big firm, but have no influence with business houses across the Atlantic (letter of 17 December 1936).

The implicit anti-Semitism is surprising in one who had taken great pains in 1921 to condemn Nesta Webster's hysterical account in *The Morning Post* of a Jewish 'occult' peril and who took great pride in Gershom Scholem's remark that Waite's books 'belong to the best that have been written on the Theosophy of the Kabbalah' (quoted in the *Times Literary Supplement* review of *The Holy Kabbalah*, 12 December 1929).

But if the financial rewards were few and if the task of writing was increasingly onerous and unsatisfactory (of the additional chapter on the Masonic Peace Memorial for a new edition of the *New Encyclopaedia* Waite wrote, 'The article may be not much worse than the alleged peace, but it seems to me pretty bad', Diary, 11 June 1934), there were other rewards. In August 1933 Waite was surprised but delighted to receive a letter from William Moseley Brown, a prominent American freemason, who wrote, 'as one of your American admirers and a student of your works', to ask 'whether you will do us the honour to accept an honorary degree from Atlantic University'. Waite was only too willing to accept and he advised Brown accordingly. A second letter followed on 21 September, in which Brown announced that 'it gives me the greatest pleasure to enclose with this letter the formal notification of the award of the degree of Doctor of Letters (*honoris causa*) to you. The diploma will be duly prepared and, after it has been signed by the proper officers, it will come forward to you by registered post. I hope that this action on our part will afford you a small part of the pleasure, which we have received in performing it.'

The diploma was finally issued on 7 November, duly signed and sealed—the seal showing the date of the University's foundation: 'AD 1930'. What Waite was not told at the time, and what he never learned subsequently, was that the degree was quite worthless; Atlantic University of Virginia Beach, Virginia, had existed for some eighteen months when it went into voluntary bankruptcy in December 1931, its 202 students hurriedly transferring to other institutions—to their own advantage, for the university was not formally approved by the State Board of Education as a standard college and was not accredited to award any type of degree. After 1931 it had ceased to exist in any form and could not issue even un-accredited degrees. Waite, had he but known, would have been better served by using his existing degree of 'Docteur en Hermétisme'. It had at least the merit of having been awarded in good faith.

17

THE PASSING OF ARTHUR

WAITE'S literary output was prodigious but was maintained by constant working into the small hours; his diary regularly records 'lights out at 4 a.m.' and not infrequently at 5 a.m. or 6 a.m. His health inevitably suffered and it was as much to improve his health as to mend his finances that he moved out of London in 1919 to settle permanently on the Kent coast.

Shortly after the sale of Eastlake Lodge in 1899, Waite had moved to the far side of Gunnersbury Park, having acquired Sidmouth Lodge, a much less gloomy house at 31 South Ealing Road. The family remained at Ealing for almost twenty years and Waite took great pride in his home—especially in his library. Philip Wellby remembered it as 'a long old-fashioned room lined with ponderous book-cases, with more books stacked in every corner and against the wainscot—an enviable collection of rare, curious and miscellaneous volumes' (obituary of 1942). When the house was sold Waite's greatest regret was having to part with some 1,500 volumes that could not be fitted into the cottage at Ramsgate; his regret turned to distress when he discovered that Jeffery, the bookseller to whom he had sold them for £90 ('he has dealt with me as a friend'!), had promptly turned them over to the highly respected firm of William Heffer & Sons Ltd., who made the collection a special feature of their Spring catalogue for 1920—at some ten times the price received by Waite.[1]

The Kent coast had always been a refuge for both Waite and Ada, and when, after the outbreak of war in 1914, they began actively to seek a house outside London they turned first to Ramsgate, where they found an ideal home in the shape of a 300-year-old cottage in the High Street. This was purchased in 1916 and over the next three years Waite made increasingly frequent trips to the coast. Financial pressures eventually forced a permanent move upon the family:

We were confronted now by the problem of keeping or parting with Sidmouth Lodge. The cost of living was high indeed, compared with pre-War days, while rates and other charges were doubling. I saw my way no longer, though I had misjudged the feared fatality concerning my future books. On the other hand, the value of available houses, in the absence of all fresh building for the space of four years, was such that incredible stories went from mouth to mouth as to prices asked and obtained for freehold property. In the end it was decided to sell; and the little old place, with its ancient yews and firs, its roof-high hollies and its summer-houses, did not indeed realise twice what it cost to purchase, but it was approaching that figure (*SLT*, p. 205).

The price obtained for Sidmouth Lodge was '£1350 + £25 for Summer House and fixtures'; but, despite the profit, Waite did not approve of the new owners: 'The purchasers of Sidmouth Lodge', he noted in his diary, 'came in the afternoon to see the furniture. They are all Russian and believe in Bolshevism' (30 August 1919).

After his books, Waite found his garden the hardest thing to be parted from. he enjoyed gardening and was fascinated by the garden's inhabitants, whether his wife's cat, the abundant bird life, or the toads; even these seemed significant in a wider sense: 'Even the toads in my garden—a great colony—have jewelled eyes which are outward signs of a grace that is somewhere to be found within, and the new black kitten on the hearth has a spirit of divine mischief, as in some wise also an "annihilative" divine power' (review of E. Underhill, *Theophanies*, in *The Occult Review*, December 1916).

But if he had lost his garden, he had also—for the moment—lost the burden of financial hardship.

Poverty, alas, was never far away. The proceeds from the house sale were invested on Sybil's behalf in War Loan stock that returned £85 per annum in interest. There was little else save income from Waite's writing and more than enough problems with the cottage: the bomb-damaged roof (Ramsgate had suffered from air raids during the war) had been inadequately repaired, and when it was finally dealt with in 1923 the rafters were found to be 'like powder' and renovation used up most of the year's interest from the War Loan. The damp cellar was a perennial problem, and Waite periodically spent many hours rescuing what he could of the papers he unwisely persisted in storing there. His solution to this problem was original, if odd; by 1924 'many hundreds' of papers had fallen to pieces, and to save the rest from a similar fate they were 'hung up in parcels from the rafters' (Diary, 7 October 1924).

And at Ramsgate Ada died. Her relationship with Waite had been a curious one. They had little in common—she had no interest whatsoever in his esoteric pursuits and remained content with her devotion to the Anglican Church—but they were genuinely fond of each other. Waite's multitude of activities, however, left him with little time for his family and his unconscious neglect came home to him only when he perceived, finally, that Ada was desperately ill. Her periodic bouts of illness had not troubled Waite—she always recovered—and his only real anxiety had been caused by Sybil's attack of double pneumonia in 1919. But when Ada's father, W. H. Lakeman, died early in 1924, Waite noticed how 'very ill' she looked at the funeral; by June she was extremely ill, 'perhaps worse than I dare as yet put down', and, inevitably, cancer was diagnosed. For ten weeks Waite alternated between bursts of hope at new treatments and an underlying blank despair; then, on 18 September, Ada died and Waite threw himself back into his writing and his Order to escape at once from his sorrow, his guilt, and his loneliness.

Waite's own health was somewhat unstable. Chronic overwork and a pronounced tendency to hypochondria often laid him low, but the medical members of his order usually succeeded in restoring him to health. In 1913 he had been introduced to Dr Elizabeth Severn, a psycho-therapist (in the sense of one engaging in psycho-spiritual healing) who had joined the Independent and Rectified Rite (as Soror Prudentia in libramine) and offered to restore his physical balance. Whatever process she used, it worked: 'That is no ordinary power which works in her simple processes, and the result is an almost startling restoration, accompanied by renewed mental freshness. To bear this testimony is a matter of common justice, more especially as I brought with me no living faith, except in her utter sincerity, and my detachment could not have been encouraging' ('The Way of the Soul in Healing', in *The Occult Review*, January 1914). Dr Severn's pupil, Helen Worthington, maintained the role of 'personal physician' to Waite—in his *persona* of Frater Sacramentum Regis—for the rest of his life.

An unspecified illness, probably physical exhaustion, prostrated Waite for some three months at the end of 1927, but the enforced idleness hindered his recovery because of the intense frustration it caused him. He followed this with a series of accidents: in March 1928, while staying at Cricklewood as the guest of the photographer F. C. Stoate (who was also an Order member), Waite collapsed in the bathroom where he had been overcome by gas fumes, and on recovering consciousness became 'hysterical for the first time in [my] life' (Diary, 2 March 1928). Later in the same year he burnt his hand badly and was unable to write for four weeks. Fire indeed, or rather smoke, caused him more than one problem: in 1933 the New Year came in with a chimney fire at the Ramsgate cottage, which Waite later learned had been smouldering for some weeks and was only discovered when 'smoke from one of our chimneys was filling the street'.

Some months later 156 High Street was sold, and Waite and Sybil moved to Betsy Cottage at Broadstairs, where in 1936 he was again affected by smoke. He had fallen asleep one night, leaving a bedside lamp, 'which never smokes', 'burning quietly'; but it was a false sense of security, for he 'awoke at 4, nearly strangled by black smoke filling the whole room'. An 'awful day' followed, spent entirely in cleaning up after the 'foul lamp grease'.

But Waite's ill-health, real or imagined, was exacerbated by domestic stress. In April 1916 a young schoolmistress, Mary Broadbent Schofield, had joined the Fellowship of the Rosy Cross and taken the motto of 'Una Salus'. She idolized both Waite and his work, and after Ada's death she took it upon herself to act as his private secretary—much to the annoyance of Sybil Waite, who saw her father as her own private preserve, at least as far as female company was concerned. The closeness between Waite and Mary Schofield continued to grow, however, and led to frequent jealous outbursts on the part of his increasingly neurotic daughter (he was advised by his local physician of the 'need of rest and change for Sybil and myself, apart from one another' and told that her state was partly due to thyroid poisoning). In spite of the intolerable atmosphere in Waite's home they eventually married, on 15 August 1933, and Mary moved to Ramsgate—only to live apart from her husband: 'All is peace at Westfield Lodge, where Mary is', wrote Waite in his diary on 15 December, 'and all is dreadful at my supposed home.'

When the F∴R∴C∴ moved to 104 Maida Vale, Mary occupied a flat in the building where Waite was able to stay when in London, and thus gain some peace from the querulous Sybil, but even here there were problems. In October 1937 Waite 'fell heavily from steps to path and was much bruised and hurt'; he had, in fact, badly gashed his leg and was bed-ridden for two months. He returned to Broadstairs for Christmas but Mary remained in London, diplomatically 'too ill' to join them. She could also be difficult herself. Those who knew both Waite and his second wife all recall her as being 'perpetually ill', and when in 1938 the property adjoining Betsy Cottage was bought (cheaply, because of its ruinous state) with the intention of providing a second home for the Order and also a separate home for Waite and his wife, she 'decided suddenly that she would have nothing to do with housekeeping'. The old shuttling from one ménage to another continued.

Waite was already used to such changes. In 1927 Sybil Waite had purchased, in addition to their Ramsgate home and at her father's suggestion, a small house at Bishopsbourne near Canterbury, known as The White Cottage, where they spent much of their summers. Waite created regular chaos by insisting on a large part of his library travelling with him—to Bishopsbourne in the Summer and back to Ramsgate or Broadstairs at the end of the season. But although it was a working second home, Waite enjoyed the tranquillity of village life while welcoming the occasional visitor: Moseley Brown from Virginia, and Colin Summerford with his news of Arthur Machen, in particular. He did not neglect his old friends and enjoyed to the full his rare opportunities of meeting them.

Since leaving London, Waite had seen little of the Machens, visiting them annually—more often when possible—until 1925, after which year the intervals between meetings became ever longer: when he lunched with Machen and Colin Summerford in April 1933 it was his 'first sight of Machen for six years'. Their next meeting was not until 3 March 1937—although they continued their joyously controversial correspondence—when Waite and Mary were guests at a civic luncheon in Newport arranged to celebrate Machen's 74th birthday. The Waites stayed at Brynhedydd with their mutual friend, Ada Forestier-Walker (whose son Jocelyn had been a pupil of Mary), and returned for a longer holiday in July 1938. On that occasion Jocelyn Forestier-Walker took Waite and Mary for an extended tour of central Wales, stopping at Nant Eos to see the 'Sacred Cup of Tregaron'. When they arrived at Nant Eos, 'Mrs Powell, Keeper of the Cup and last of her line, gave us a most warm welcome'. They stayed for three days, during which they saw 'the fragments which remain of the Cup and certain records chiefly concerned with cases of its healing powers' (Diary, 16 July 1938), and on their return to Brynhedydd Waite enjoyed himself immensely, arguing over the question of eternal life with the younger Forestier-Walkers; it was the kind of argument he had with Machen on his rare visits to Amersham—where Machen and Purefoy then lived—and provided a stimulating change from the stresses of living in a state of armed truce at Broadstairs.

There had been an earlier visit to Monmouthshire in 1920, when Waite stayed for a week during October with an American Baconian, Dr William H. Prescott, who was convinced that both lost Shakespearean manuscripts *and* the Holy Grail were to be found within the walls of Chepstow Castle. Prescott enthusiastically dragged Waite around the castle, showing him the various landmarks he believed he had identified from his cipher, and asked Waite to write a report that would encourage the owner to believe that excavation was worthwhile. After days spent sight-seeing at Tintern and Caerleon, Waite accompanied Prescott on his visit to Mr Lysaght (the owner), read to him his 'non-committal effort' in support of Prescott's notions (the sanity of which he privately doubted), and returned, somewhat bewildered by the whole affair, to Ramsgate. For Waite, 'The Arthurian Caerleon is not on this earth'—nor was the Holy Grail.

As he passed his eightieth year, Waite's travels grew less in number and he relied on his friends and Order members to come to him. When they did, they found that his health was failing—and it was not, as it had often been in the past, a *malade imaginaire* (in 1931, the year in which he began his 350,000 word revised version of *The Holy Grail*, he entered his occupation on the census form as, 'occasional literary work as age and health permit'). While he was at Maida Vale with Mary he was approached by the publishers Selwyn & Blount with a request to write his memoirs, and in February 1936 he began his first draft, unsure whether he would be able to finish it and even less sure that it was a book worth writing. By May 1937 the memoirs were well advanced but he found his work increasingly tiring: 'I fell asleep over them', he wrote, 'and who will keep awake?' By careful and continual prodding, Erle Lunn, Selwyn & Blount's manager, ensured that *Shadows of Life and Thought* was completed; in Lunn's copy of the book Waite wrote: 'It was undertaken at his instance. It is owing to his unfailing encouragement that it ever reached completion.'

It was to be his last book. By 1938 Waite had written forty-six books; translated, edited, or introduced forty others; and written more than forty distinct rituals for the two Orders he had controlled. He dreamed of other works—a revision and expansion of his Fairy Tales and a completely new edition of his poems. In the latter project he was encouraged by Ethel Archer, a former devotee of Aleister Crowley who had developed a great admiration for Waite's poetry and had written an eulogistic article on it for *The London Forum* (June 1935; this was a new name for the old *Occult Review*). It came to nothing and, as with all of Waite's other projects, remained a dream.

Waite had long been convinced that his heart was failing, despite assurances to the contrary from his medical friends until he was well past seventy years of age, and by 1940 he was proven correct. He wrote to Harold Voorhis, his American correspondent and avid collector of his books, on 16 March to tell him that, 'I have been seriously ill during most of this year, owing to a distended heart and Aorta worries'. Over the following two years he grew steadily worse and hardly moved beyond the new home that Sybil had acquired (Gordon House, at Bridge near Canterbury; Betsy Cottage was sold in 1941). His last regular visitors were members of the Order for whom he was still working on revised rituals; two of them, Thomas Wild and his wife, were raised to the Grade of Adeptus Minor on 24 February 1942. It was the last act of the Fellowship of the Rosy Cross during Waite's lifetime. The Wilds went home to Glastonbury but returned to Bridge on 15 May. They found him, as Wild later wrote to Jocelyn Forestier-Walker,

> In his usual rather uncertain state of health, but with the addition of a chill, which the next day began to affect his heart. I was with him during the greater part of the last day of his life. His thoughts were with his work almost to the end. I left him about an hour before he died, since the nurse wished him to be quiet, but she told me that he asked for a pencil and traced what he said was a Latin word upon the counterpane—he thought he was writing on paper—and then said: 'That's the end.' We can only guess what that word may have been (letter of 8 June 1942).

The end had come at 11.30 p.m. on 19 May 1942. For Waite the end of the mystical quest was not union but Unity; his last word could only have been 'Unitas'.

The obituaries were dutiful and praiseworthy, but they did not convey any sense of Waite's true importance. It has been so also with would-be historians of the occult ever since; when Waite is mentioned he is praised for his translations of Eliphas Lévi, for his work on the Tarot, and for his alchemical studies; his *New Encyclopaedia of Freemasonry* is rightly dismissed; his major studies of the Kabbalah, the Holy Grail, and the Rosicrucians are respected and quoted from; his poetry and literary style are both derided; of his mystical works nothing is said at all. In this way latter-day critics emulate the unthinking, obsessional attacks upon Waite so often made by Aleister Crowley; like Crowley they also invent what they do not know. With no more evidence than her own fertile imagination Ithell Colquhoun claimed that in 1929 'there was current gossip that he had already taken to the bottle'; more feasibly, but with equal lack of evidence (his own senses were clearly unreliable), J. G. Bennett claimed that he 'was among those who found it amusing to hear A. E. Waite, a well-known author, rise to his feet and say: "Mr. Ouspensky, there is no love in your system," and walk solemnly out of one of the meetings' (*Witness*, 1962, p. 95). Waite never read Ouspensky, never mentioned him, and never attended his meetings.

Waite's name has survived because he was the first to attempt a systematic study of the history of western occultism—viewed as a spiritual tradition rather than as aspects of proto-science or as the pathology of religion. His codification of what he termed the Secret Tradition was a pioneering effort that established 'rejected knowledge' as a fit subject for study within the History of Ideas. His idiosyncrasies and carelessness over minor details do not weaken the foundations he laid; his work was sound enough for it to carry the superstructure of modern scholarship when it begins to build, as it must, upon his researches.

But the outer form of the Secret Tradition, fascinating though it is, is not its essence. Arthur Machen knew that essence, and although he approached spiritual reality by a road very different from that of Waite, he knew where Waite's greatness lay. It was the loss of a great mystic as much as the loss of a friend he had loved that grieved him when he learned of Waite's death; and it was a sense of that double loss that led him to express his grief in 'a silence and a sadness' that went beyond mere words.

Waite's true legacy is in his philosophy of mysticism, but until such time as it is analysed in something more than a superficial manner, and its originality and genius recognized, he will not be accorded the place in the history of thought that he deserves. Until then his reputation will be shrouded in a manner analogous to that of his grave at Bishopsbourne: a grave that has for many years been covered by a rank and spreading growth of Deadly Nightshade.

Afterword

THE FAITH OF A. E. WAITE

'I HAVE known my very dear friend A. E. Waite for 38 years; and I have not the faintest notion as to his real beliefs. In hopeful moods I am inclined to think that he is a Deist; but in stern fact I should think that Pantheism is his veritable label.' So Machen wrote to Colin Summerford in 1925. But he was quite wrong. Waite was far from being a Pantheist; he referred scathingly to 'the false teachings of pantheistic identity' in his Introduction to Vaughan's *Lumen de Lumine* (1910, p. xxxii). A more accurate assessment of Waite's beliefs was made by Ralph Shirley; in his editorial for *The Occult Review* of January 1914 he posed the question 'Is Mr. Waite a Catholic?' and gave this answer:

> Perhaps the question could be answered both in the negative and in the affirmative. It might sum up the position more adequately if I were to say that Mr Waite would like to be a Catholic if the Catholic Church filled that place in the world which our author would hold to be its true inheritance. An all-embracing Church, in short, with full pontifical authority, is his ideal—a Church which, while it teaches to the people that which they can understand, or alternatively that which without understanding, they may accept on its authority, at the same time has as its highest mission the handing down through the ages of a secret mystical truth of which it is the divinely appointed repository. The following out of this secret tradition in the various phases and forms in which it has been embodied, from the commencement of the Christian era up to the present time, disfigured sometimes by superstition and distorted at others by bigotry and prejudice, but still, in whatever guise, containing as its kernel the mystical meaning of the history of mankind from its creation to the divine reunion which is its term—this has been Mr Waite's life task. Personally, I would describe him as a Sacramentalist rather than a Catholic.

But was Waite a Christian? From what he wrote to Robertson Nicoll (see p. 134) it is clear that he believed in the atonement, albeit as a Universalist who accepted that *all* men would ultimately be saved. As to the person of Christ, he made one dogmatic statement on the nature of the Trinity: 'The Christ is God immanent in the universe and man. The Father is God in the transcendence. The Holy Spirit is the bond of unity between them.' But he promptly qualified it by adding that 'these points are of personal understanding (*The Way of Divine*

Union, p. 244). In the same work he set out his idea of the nature of Christ: 'Meanwhile, as one who is assured that there have been many saviours, I feel on my own part that He whom we call Christ, being last, is also the first. He carried with Him throughout the whole crucifixion, which was also the concealed glory of His earthly life, a consciousness of His Divine Nature and Destiny. As real man He suffered, but as Divine Man He knew'—knew, that is, 'whence He came and why; He knew that it was for the working of a mystery; He knew that this mystery was an epitome of the experience of each individual soul on the way of return Godward. He went through the high dramatic enactment with a conscious and plenary realisation of every element therein, from the most even to the least; and hence for us there is vitalism and grace in all' (pp. 185–6). Redemption is 'by the finding of life in God' and it is a continuing process, not a once for all event. Waite *was* a Christian, but he was certainly not orthodox.

The mystic, specifically the Christian mystic, seeks Divine Union, which is 'realization in God'; but this can only be obtained, for Waite, by an act of Mind. But this is not mind as the rational, thinking part of our being, rather it is 'the state of pure intelligence in deep contemplation [which] is a state of essential love in the highest, as at an apex of Mind. The Mind is love, the Mind is high desire, the Mind is Soul, unless we talk of the Soul as a kind of psychic body or vesture of the next life: in this case Mind is Spirit' (*SLT*, p. 238). And, Waite maintains, we can know God only by way of the Mind:

> All whatsoever which we know, shall and can know of God, lies within these measures—the measures of human Mind. It follows that the search after God is a Quest in our own being; and, *linea media* or otherwise, supposing that there is a way to God, this way is within. The reason is that obviously there can be no other, seeing that it is we who ascend the heights, as it is we who explore the deeps (*SLT*, p. 237).

In one of his few fully dogmatic statements, Waite concludes that 'there is no revelation of God except through us as channels'.

The state of Divine Union can be attained by contemplation, but it is not a permanent state, nor can it be while we are in the material world; it can also be attained through the use of ritual but this is not the way for everyone. Referring to his 'Last Grade of the Great Mystery', Waite says, 'It is of necessity for those only who have a state of real inward illumination, in what is called the mind at least. To others it will not be intelligible. It is difficult to myself when I am not in the mood of life' (Diary, 9 August 1926). For the mystic who has attained Divine Union, return to this world brings a sense of loss, but the mystic *must* return for he has a duty to guide others on the same path of attainment. 'And those who enter into this state come back into the world, with the yoke of the kingdom upon them in a law of service. Then God shall give them work' (*Lamps of Western Mysticism*, p. 329).

It was this threefold conviction—that Divine Union can be attained; that it can be attained only through the Mind; and that, once attained, it lays a duty upon us to guide others in the same path—that constituted Waite's faith. He saw himself as Christian and his Order as a body devoted to propagating Christian mysticism—as experience rather than learning. Waite spent his life on a spiritual quest for his own identity in God; he had no personal roots in the material world and sought them instead by turning within himself, where against all expectation he found a unique path to the direct experience of God. All mystics turn within, but Waite was alone in grasping what he found and bringing it back so that all mankind could understand its nature and be offered a means of attaining it.

It is our failure, not his, that we have not taken what he offered.

Appendix A

(I)

THE NEW LIGHT OF MYSTICISM: ORDER OF THE SPIRITUAL TEMPLE

FIRST CONSTRUCTIVE PERIOD

F. HILDEBRAND ROTHWELL.,
Hon. Sec. (*pro tem.*) to 'The Triad'
85, SINCLAIR ROAD, KENSINGTON, W.

I

The psychological phenomena of the nineteenth century have directed the attention of many earnest students to the Spiritual Mysteries of the past, and the present epoch of humanity may be deemed a ripe time for the more general diffusion of the important philosophical conclusions which have taken shape in the minds of a large section of patient investigators.

II

It is bêlieved that the lost keys of the ancient secret sciences may yet be recovered. Modern facts, regarded in the light of old theories, and old theories explained by modern facts, seem to have brought already a number of individual and unassisted seekers to the threshold of the Ancient Wisdom.

III

Those who are convinced of the permanence, reality, and proximity of an unseen world, and who believe in the possibility of communication therewith, are invited to co-operate in the first systematic attempt to establish a direct correspondence of an advanced kind between that world and the whole body of humanity.

IV

Certain circles of investigation, and certain unattached students working on individual lines, have set themselves to discover in the literature of Western Mysticism a solution of the great problems of existence.

V

The religious aspirations of the age are distracted by the conflict of the sects, and those principles which are at the base of all religion must undoubtedly be sought as the source of illumination by the many minds which are weary of vain speculations and disputes that have no end.

VI

To these it may be stated that a method of transcending the material world, of penetrating the veil of appearances, and of entering into the realities which underlie sense-delusions does not seem beyond the reach of the age. An acquaintance with this method will destroy the philosophy of the materialist; it will realise spiritual aspirations and the hopes of a larger life.

VII

While the existence of a Supreme Intelligence is being relegated to the rank of superstitions, that process is in course of construction, by which the God-illuminated seers of old—Plato, Plotinus, Ammonius, Bonaventura, Eckart, Tauler, Vaughan, Theresa, Saint-Martin, and Jacob Böhme—accomplished an individual reversion to the fontal source of souls, and entered into an ecstatic communion with the universal consciousness.

VIII

In view of these facts, in view of the actual discoveries which have been made in the domain of psychology by various circles of investigation, in view of the singular fields of experiment on the threshold of which the age now stands, in view of the needs of the age to which these discoveries and these experiments can alone truly minister, we invite the co-operation of all persons who are enthusiasts for God and the Soul, who believe that the revelation of the indwelling Spirit and the overshadowing Deity can alone accomplish a conversion in the life of mankind; we invite them in the name of their divine and sacred zeal to co-operate in the first mystic propaganda which has been seriously attempted in this century.

IX

To such we would proclaim, on the faith of an unbroken historical testimony, and on the evidence of innumerable witnesses, that it is possible in this life, and in this body, to know God, and that the process is enshrined in the secret language of so-called alchemy, in the allegories of transcendental Freemasonry, in the occult initiations of the Mysteries, and in the books of the Christian mystics.

X

From the same circle of esoteric literature it is believed there may be elaborated the true methods for the

(*a*) Interior regeneration of humanity.
(*b*) The manifestation of the soul in man.
(*c*) The unification of the soul and spirit, which are *Pneuma* and *Psyche*.

(*d*) The transfiguration of the body of man by the splendour of spirit and soul.
(*e*) The physical glorification of humanity.
(*f*) The evolution of the perfect man.
(*g*) The elaboration of the Christ in man.
(*h*) The attainment of the crown of evolution.

All aspirations of religion, all dreams of idealism admit of realization by the application of the arcane instruments which were known to the mystics, and the gulf between actuality and poetry can be bridged by their means.

XI

A society, brotherhood, or club, is in course of formation for the diffusion of the scientific and philosophical doctrines of the Light and the interior religion of the Light, as they have been expounded by the children of the Light, who are the mystic seers of old, and for the exercise of the spiritual methods of perfection on the transcendental plane. The number of postulants or members which the existing circle is at present prepared to receive is of necessity limited, and earnest seekers after the interior knowledge of the soul, men and women of culture, intuition, and aspirational nature will alone be eligible.

XII

It is designed in the first instance to take possession of a suitable Mansion in a convenient, London centre, which will be made use of as a nucleus for the propagation of the New Mysticism and of those high doctrines of Transcendental Religion which are destined for the conquest of the world. It will combine at the same time all the conveniences of an institution, to which members may resort for the more ordinary purposes of life, and for harmonious communication within the bonds of a common sympathy.

XIII

The private objects of prosecution on the part of associates and members will be the attainment of the following exalted interior states:

(*a*) The Manifestation of the Divine Virgin.
(*b*) The Manifestation of the Dual Flower.
(*c*) The Vision of Diana Unveiled.
(*d*) The New Birth or Interior Regeneration.
(*e*) The Revelation of the Holy Graal.
(*f*) The Interior Translation.
(*g*) The Mystic Marriage.

XIV

By the exercises which give entrance to these states, it is intended to qualify and prepare at all points an elect, esoteric circle for the Regeneration of Humanity, the propaganda of the New Mysticism, the erection of the first temple, and the creation of the coming man.

XV

The erection of the first temple of the soul as a visible witness of the way of positive truth is the grand design of the order, and it is to assist in its promotion that this present invitation is extended to all persons who have received the mystic gospel and have been illuminated by the interior Light. The rituals and liturgies of this Temple, by which humanity at large is to be led to the threshold of the New Life, are already in course of development.

SYNOPSIS OF THE NEW SCIENCE OF LIFE

The creation of the perfect man can be accomplished solely by correspondence with Evolution, which is the abiding law of life.

The law of evolution may be sub-divided into—

The laws in the development of physical beauty and perfection.
The laws in the development of the higher morality.
The laws in the development of intellectual aspiration and the realization of intellectual ideals.
The laws in the development of the spiritual principle in the direction of the perfect rest and the perfect activity in God.

PERFECTION CONSISTS

In the physical order: In the realization of the dream of beauty.
In the moral order: In the realization of the dream of love.
In the intellectual order: In the realization of the dream of poetry.
In the spiritual order: In the realization of the dream of the mystics.

[Note: The prospectus was issued in 1891. I have been unable to identify Mr Rothwell or to determine his relationship with Waite. RAG]

(II)

'A TENTATIVE RITE' FOR 'AN ORDER OF THE SPIRITUAL TEMPLE'

WE ARE told by the Mystics that there is an exterior evolution on the physical plane, and an interior evolution on the psychic plane. There is a promise to the outward man and a promise to the inward man. They prophesy unto us of a glory to be revealed outwardly and of a glory to be realized within—of an exterior splendour and an interior light. This two-fold evolution will be represented in the ministry of devotional Mysticism by the liturgy and the ritual. The liturgy will be concerned with the inward man; in the symbolic ritual there will be a service of the outward senses, and as there is a solidarity between the two evolutions, so there should be a solidarity between the liturgy and the ritual. There are also four chief processes in Mysticism—Regeneration, Illumination, Dedication, and the Mystic Marriage, or communication with Deity. These will be represented in the four divisions of the service—Regeneration through Aspiration by an opening aspirational rite, Illumination by the instruction of lessons and discourses,

Dedication by a sacrificial service, the Mystic Marriage by a Eucharistic rite. Three other ideas would also be involved by the Ministry of a Mystic service—a possibility of communication with the Divine, and the way and the means thereof, with the two who seek to communicate, namely, Pneuma and Psyche—the Spirit and the Bride. If we educe these processes and ideas into form on the exterior plane, we shall have definite points for our guidance:

(*a*) The Temple into which all retire to establish correspondence with the Divine—and this is the Interior Sanctuary.
(*b*) The visible body of the Church, corresponding to the physical body, and represented by the concourse of worshippers.
(*c*) The Ritual of the Temple, which creates the conditions that are required in the exterior man.
(*d*) The Soul and the Spirit which do reside in the interior man, and wherewith the outward man must be unified. These are represented within the interior sanctuary by the ministry of a man and a woman.
(*e*) The Liturgy, or devotional service, by which it is sought to unite the three principles of man in a common aspiration and outreaching towards the Divine.
(*f*) The high priest, also within the Sanctuary, who is the chief celebrant, the sign of the possibility which exists, the type of communication, the living symbol of the bridge between the seen and the unseen, the representative of God, the speaker who, symbolically, is commissioned from the other side of life.

In the order of mystical ideas, the priest ministers to the Three Principles, but especially to the Spirit; the Spirit ministers to the Two inferior Principles, but especially to the Soul; the Soul ministers to the whole body. Our Mystic service will be shaped along these lines; they are not arbitrary; they are the order of spiritual procedure. The liturgic portion of the service will be compiled from the Mystics. It will be wholly aspirational and devotional, and will embody the aspirational Mysticism of the Old and New Testaments of all religion. There will be a hymnal portion, selected from the metrical literature of Mysticism. The instructional section will be derived mainly from the lives and teachings of the Mystics. We shall select from the concourse of the Sages fifty-two representative men, taken in historical order, beginning with Pythagoras and Plato. The lessons of each week will be taken from the works of one of these men, and the discourse will interpret his wisdom, or some important factor in mystical philosophy which may be said to take shape in him. During seven days he will rule our thoughts, and will be therefore the ascending star which will govern during that period in the spiritual sky. The lessons and discourses which constitute the second division of the service will be followed by a dedicatory rite, which will open with a choral hymn and a devout invocational litany. A solemn act of Dedication will then be made, and the seven-branched candlestick, which now overshadows you, will be lighted on the altar, representing the five senses, or faculties, and the two principles of the interior man, among other profound significances. The symbolic sacrifice of incense and perfume will be offered to the Divine Substance, representing the aspiration of the worshippers. Acts of Mystic Renunciation will then be made by all present, after which the priest, as the ambassador of the superior world, will proceed to the consecration of bread and wine, symbolical of the divine principles which constitute the food of the interior man. After the consecration, the priest will partake of the elements, and then all present, to signify the communication with Deity, which is the end of the Mystic process. The order of procedure will be as follows: The elements will be received by the deacon from the hands of the priest himself, for he stands as the Spirit in Man. The lady sub-deacon will receive them from the hands of the Pneuma, who is the proper mediator to the Soul, and she in turn will communicate them to the body of the worshippers, as she is the proper ministrant to the Body. After an interval of interior recollection, the service will conclude with an act of thanksgiving, a solemn charge, a benediction, and a final jubilatory hymn.

When prompted by genuine enthusiasm, propositions like these are pleasing, but of little practical value. The church of the future can become actual only by evolving, and the modes of its ministry must be left to evolve with it. The essential quality of life escapes in the ready-made ritual. We are not afraid of the development of another priestcraft, we believe in the magnificence of the exterior sign, and in the grandeur of outward worship; but, with full sympathy for the spirit which governs them, we must deprecate these designs, which have only the elements of failure. At the same time, it is pertinent to draw attention to their existence, for they are part of that spiritual ferment in which we all of us breathe and move.

[From *Azoth: or the Star in the East*, pp. 126–8.]

Appendix B

THE CONSTITUTION OF THE SECRET COUNCIL OF RITES

(1) The S. C. R. was constituted on December 2nd, 1902 for the determination in a particular direction of existing Mystic Interests, more especially in connection with Masonry and the Orders which are connected with and dependent upon it.

(2) The work of the S. C. lies entirely outside that of any legislative bodies, Grand Lodges, Grand Chapters or Supreme Councils; it does not seek to intrude among them and it will not tolerate their interference in its concerns.

(3) The S. C. will for its better protection vigilantly conserve an occult and anonymous character and, save in the Supreme Degrees of the Council, will at no time divulge the names of its Members to any person in the world.

(4) The S. C. consists of the following brethren. Frater L. S.; Frater M. W. θ.; Frater S. R., under the conditions now to be set forth:—The S. C. of R. does not exist and no person is, therefore, a Member of it, except when it is called into being and declared to be in activity by some one or more of the above mentioned Fratres or their successors for executive or consultative purposes and on the completion of the work in hand, or before if so declared, it automatically lapses until again in like manner revived. Membership of the S. C. R. is therefore to be understood in the sense just defined whenever referred to in this Constitution.

(5) Frater L. S., Frater M. W. θ. and Frater S. R. being members *ab initio* by whom the C. was constituted simultaneously, there is no priority or precedence in respect of them and this fact is to be borne in mind more especially by the Frater S. R. who first suggested the constitution of the Secret Body for those objects which are known to the C.

(6) The Members of the S. C. can work only in common for the furtherance of the objects which it proposes and therefore no action must be taken by one independently of the others in respect of any C. matters.

(7) The S. C. has no power to add to its numbers and the absence of any Member from the country of its present location does not constitute a vacancy, since an efficient inter communication can always be preserved. This rule is absolute and invariable in respect of both its clauses.

(8) Vacancy is constituted by death or permanent alienation as also by insanity or unfitness to act; agreement on the part of the other two Members as to the existence of either

disability being alone necessary in order to take action. Each Member has the right to nominate his successor, who shall be of the male sex and a Royal Arch Mason. Such nomination may be made absolute prior to decease by the approval of the other Members and ranks alternatively as a very serious and urgent recommendation to be adopted if possible, failing which, the appointment rests with the survivors.

(9) In the event of permanent alienation, insanity or unfitness to act without a successor having been nominated previously, the other Members shall appoint a suitable Mystic Mason to complete the Triad at such time as may be advisable and in any case within a period of twelve months.

(10) In the event of the death of a Member suddenly and without nomination, similar procedure shall be adopted, as two Members cannot constitute a complete C.

(11) The C. as it now stands is complete, perfect and permanent, without power of expulsion or the right to insist on resignation.

(12) The S. C. will always deprecate resignation on the part of a Member, but it must not disallow it altogether. In such event the right of nomination is abrogated but one of counsel remains, such counsel to be regarded with great respect and followed if reasonable and desirable.

(13) In the event of two Members resigning simultaneously, the C. would cease to exist, and this therefore is interdicted by the honourable pledge which has been taken by each Member, as will appear hereinafter.

(14) As it is necessary for the furtherance of its objects that the S. C. shall have a certain acknowledged existence, it has appointed the Frater S. R. as its present Envoy-Extraordinary with full powers in conjunction with the whole C. only.

(15) The Envoy-Extraordinary is not as such a Member of the C.

(16) The S. C. may and will appoint Envoys-Subordinate for different countries or districts for the spread and representation of the Rites conserved by the C. but such Envoys shall represent special Rites only.

(17) The Frater S. R. is at this time the sole Envoy-Extraordinary representing all Rites of the C., under the obedience of the C., with the special Envoys to him subordinate, also under the obedience of the C., and this rule shall be absolute henceforward for every Envoy-Extraordinary successively appointed and for the Envoys-Subordinate.

(18) The S. C. will obtain and exercise jurisdiction over Independent Lodges, Chapters and Temples of the following Rectified Occult Orders and Masonic Rites:

The Occult Orders.

(a) The Independent and Rectified Rite of Martinism.
(b) The Reformed Order of the G. D. Masonically reconstituted.
(c) The Rectified Rite R. R. et A. C.

Masonic Rites

(a) The Rectified Rite of Swedenborg.
(b) The Independent Order of the Illuminati.
(c) The Order of the Novices and Knights Beneficent of the Holy City of Jerusalem.

(d) The New and Reformed Rite of Adoptive Masonry.
(e) The Incorporated Order of the Eastern Star.

(19) Members of the S. C. are Members of these Bodies and will work them in a constitutional manner for the purposes of the C., and all other Rites and Orders which it may subsequently acquire for the same purposes in like manner.

(20) The Members of the S. C. will if possible obtain their reception into the Secret Order 7..16., as it is requisite for the purposes of the C.

(21) The S. C. will if necessary and desirable acquire other Rites and Orders, Masonic and non-Masonic, to work in connection with its purposes and will at the proper time constitute two further Rites for the completion of the existing series as follows:

(a) The Order of the Daughters of Zion.
(b) The Third Order R. R. et A. C.

(22) The C. will distribute these Rites upon an ascending scale as follows:

(a) Rite of Martinism, referred to Malkuth.
(b) Rite of the G. D., referred to Jesod.
(c) Rite of Swedenborg, referred to Hod (with its complement).
(d) Rite of the Eastern Star, referred to Netzach.
(e) Rite of the R. R. et A. C., referred to Tiphereth.
(f) Rite of the Illuminati, referred to Chesed (with its complement).
(g) Rite of Adoption, referred to Geburah.
(h) Rite of the Novices and Knights of the Holy City, referred to Chockmah (with its complement).
(i) Rite of the Daughters of Zion, referred to Binah.
(j) Rite of 7..16, (intermediate) referred to Daath.
(k) Rite of the Supreme Crown or Third Order R. R. et A. C., referred to Kether.

(23) This distribution is in part a matter of convenience and in part arises naturally from the ascent of the Grades. Its design and arrangements are entirely a C. Secret, as ostensibly there will be an independent working of all the Rites.

(24) The scheme of Rites belonging to the Pillar of Benignity can be entered only through Martinism, with the exception of that referable to Daath.

(25) The Masonic Rites can be entered independently without passing from one to another.

(26) The Adoptive Rites can be entered only through the Order of the Eastern Star.

(27) By the design of the S. C., the Rite of Martinism will act as a drag net for all the Rites, but especially for those of the Central Pillar, and the most suitable Members who had drifted independently into the Masonic and Adoptive Orders will ultimately be absorbed by the Androgynous Centre.

(28) With the exception of the Third Order R. R. et A. C., all Rites will meet and recognize each other in Daath, and so far the Scheme of the S. C. will be at last unveiled.

(29) Those who attain the Third Order will meet the C. for the first time face to face, and it is hoped that in the course of Nature the C. will be recruited therefrom.

(30) The Members of the S. C. pledge themselves hereby to communicate to one another

all occult knowledge and all knowledge concerning occult Orders which they may possess now or obtain hereafter, and in the case of such knowledge being communicated to them individually under binding obligations, each will do his best to obtain for the two others a participation of such knowledge and reception by such Rites.

(31) The Members also honourably pledge themselves, each to each and all to all, to work seriously and in harmony for the objects of the S. C., to keep their names unknown, not to desert one another, to resign only by necessity, simultaneous resignation being interdicted unless it be unanimously determined to dissolve the C., and to bear in mind the desirability of finding someone to succeed them if possible.

(32) The objects of the S. C. of R. are the stimulation and the nourishment of Mystic Aspiration, more especially in Freemasonry, towards the Great Work of Reintegration with the Centre, or Union with the Divine as the Supreme End of all research, such objects to be pursued by all legitimate means, from which any identification with social or political movements is expressly excluded, the same being neither means nor ends.

★ ★ ★ ★ ★ ★ ★

These are the 32 Paths of the Absolute in respect of the S. C. of R. and are the irremovable Landmarks thereof, to which, in token of their agreement, the contracting parties here append the initials by which they are known to each other within the C.

Dated this 25th day of May, in the year of our Lord 1903.
L.S. [i.e. Lucem Spero = Ralph Palmer-Thomas]
M.W.θ [i.e. Ma Wahanu Thesi = Marcus Worsley Blackden]
S.R. [i.e. Sacramentum Regis = Arthur Edward Waite]

Appendix C

(I)

THE MANIFESTO OF 24 JULY 1903

WE, the undersigned, Members of the Order R.R. et A.C., having been asked to state the grounds on which we demand independence, hereby affirm as follows:

We object to return of the status quo ante 1890 along the lines proposed by the Draft Constitution 1903.

We will not be committed definitely to any expression of opinion regarding our past connection with a Third Order.

We object to the principle of practical examination within the Second Order.

We object to the continued use of the original defective rituals and we require them re-edited in strict accordance with the cipher manuscripts.

We are of opinion that Grades within the Second Order should either cease or advancement therein should take place otherwise than by the present system of examination, more especially in practical subjects. We do not consider that any person competent to confer the higher grades is now amongst us. We regard the examination of one 5 to 6 member by another as childish. We confirm clause 9 of the Draft Constitution 1903, with such modifications as may seem desirable. The clause is as follows:

Having regard to the fact that the secret knowledge of the Second Order has been and is in possession of certain Adepti independently of grade and that for the present the side grade of Theoricus has no special knowledge of importance the existence of grades shall cease and there shall be an absolute equality of membership apart from official position; any special knowledge of the Theoricus Grade shall be attainable by 5 to 6 members as such.

We consider that the expectation of an established or renewed connection with a Third Order cannot be too carefully controlled and if such a connection should be affirmed by any Chief or 5 to 6 Adept we do not regard the Theorici as the sole or necessarily the best judges of the evidence.

We object to the statements which have been circulated by which we are represented as having affirmed the restoration of the status quo ante 1890. At the Annual Meeting in 1902, a temporary and experimental coalition was formed to last till May 4, 1903, to prevent the entire paralysis of all business, but the two sections of the Order were obviously not in agreement then and they are not in agreement now.

We consider that all in our power should be done to corroborate and extend our knowledge and not to restrict it within the present narrow limits. We consider that special attention should be given to historical and mystical research.

We hold that the Order should be reconstituted and desire to reconstitute it on its original basis prior to the ascendency obtained by a single Chief. The Order was established about 1885 by Chiefs who were Masons and possessed high grades in the Masonic fraternity. If these Chiefs were warranted by a Third Order, they were in our opinion warranted as Masons. The Order at that time was ruled from within a body in which the Masonic qualification was required of joining members. The Order in respect of its rituals as well as of its government was Masonic at that period and is still Masonic by its rituals. It has become divorced from Masonry solely through the dissensions of the original Chiefs. The period of harmony and progress was the Masonic period and the difficulties began when the Chiefs forgot that they were Masons. We affirm the necessity of restoring the Masonic rapport by electing certain Masons as Chiefs and encouraging, as regards men, the admission of Masons rather than non-Masons to the Outer and Inner Grades of the order. We believe also that the extension of our knowledge and the communication with a Third Order must be sought in those fraternities which some of us know and others believe to exist behind Masonry.

We affirm that the earliest status of the Order was mystical and that the trend of the Order practice towards the lower occultism rose with the rise and grew with the growth of the ascendency of a single Chief. Attention was originally paid to the mystic way, more especially when the studies were chiefly directed by S. A. We desire to give prominence to this method of progress.

We are of opinion that our objects will be best attained by the constition of an independent branch of the R.R. et A.C. working under a Masonic regime and that this course does not involve hostility to those whose requirements are met by the practical part of the Order knowledge. We have no idea of excluding women from membership or from office within the Order, apart from the Masonic Chieftainship, which is a business and working headship. We believe that our scheme is calculated to increase the number of male members and thus ensure the equality of the sexes; and we affirm in conclusion our intention of insisting on the literal fulfilment of all our requirements for which purpose We Hereby Declare Our Independence From The Date Hereof To Be Reconsidered If Our Demands Are Granted.

VIRTUTE ORTA OCCIDUNT RARIUS [i.e. Revd W.A. Ayton]
MAWAHANU THESI [i.e. Marcus Worsley Blackden]
SACRAMENTUM REGIS [i.e. A.E. Waite]
VIGILATE [i.e. Mrs Helen Rand]
A POSSE AD ESSE [i.e. Miss Harriet Butler]
SHEMEBER [i.e. Mrs Pamela Bullock]
CAUSA SCIENTIAE [i.e. Julian L. Baker]
SILENTIO [i.e. Mrs H. Fulham-Hughes]

PERSEVERA [i.e. Miss K.E. Broomhead]
ALTA PETO [i.e. Mme Isabelle de Steiger]
TEMPUS OMNIA REVELAT [i.e. Miss Maud Cracknell]
VOLO ASPIRARE [i.e. Mrs Ada M. Blackden]

(II)

CONSTITUTION OF THE R.R. ET A.C. (PROCLAIMED AT THE MEETING HELD ON 7 NOVEMBER 1903)

1. The name of the order shall be the Independent and Rectified Order R.R. et A.C.
2. The Order is the custodian of certain knowledge a part of which only can be found in printed books or known manuscripts. There is further knowledge obtainable along the same lines.
3. The Independent and Rectified Order believes that there is a higher or mystical sense of the entire Order knowledge.
4. It affirms individually and collectively its earnest desire for advancement in spiritual knowledge by which alone a connection can be established with Masters in Secret Science.
5. The original connection of the R.R. et A.C. with such Masters under the name of the Third Order is a matter of opinion but the existence of special knowledge within the Second Order, however derived, is not a matter of opinion and is its title to continuation and diffusion.
6. The Chiefs of the Second Order shall be Master Masons of the 3rd, Degree in accordance with the tradition of the Order holding under the Mother Grand Lodge of England or some other Grand Lodge recognized by her.
7. All authority within the Order is vested in the three Chiefs. The existing Chiefs are VIRTUTE ORTA OCCIDUNT RARIUS, MAWAHANU THESI, SACRAMENTUM REGIS. In the event of the death or demission of a Chief his place shall be filled by another Mason from within the ranks of the Second Order.
8. The power of appointment in this case shall rest with the remaining Chiefs.
9. The special Grade of Theoricus is abrogated and the knowledge possessed thereby is placed at the disposition of the Second Order as a whole.
10. There are no examinations within the 5=6 Grade which is the sole Grade of the Second Order.
11. The advancement of new members in the knowledge possessed by the Second Order takes place at the discretion of the Chiefs.
12. The instruction of new members may be delegated to experienced Fratres or Sorores at the discretion of the Chiefs.

13. The V. H. Soror VIGILATE is hereby appointed Keeper of the archives of the Independent and Rectified Order with the title of Recorder.
14. The V. H. Soror SHEMEBER is appointed the Bursar of the Order.
15. The Order shall as soon as possible acquire a permanent habitation which shall be placed under the control of a librarian to be hereafter appointed.
16. There shall be a special meeting of the Order in January of each year when the Recorder shall present the Report of the progress of the Order and the Treasurer the financial statement.
17. All disputes and complaints shall be in the sole jurisdiction of the Chiefs and in the case of differences between members they shall be determined as privately as possible.
18. Every member of the Independent and Rectified Order shall be honourably bound to abide by the constitution and the regulations.
19. Simple resignation or demission from the Second Order shall not of itself involve the forfeiture of manuscripts. All manuscripts are however held by members at the will of the Chiefs.
20. Expulsions can only take place by fiat of the Chiefs or at their discretion by a vote in the Vault of the Adepts with a 3. 4ths majority, notice having been sent seven days before the meeting to every member.
21. The C. C. Ceremony will be retained but will undergo a certain slight revision in order to bring it more into harmony with the traditions of past ages.
22. The subscription of the Second Order is (Xs) per annum which can be remitted at the discretion of the Chiefs in certain cases.
23. The Trustees of all the Properties of the Inner and Outer Orders are MAWAHANU THESI and VIGILATE.
24. The regular meetings of the Second Order are the first Saturday in January, April, July and September at such times and places as may be appointed.

Appendix D

THE 'MOST FAITHFUL AGREEMENT AND CONCORDAT'

BETWEEN THE INDEPENDENT AND RECTIFIED RITE AND THE STELLA MATUTINA TEMPLE

[From Waite's summary of the controversy with Felkin over the Concordat ('Notes upon certain points dwelt upon by F.R.') the following clauses of the Concordat can be reconstructed.]

Clause 4: The full membership of each section shall be known to the Chiefs of each section. [Felkin proposed to add the words, 'Solely and under pledge of secrecy'.]

Clause 5: The Rolls of the two Orders which are now in possession of Finem Respice shall be used in common.

Clause 6: [This clause evidently related to the exclusion of certain members from both Orders.]

Clause 12: The password of each Equinox shall be arranged between the Chiefs of the two sections and shall be one password.

Clause 15: No member shall be permitted to work with both sections simultaneously in so far as the degrees recognized up to the separation are concerned.

Clause 17: Subject to the independence and autonomy of each section there shall be no reserve of doctrine, instruction or means of ceremonial working between the Chiefs of the two sections.

Clause 18: There shall be no secrecy between the two sections in respect of those grades of the Order known and recognized up to the time of the separation of the sections but grades and rites worked subsequently by one section if any shall be communicated only under the rules by which they are governed.

[A further clause (the number of which cannot be identified) 'affirms that in the one case there is a triple Headship and in the other that the Head is "the Most Honoured Frater Finem Respice, 7=4," and him only'.]

Appendix E

THE FELLOWSHIP OF THE ROSY CROSS

(I)
CONSTITUTION & LAWS OF THE FELLOWSHIP

1. The Fellowship of the Rosy Cross is the guardian of a path of symbolism communicated in Ritual after the manner of the chief Instituted Mysteries, past and present.
2. The symbolism is concerned only with the quest and attainment of the human soul on its return to the Divine Centre: it is sought thereby to recall its members to the true object of research and the living method of its attainment.
3. The Fellowship does not profess to communicate knowledge of the soul and experience in the path of return otherwise than by the mode of symbolism; but this way is sacramental and those who can receive into their hearts the life and grace of the symbolism may attain both knowledge and experience thereby and therein.
4. The symbolism of the Fellowship implies a Doctrine and Practice of Mystical Religion, understood in its universal sense.
5. It has a message to those who are prepared in Christendom, though the lower Grades of the Fellowship are not explicitly Christian Grades.
6. The tradition and symbolism of the Fellowship are a derivation from the Secret Doctrine of Israel, known as Kabalah and embodied in the SEPHER HA ZOHAR.
7. The mode of interpretation in respect of Kabalistic Tradition is a Christian Mode.
8. It is to be understood that the Fellowship is similar to other Instituted Mysteries working under particular veils, the Masonic Brotherhood, for example, which uses building symbolism to produce upright and honourable members of the Speculative Art, while the Fellowship of the Rosy Cross uses theosophical symbolism of Israel and seeks to lead thereby into a deeper knowledge of the soul and its relation to GOD.
9. The Fellowship is open to all who desire the knowledge of Divine Things and union with GOD in Christ, and its path of symbolism is a true light of understanding on the Path of Union.
10. The common aspiration of its members is a living bond between them, the Fellowship

is a living body, and to those who are properly prepared it should be a source of spiritual life.

11. Initiation and advancement in the Fellowship take place under pledges of secrecy, being (*a*) the condition imposed invariably by all Instituted Mysteries; (*b*) the outward indication of the inward way of the spirit, which is secret and apart from the world; (*c*) a sacrament of the analogy between birth into physical life and the new birth or regeneration of mystical life, which are both secret processes, as are also those of physical and spiritual growth; (*d*) the proper method by which things appertaining to the Sanctuary are reserved to the Sanctuary alone.

12. The Brethren of all Grades are covenanted (*a*) to remember that if they seek first the Kingdom of GOD and His Justice, all other things shall be added unto them which are needful for the soul's progress and its attainment of the Divine Term; (*b*) to seek the knowledge of Divine Things and conscious union with GOD, so far as it may be possible in that sphere of life in which it has pleased GOD to call them; (*c*) to maintain the veil of secrecy; (*d*) to live in peace with one another; (*e*) to help each other in spiritual things, as they would wish to be helped themselves; (*f*) to avoid all interference with the Official Religion professed by their co-heirs in the Fellowship and to discourage it when attempted in their own case, (*g*) to endeavour before all things to realize in their own hearts those high intimations which are contained in the symbolism of the Grades.

13. The Constitution of the Fellowship is hierarchic and not elective, its government being vested in the Imperator of the Rite, who has power to appoint his successor, subject to confirmation by the body general of Adepti Exempti, and also to appoint substitutes for the government of the Temple.

14. The conditions on which persons are received into the Fellowship are embodied in the Form of Profession supplied through their Sponsors to Postulants and such persons may be of either sex. The decision as to reception rests solely with the Imperator.

15. This general principle being recognized as irrepealable, it shall be lawful to establish Temples consisting of men or women only, under proper warrant from the Imperator, should a sufficient reason be forthcoming.

16. The conditions of advancement from Grade to Grade in the Fellowship are: (*a*) the Warrant of the Imperator or his substitute; (*b*) the desire of the Postulant on his own part; (*c*) sufficient evidence that he or she has fulfilled the duties of the Grade to which he belongs.

17. No transcription of manuscripts is permitted without authority, which must be applied for and obtained in writing.

18. All copies of Rituals and other papers in the possession of members shall be kept in a locked case or box, bearing the label issued by the Fellowship and certifying that the package must be returned unopened to the address given thereon at the death of the member.

19. Members are covenanted to return all Rituals and papers in the case of their resignation or dismission.

20. The Obligatory Meetings of the Fellowship are the Festivals for the celebration of the Vernal and Autumnal Equinox, under reasonable reserves in respect of sickness, prohibitive distance and real inability of other kinds. Attendance is a matter of duty when there is no absolute hindrance.
21. The history of the Fellowship is communicated in the Third Order only but in one of its forms it is referable to the third quarter of the 18th century, without such antiquity being regarded as *per see* a test of value.
22. The construction of the Constitution and of these laws rests in the authority of the Imperator, it being laid down that alterations herein or additions hereto shall be made only with the concurrence of the body general of Adepti belonging to the Third Order.

(II)

THE OFFICERS OF THE F∴R∴C∴ AND THEIR REGALIA

1. THE HONOURABLE FRATER PHILOSOPHICUS,
   id est, Propositum Conscium Dei
   Master of the Temple
2. THE HONOURABLE FRATER PRACTICUS,
   id est, Desiderium Conscium Dei
   Warden of the Temple
3. THE HONOURABLE FRATER THEORETICUS,
   id est, Mens Conscia Sponsi
   Guide of the Paths and Grades
4. THE AUXILIARY FRATER ZELATOR,
   id est, Terra Illuminata
   Proclamator et Lucifer
5. THE FRATER THURIFICANS,
   id est, Thuribulum Ferens
   Thurifer
6. THE FRATER AQUARIUS,
   id est, Aquam Benedictam Ferens
   Aquarius
7. THE FRATER OSTIARIUS,
   id est, Custos Liminis, A Novice of the Rosy Cross
   Guard

N.B. The Imperator, or Chief of the Rite, presides *ex officio* in all Grades of the Fellowship, either personally or by his appointed Substitute.

In those cases where certain Offices are taken by Sorores of the Fellowship, the necessary alterations are made in the modes of address.

THE CLOTHING OF CELEBRANTS AND OFFICERS

1. THE HONOURABLE FRATER PHILOSOPHICUS wears a green robe over his black habit and a collar of red silk, from which depends a circular lamina, inscribed with the letter YOD. The green colour of the Master's robe represents the growth in life which is of GOD. The symbol of the Lion is embroidered thereon, upon the left side, with the inscription: FACIES TERTIA, FACIES LEONIS. The Master bears a Wand, surmounted by a Calvary Cross, having four circles at the end of the four arms and one circle toward the centre of the lowermost arm.

2. THE HONOURABLE FRATER PRACTICUS wears a yellow robe over his black habit, symbolizing the beginning of transmutation in GOD. The symbol of the Eagle is embroidered thereon, upon the left side, with the inscription: FACIES QUARTA, FACIES AQUILAE. His collar is of violet silk, from which depends a circular lamina, inscribed with the letter HE, being the first HE of the Divine Name. He bears a Wand surmounted by a flaming heart.

3. THE HONOURABLE FRATER THEORETICUS wears a blue robe over his black habit, symbolizing the aspiration and desire which initiate the great quest and reflect things unrealized. It bears the symbol of the Man embroidered thereon, upon the left side, with the inscription: FACIES SECUNDA, FACIES HOMINIS. His collar is of orange silk, from which depends a circular lamina, inscribed with the letter VAU. He bears a Wand, surmounted by an open eye, signifying the eye of mind.

4. THE AUXILIARY FRATER ZELATOR wears a cloak of reddish brown, corresponding to the Adamic earth and symbolizing the first movement of the Divine Spirit toward the making of a living soul. The symbol of the Ox is embroidered thereon, with the inscription: FACIES UNA, FACIES CHERUB. His collar is of blue-green silk, from which depends a circular lamina, inscribed with the letter HE, being the HE final of the Divine Name. He bears a Wand, surmounted by a Calvary Cross, having a crown upon the upper arms. The Frater Zelator is in symbolical correspondence with the Guide of the Paths and Grades.

5. THE FRATER THURIFICANS wears a red surplice and a collar of green silk, from which depends a circular lamina, inscribed with an equilateral △, having the apex upward, as a symbol of Fire. He is in symbolical correspondence with the Master.

6. THE FRATER AQUARIUS wears a blue surplice and a collar of orange silk, from which depends a circular lamina, inscribed with an equilateral ▽, having the apex downward, as a symbol of Water. He is in symbolical correspondence with the Warden.

7. THE FRATER OSTIARIUS, who is not strictly an Officer, has no special vestments. he carries a Wand, surmounted by a Dove of Peace. There is no Sword in a Temple of the Rosy Cross.

8. In addition to the black habit, the Frater Ostiarius and all unofficial members wear a collar of white silk, emblematic of purification in progress, from which depends

a crimson Calvary Cross. It is the general jewel of the whole Fellowship on the external side.

9. In Grades below the Third Order, the Imperator wears the general Rose-Cross of the Third Order and the clothing of an officiating Adeptus Minor. He carries a Wand surmounted by a triple Sephirotic Cross.

[Printed before the text in *The Ceremony of Reception into the Grade of Neophyte*, 1916.]

NOTES

CHAPTER 1

1. Waite: letter to Harold Voorhis, 24 September 1936. Voorhis visited the site of 206 Washington Street on 7 March 1937 and sent his description to Waite on the same day.
2. Reuben H. Walworth, *Hyde Genealogy; or the descendants, in the female as well as in the male lines, from William Hyde of Norwich* (Albany, 2 vols., 1864). The entry relating to the Waite family is in vol. 2, p. 905.
3. The Thomas Waite who signed the death-warrant of King Charles I in 1649 was imprisoned at the Restoration and died in 1668. For genealogical information on the Waite family I am indebted to Mr Charles J. Jacobs of Bridgeport, Connecticut; he has traced one line of descent from Alice Southworth, who sailed on the *Mayflower* and became the second wife of William Bradford, the first Governor of Plymouth Colony.
4. See C. P. Magrath, *Morrison R. Waite: the Triumph of Character* (New York, 1963), p. 25.
5. For a more detailed account of *A Soul's Comedy*, see ch. 5. The passages referring to Lyme are on pp. 23 and 189; the date 1857 can be deduced from references to the Civil War and to a period four years previously; see pp. 202 and 145.
6. Harleian Society Publications, vol. 25, *The Register Book of Marriages belonging to the Parish of St George, Hanover Square, in the County of Middlesex*, p. 19. My attention was drawn to this entry by Charles Jacobs.
7. Waite, Diary, 29 September 1937.

CHAPTER 2

1. This was evidently Trinity Church, Kentish Town, where the Revd T.W. Hathaway was curate during the early 1860s.
2. The Revd Seton Patterson Rooke (1824–1901) was a graduate of Oriel College, Oxford, who seceded to Rome in 1851 and became a Dominican Friar. See W. G. Gorman, *Converts to Rome* (1910), p. 236. The date of the baptism was supplied by Fr Hubert Edgar, O.P., of St Dominic's Priory, Southampton Road, Haverstock Hill.
3. St Joseph's Retreat was founded in 1858. By 1863 a permanent building had been completed and it was this that Waite remembered. The present structure dates from 1889.
4. Waite lists a number of them: 30 Windsor Road, Holloway, then Angler's Lane,

Torriano Avenue, Prince of Wales Road (above a chemist's shop), and a cul-de-sac near Ferdinand Street.

5. George White was successively Headmaster of the Abbey Street Schools, London; Tutor of St Edmund's College, Ware; and Principal of Bellevue Academy. He wrote at least four text books and six devotional and church-historical works.
6. S. J. Kunitz and H. Haycraft, *Twentieth Century Authors: a Biographical Dictionary of Modern Literature* (New York, 1942), p. 1462. Waite's mother learned her French at a school in Chiswick (*SLT*, p. 14). In 1874 St Charles's College was moved into magnificent new buildings in North Kensington; these made way for a modern school in the 1960s but the original five-storey building in Bayswater still stands.

   The Revd Dr Henry Augustus Rawes (1826–85) was a graduate of Trinity College, Cambridge, who seceded to Rome in 1856. He became Prefect of Studies at St Charles's College in 1870, and in 1879 was elected Superior of the Oblates of St Charles at Bayswater. Of all his twenty-five published works—largely devotional and controversial, with a scattering of verse—Waite was most impressed by *Homeward: a Tale of Redemption* (1873). For Fr Rawes's life, see J. Gillow, *Bibliographical Dictionary of the English Catholics*, vol. 5 (1900—), pp. 394–5.
7. Frederica died on 15 September 1874 at 45 Richmond Road, a house in which the family lodged on a number of occasions. It was owned by a Miss Bibby, 'an Irish lady, sunk in an abyss of Protestantism and Bible Christianity' (*SLT*, p. 50).
8. 'Laban Rewell' (i.e. A. E. Waite), 'A Recollection of Robert Browning', in *Horlick's Magazine*, vol. 1 (1904), p. 42. It is possible that the 'friendly hand' was that of the Revd Greville Chester rather than James Smethurst; in which case it could not have been earlier than 1877.
9. ibid. pp. 39–40.
10. *The National Magazine* was edited by S. H. Harding of Liverpool, who issued seven numbers in 1877 and 1878. Waite's letter appeared in no. 7, June 1878.
11. Waite, *The Way of Divine Union* (1915), p. 302.

CHAPTER 3

1. Waite, 'Byways of Periodical Literature', in *Walford's Antiquarian Magazine and Bibliographical Review*, vol. 12 (July 1887), p. 74.
2. See *A Catalogue of Books*, for sale by Auction by Hodgson & Co., no. 18 of 1932–3 (28 June 1933). The 'Early Victorian sensational literature, from the Library of A. E. Waite'comprised lots 815 to 828 and contained 373 volumes. By contrast, 'Barry Ono's' collection, which was bequeathed to the British Museum Library in 1946, contains some 500 volumes.
3. Letter of 4 August 1923. Waite's letters to Partington formed a part of the correspondence files of the *Bookman's Journal*, which were sold at auction on 29 July 1977 by Sotheby Park Bernet & Co.

CHAPTER 4

1. [Waite], 'A Recollection of Robert Browning', p. 41. The second letter is on pp. 41–2 and the final letter on pp. 42–3.
2. Very few of the 'amateur' magazines have survived—none of the manuscript

journals—and information about them is sparse. Among the printed magazines to which Waite contributed were *The Idler, The London Amateur, Green Leaves, The Gloucestrian, Echoes from the Lyre, The Sentinel*, and *The Central Review*. Manuscript magazines included *The Rambler, Amateur Standard*, and *The Golden Pen*.

3. See *Echoes from the Lyre*, vol. 1, no. 7 and no. 8 (September and October 1878), and *The Poet's Magazine*, vol. 4 (1878).
4. The Amateur Conference was the brainchild of Arthur Loseby, a Leicester solictor. The solitary issue of *The Central Review* appeared on 15 October 1878, priced at 1*d*.

CHAPTER 5

1. James Henderson was both founder and editor of *Young Folks Paper*. It started life at Manchester in 1870 as *Our Young Folks' Weekly Budget*, changing its title in 1879. Later still it was known as *Old and Young* and finally as *The Folks at Home*. Henderson died in 1906 at the age of 83.
2. *Aunt Judy's Magazine* was founded in May 1866, by Mrs Margaret Gatty (1809–73), the name being taken from the nickname of her daughter, Juliana Horatia Ewing, the author of *Jackanapes*. Publication ceased in 1885.
3. For Chester's life, see the anonymously edited *Obituary Notices of the late Rev. Greville John Chester, B.A.* (Watlington, 1892). The account of his life in Sheffield was contributed by the Revd Alfred Gatty.
4. Printed in *Strange Houses of Sleep* (1906), pp. 93–6.
5. The Revd James Scratton M.A. was a graduate of St John's College, Cambridge. He had seceded to Rome in 1851.
6. These 'fragments' extend to 28 quarto pages. They are preserved in the *Collectanea Metaphysica* volume.
7. Mr Timothy d'Arch-Smith, the author of *Love in Earnest* (1970), the classic study of Uranian verse, read—at my request—*A Soul's Comedy* and agreed with me over its Uranian content. He suggested that Waite was portraying what Freud believed to be 'a natural homosexual phase in adolescence' and that one should not over-emphasize such behaviour. However, in 1881 Waite was 23 years of age, and at the time I discussed this with Timothy d'Arch-Smith neither of us had seen the manuscript 'fragments'.
8. *Israfel. Letters Visions and Poems* (E. W. Allen, 1886). Waite presented a copy to Chester, to whom he also gave a copy of *A Soul's Comedy*. Both copies are in the collection of the author.
9. 'Mysticism: its use and abuse', a review of *A Book of Mystery and Vision*, printed in *The Speaker* (31 May 1902).

CHAPTER 6

1. It can be dated by Waite's reference to the reprint of Godfrey Higgins's *Anacalypsis*, which James Burns 'had begun to reprint'. The incomplete reprint was issued in 1878.
2. This is the definition adopted by the National Spiritualist Association of America. It is quoted in full in Fodor, *Encyclopaedia of Psychic Science* (1933), p. 360.
3. James Burns (1833–94) was the proprietor of *The Medium and Daybreak*, which periodical he founded in 1869; it did not survive him. The Revd William Stainton

Moses (1839–92) was converted to Spiritualism in 1872 and became a 'powerful' medium; his principal guide, who was known as Imperator, was allegedly responsible for two volumes of automatic scripts, *Spirit Teachings* and *Spirit Identity* which were issued under the pseudonym of 'M. A. Oxon'. He founded the journal *Light* (with Dawson Rogers) in 1881 and was editor until his death.

Captain John James (1804–94) was a retired guardsman and an enthusiastic if uncritical, proponent of Spiritualism. He published a small book on Mesmerism in 1879.

E. Dawson Rogers (1823–1910) was the co-founder, with Stainton Moses, of *Light* (which he edited after Stainton Moses's death) and of The London Spiritualist Alliance (1884). By profession he was a journalist.

4. Monck began his career as a Baptist minister, but in 1873 he embraced Spiritualism and became a professional medium. Archdeacon Colley was a firm believer in the reality of the phenomena produced by Monck and his accounts can be interpreted either as hallucination pure and simple, or as a record of materializations more remarkable than any other—before or since.
5. The friend was Gilbert Bryant, also an amateur poet, under whose name some of Waite's early poems appeared. They continued to meet occasionally until Bryant's death in 1915.
6. William Eglinton (1857–1933) began his career in Spiritualism by giving remarkable materialization seances (described in Farmer, *Twixt two Worlds*, 1886, with startling paintings of the 'spirit' figures by James Tissot, who was later more profitably employed in painting scenes from the life of Christ). He turned to slate-writing in 1884 after returning from India under a cloud following the production of spurious 'Mahatma' letters which may have been the result of collusion with Mme Blavatsky.
7. Mr A. Rita was notorious for holding seances only in darkness. In 1878 at Copenhagen he had been caught red-handed with a confederate (who was found to have masks, a false beard, and white muslin secreted upon him) but was yet accepted as genuine by the English Spiritualist establishment. He had been a protégé of Captain James.
8. The interview is recorded in 'LSA Comments and Records' by Mercy Phillimore (*Light*, 25 June 1942).
9. The lecture was delivered on 16 December 1890; it was printed in *Light* (27 December 1890) and later reprinted in pamphlet form.
10. Printed in *The Christian Commonwealth* (6 January 1915), under the title 'If a Man Die, shall he Live Again?' Waite was among a number of authorities on theology, mysticism, and psychical research to whom the question was put.
11. The event is recorded in Waite's diary, in the entry for 23 March 1936.
12. The table-tipping (if such it was) took place on 30 July 1919 while the comment about automatists appeared in 'Christianity and Spiritualism' (a review of Stoddart, *The Case against Spiritualism*) in *The Occult Review* (February 1920). His attack on ouija boards is in 'Periodical Literature' in *The Occult Review* for April 1920.
13. Letter: Sybil Waite to the author, 14 November 1977.
14. D. D. Reese, 'Is there an Anti-Spiritualist Movement?', in *Reason* (March 1924).
15. op. cit., *Light* (25 June 1942).

CHAPTER 7

1. *Beyond the Ken: a Mystical Story of Styria*, was published in 1886. Miss Corner had previously published one volume of fiction and two books on travels in Germany. Waite's article, 'Nuremberg', was printed during 1891 but I have been unable to ascertain the exact date.
2. Granville belonged to a cadet branch of the Stuart-Menteath family. None of his children married, and with the death of Ludivina—his and Dora's daughter—the branch became extinct.
3. The information about W. H. Lakeman and the Queensbury Nursery was supplied by Mr S. J. Relf of James Relf & Sons Ltd., Sanderstead, through the kind offices of the Horticultural Trades Association.
4. Letter of May 1942. Quoted in A. Reynolds and W. Charlton, *Arthur Machen* (1963).
5. Two catalogues are attributable to Machen: 'The Literature of Archaeology and Occultism' of 1885; and 'List of books chiefly from the library of the late Frederick Hockley, Esq.' (1887). He also wrote some of the brief paragraphs of 'Notes and News' in *George Redway's Literary Circular* (1887–8).
6. Letters of 19 December 1935 and 17 August 1940.
7. Letter of 21 February 1906. The texts of all these letters are printed in the forthcoming *Selected Letters of Arthur Machen* (Wellingborough; Crucible, 1988).
8. This 16-page pamphlet was issued in 1887; the text was later reprinted in the American edition of *The Shining Pyramid* (Chicago, 1923), pp. 63–71.
9. Letter of 7 October 1887, now in the Gwent County Library at Newport. I am indebted to Mr Godfrey Brangham for a transcript.
10. *Avalon* was published in 1894. An advance copy of the book exists with the author's name omitted from the title-page. Waite revised the text extensively in 1941 and the original manuscript also has many alterations. I suspect that Dora's contribution did not go beyond putting her name to the poem.
11. Letter to Munson Havens, 1 December 1924; quoted in Reynolds and Charlton, op. cit., p. 74.

CHAPTER 8

1. Frank Benson (1858–1939) founded the Benson Company in 1883. He was knighted in 1916.
2. Waite's records of the Order are bound up with his *Annus Mirabilis Redivivus* diary. He lists the Lords Maltworm as Arthur Llewellyn Jones Machen, Hugh Christopher Wilson, Frederick Randle Ayrton, Garnett William Holme, Harry William Hubert, Ernest George Harcourt Williams, Edward Mall Swete, and Leonard Bultress.
3. The MS is bound up in the same diary as the 'minutes' of the Rabelaisian Order.
4. Letter of 11 April 1936. I have been unable to determine the date of the incident itself.
5. Letter of 9 October 1928. The incident is also referred to, more briefly, in Machen's letter to Waite (see Note 4).
6. Diary, 12 February 1903. The reviews appeared between February and August of that year.
7. Letter to the author, 3 December 1986. Mr Machen did not indicate the date of the 'glorious occasion'.

CHAPTER 9

1. Alfred Percy Sinnett (1840–1921) had taken up the editorship of the *Pioneer* in 1872. He met Mme Blavatsky and Col Olcott in 1879 and was immediately impressed—and favoured, for he became the recipient of the majority of the allegedly 'precipitated' letters of the Mahatmas (or of H. P. Blavatsky, if one is sceptical). His two books, *The Occult World* (1881) and *Esoteric Buddhism* (1883), did much to promote Theosophy in Britain. Sinnett has often been claimed as a member of the Golden Dawn although he had no connection with the Order; the mistake arose because simple-minded writers on occultism assumed that the initials A. P. S. referred to Sinnett, whereas they are those of Frater Anima Pura Sit (i.e. Dr Henry Pullen Burry).
2. Dr Richard Hodgson was sent to India in 1884 by the Society for Psychical Research to investigate the claims of wonder-working associated with H. P. Blavatsky. He found abundant evidence of fraud and set it out in his Report, which was published in 1885. Theosophists have attempted ever since to discountenance his findings, but with little success save among their fellows.
3. Anonymous review in *The Theosophist* (February 1887).
4. The 'occult' review is that of Mrs Sinnett, in *Lucifer* (November 1887). The anonymous review in *Nature* appeared in the issue of 29 December 1887.
5. Horatio William Bottomley (1860–1933), financier, Member of Parliament, newspaper proprietor, and swindler, was among the most charismatic rogues of this century. He was not considered fit to grace the pages of *Who's Who* after his death, but there is an entertaining biography of him by Julian Symons (1955).
6. Ruland's *Lexicon of Alchemy* was printed, in an edition of six copies, in September 1892, but it was not intended for public distribution and *The Hermetic Museum* was technically Elliott's first publication.
7. Emma Waite died on 14 December 1893. Her entire estate—of £736. 6*s*. 10*d*.—was left to her son. One of the witnesses to her Will was Charles Granville Stuart-Menteath, shown as living at 31 Harvard Road; presumably he was then living with the Waites.
8. Some of the stock had also passed to John Watkins; in 1897 both Quaritch and Watkins issued identical catalogues of the alchemical translations.
9. For the events surrounding this book, see pp. 125–6 below.
10. The pamphlets comprised: *Horlick's Malted Milk versus Cow's Milk*, *Ordered to the Front*, *The Medical Profession on Horlick's Malted Milk*, *Horlick's Malted Milk and the Nursing Profession*, *The Cyclist's Friend*, *The Eulogy of Horlick's Milk*, *Little Miss Muffet*, and *Freddy's Diary*. No copies of the last two, which were written for children, have been traced.
11. The most prolific contributors of 'colonial' stories were Mrs Chan Toon, W. B. Koebel, and V. B. Paterson. Edgar Jepson's *The Horned Shepherd* first appeared in the magazine, while Machen contributed *A Fragment of Life*, *The Garden of Avallaunius*, and *The White People*.

CHAPTER 10

1. Waite's letter, 'Eliphas Lévi and the Antiquity of the Tarot', was printed in *Light*

(18 December 1886). Macbean's 'Criticism' appeared in the *Transactions* of the Metropolitan College, S.R.I.A., for 1888–9.

2. Waite's letter on 'Count Cagliostro' was printed in July 1888; his two letters on 'A New Light of Mysticism' appeared in September and October of the same year.
3. The letters of both Waite and Mr Pfoundes appeared in *The Medium and Daybreak* during March and April 1889.
4. *A Suggestive Inquiry into the Hermetic Mystery* was reissued in 1918 with an Introduction by W. L. Wilmshurst and an Appendix containing Mrs Atwood's 'Memorabilia'.
5. Among Waite's lectures were two to the London Occult Society: 'Alchemy' on 16 December 1888 and 'History of Rosicrucianism: an elucidatory Sketch' on 23 October 1887. He also addressed the Revd G. W. Allen's 'Christo-Theosophical Society' on three occasions; the lectures were: 'Transcendental Science and Transcendental Religion', 5 March 1891; 'The Agnostic Standpoint as the Threshold of Mysticism', 14 May 1891; and 'The Catholic Doctrine of Theosophy and Mysticism', 28 January 1892.
6. Waite's introductions varied in length from a brief two-page note in *Collectanea Chemica* to a fifty-page study for *The Alchemical Writings of Edward Kelly.*
7. *The Zodiac of Life*, by Marcellus Palingenius Stellatus, 'now for the first time rendered into English prose', was prefaced by Waite's 'Introductory Remarks on Hermetic Poetry'. The unbound sheets were taken over by Redway and bound up after he acquired his share of Elliott's stock.

CHAPTER 11

1. A substantial portion of the text had previously appeared in the form of articles in both *Horlick's Magazine* and *The Occult Review.*
2. George Robert Stow Mead (1863–1933) was a classical scholar and a pioneer in the study of Gnosticism. His translation of *Pistis Sophia* catches the spirit of Gnostic thought in a way that is absent from the quite unreadable translations made by more orthodox academics. Later in life Mead became increasingly interested in spiritualism. The initial suggestion for the founding of The Hermetic Text Society came, unwittingly, from Mead. In 1903 he had reviewed the reissue of *The Cloud upon the Sanctuary* and was so impressed by Waite's introduction that he wrote: 'If only someone—and why not the scholarly mystic who writes this Introduction?—would play Max Muller to the "sacred books" of the Christian mystics from the XIVth to the XVIIIth centuries, what a feast there would be for hundreds of thousands of starving souls!' (*Theosophical Review*, January 1903).

CHAPTER 12

1. William Wynn Westcott (1848–1925) was orphaned at an early age and brought up by an uncle who was a physician at Martock in Somerset. Westcott followed his uncle's profession, developed a keen interest in occultism and Freemasonry, and wrote extensively upon both subjects. His career in the Golden Dawn has been related often but there has, as yet, been no substantial study of his life. A collection of his essays, under the title *The Magical Mason*, was edited by the present writer in 1983.

2. Samuel Liddell McGregor Mathers (1854–1918) was eccentric, autocratic, and extremely learned in the practice of magic. He published two important magical texts. *The Key of Solomon the King* (1889) and *The Book of the Sacred Magic of Abra-Melin the Mage* (1898), and suffered for his pains under Aleister Crowley, who took the credit for Mathers's labours in 777, a collection in tabular form of correspondence between various systems of occultism. Mathers has received little critical or biographical attention, the only book devoted to him being the hagiography of Ithell Colquhoun, *Sword of Wisdom: MacGregor Mathers and the Golden Dawn* (1975).
3. The definitive history of the Golden Dawn is Ellic Howe's, *The Magicians of the Golden Dawn*, (1972; reprinted 1985) in which the question of the cipher manuscripts and the Anna Sprengel letters is treated exhaustively. The official documents of the Order, an account of its structure, workings and membership, and a list of all known members, are given in my own study, *The Golden Dawn Companion* (1986). For the rituals, the most extensive study—which prints most of the rituals—is Israel Regardie's *Complete Golden Dawn System of Magic* (1984). The instructional papers of the Second Order, known as 'Flying Rolls', are printed in *Astral Projection, Magic and Alchemy* ed. by Francis King (2nd edition, 1986).
4. Florence Farr (Mrs Edward Emery, (1860–1917) is better-known as an actress, friend of W. B. Yeats, and as Bernard Shaw's 'New Woman' than as a magician. But the Golden Dawn was an important part of her life during its years of activity and influenced both her writing and her social attitudes. In 1912 she left England to teach in Ceylon, where she died in 1917. A biography of her, *Florence Farr, Bernard Shaw's 'New Woman'*, by Josephine Johnson, was published in 1975.
5. Percy Bullock (b. 1868) was a solicitor and enthusiastic student of alchemy, who married within the Golden Dawn; his wife, Pamela Carden, had followed her parents into the Order and played a prominent role in Isis-Urania during its most active period.

   Robert William Felkin (1858–1922) practised medicine in Africa and later in Edinburgh, where he joined the Amen-Ra Temple. He moved to London and transferred to Isis-Urania, coming to prominence in the Order during the 'interregnum' of 1900 to 1903. His later years were spent in taking the Stella Matutina down ever more eccentric paths in search of the Chiefs of the Third Order. Eventually he believed that he had found them in the person of an imaginary being whom he called Ara ben Shemesh; when he emigrated to New Zealand—to propagate further Stella Matutina Temples—he took Ara ben Shemesh and his teachings with him.

   John William Brodie-Innes (1848–1923) practised as a lawyer in Edinburgh and was active in the Scottish Lodge of the Theosophical Society before founding the Amen-Ra Temple. He was one of the few genuine scholars in the Order but wrote principally on occult subjects (both as fact and as overt fiction). He believed firmly in the Secret Chiefs and established his own Solar Order in 1896 with the aim of propagating their teachings.

CHAPTER 13

1. Marcus Worsley Blackden was an artist and Egyptologist who later took up

journalism. He prepared many coloured drawings of wall paintings from tombs at Beni Hasan and El Bersheh for the Archaeological Survey of Egypt. It seems to have been his Egyptian enthusiasms that drew him to the Golden Dawn. He was also a keen yachtsman and moved to Fawley to pursue his hobby. In 1925 Waite visited him and together they 'burnt certain G.D. rituals and papers'. Although reconciled to Waite as a friend he made no attempt to join the F.·.R.·.C.·..

2. William Alexander Ayton (1816–1909) was not only a keen alchemist, but also a Theosophist, supporter of innumerable 'Higher Degrees' in Freemasonry, and naïve believer in the credentials of bogus occultists. His correspondence with F. L. Gardner has been edited by Ellic Howe and published as *The Alchemist of the Golden Dawn* (1985).

CHAPTER 14

1. In fact only 6,100 sets had been printed by 1931. Later printings would not have increased the total by more than another 3,000 over the next seven years. Waite may have intended to speak of 'nineteen thousand *volumes*' rather than 'sets'.

CHAPTER 15

1. There is no reference to dental operations before 1921 in Waite's diaries; but the diaries for 1914 and 1910 are missing so that his experiences can probably be referred to one or other of those years.
2. Books on the subject of Tarot Cards are legion. For present purposes the most useful are: S. R. Kaplan, *Encyclopaedia of Tarot* 2 vols.,(1978, 1986); M. Dummett, *The Game of Tarot* (1980) [extremely hostile to all esoteric interpretations; perhaps because the author is (a) a Roman Catholic, (b) a professional Philosopher, and (c) a confirmed addict of card games]; and J. Shephard, *The Tarot Trumps: Cosmos in Miniature* (1985).
3. Pamela Colman Smith probably joined the Order on 2 November 1901, but her entry on the Roll is undated (the previous signature is so dated and Neophytes often entered together), and it may have been closer to the date of the schism of 1903. By 16 April 1904 she was still in the Grade of Zelator.
4. This lecture, with others written and delivered at the same period, is printed in *Hermetic Papers of A. E. Waite*, edited by the present writer (1987).
5. This identification has been made by Mr Roger Parisious, who will elaborate the evidence in support of it in a forthcoming study of Waite's Tarot and its connection with Yeats. Mr Parisious also maintains that Waite is the model for the character of Peter Roche in Yeats's novel *The Speckled Bird*, but while certain aspects of Roche's personality could fit Waite, there are many others that do not, and I look upon the suggestion as being, at best, unproven.

CHAPTER 16

1. In deference to the wishes of the surviving relatives of members of the F.·.R.·.C.·. I have refrained from identifying more than a small proportion of the membership. In like manner I have given only a cursory indication of the nature and content of the rituals themselves; the Fellowship still survives, albeit in a somewhat reduced and altered form, and I do not intend to cause distress to its members by publishing the texts of rituals which they perceive as sacred.

2. Coburn's principal published works were: *London* (1909), *New York* (1910), *Men of Mark* (1913), and *More Men of Mark* (1922).
3. This is possibly a reference to their mutual interest in Freemasonry; Coburn was active in the Craft and in many 'Higher Degrees'.
4. In a letter to Alice Meynell, 14 July 1916. It is quoted in A. M. Hadfield, *Charles Williams. An Exploration of his Life and Work* (1983), p. 24.
5. Williams, *The Image of the City and other Essays*, selected by Anne Ridler, with a critical introduction (1958). See pp. xxiv–xxv.
6. The lecture was delivered on 12 December; the member in question, Miss M. C. Debenham, joined the Order on 20 March 1924 as Soror Via determinata.
7. Two of the Masonic lectures—'Robert Fludd and Freemasonry' (Manchester Association for Masonic Research, 29 September 1921) and 'Masonic Tradition and the Royal Arch' (Somerset Masters' Lodge, 28 February 1921) are reprinted in E. Dunning (ed.) *Selected Masonic Papers of A. E. Waite* (1987).

CHAPTER 17

1. This was not the only occasion on which Jeffery offended Waite. He had, over a number of years, acquired a collection of original manuscripts of Waite's works—largely through Waite exchanging them for books he wanted—and in 1935 he offered 24 of them ('22 in half-blue morocco cases, and 2 in bookform') for sale at £3,500. The outraged Waite advised Voorhis not to consider buying them—his own suggested valuation was £30.

Select Bibliography

(I)
THE PRINCIPAL PUBLISHED WORKS OF A. E. WAITE

Only the more important works are cited here; for a complete descriptive list the reader should refer to my *A.E. Waite: a Bibliography* (Wellingborough: The Aquarian Press, 1983).

1877 *An Ode to Astronomy, and other Poems*

1879 *A Lyric of the Fairyland and other Poems*

1886 *Israfel: Letters Visons and Poems*
The Mysteries of Magic. A Digest of the Writings of Eliphas Lévi [tr. and ed.]

1887 *A Soul's Comedy*
The Real History of the Rosicrucians

1888 *Songs and Poems of Fairyland. An Anthology of English Fairy Poetry* [ed.]
Lives of Alchemystical Philosophers [ed.]
The Magical Writings of Thomas Vaughan [ed.]

1889 *Prince Starbeam. A Tale of Fairyland*
A Handbook of Cartomancy, by Grand Orient [i.e. A.E. Waite; ed.]

1890 *Lucasta: Parables and Poems*

1891 *The Occult Sciences*

1892 *A Lexicon of Alchemy or Alchemical Dictionary*, by Martinus Rulandus [ed.]

1893 *The Golden Stairs; Tales from the Wonder-World*
A New Light of Mysticism. Azoth: or The Star in the East
The Hermetic Museum Restored and Enlarged [ed.]
A Golden and Blessed Casket of Nature's Marvels, by Benedictus Figulus [ed.]
The Triumphal Chariot of Antimony, by Basilius Valentinus [ed.]
Collectanea Chemica [ed.]
The Alchemical Writings of Edward Kelly [ed.]

1894 *Belle and the Dragon: an Elfin Comedy*

	The New Pearl of Great Price (by Petrus Bonus of Ferrara) [ed.]
	The Hermetic and Alchemical Writings of Paracelsus [ed.]
	Avalon: a Poetic Romance. By Dora Stuart-Menteath [ed., but see p. 64]
1896	*Devil-Worship in France*
	The Turba Philosophorum, or Assembly of the Sages [tr. and ed.]
	Transcendental Magic, its Doctrine and Ritual, by Eliphas Lévi [tr. and ed.]
1898	*The Book of Black Magic and of Pacts*
	The Gift of the Spirit, a selection from the Essays of Prentice Mulford [ed.]
1899	*Braid on Hypnotism* [ed.]
1901	*The Life of Louis Claude de Saint-Martin, the Unknown Philosopher*
1902	*A Book of Mystery and Vision*
	The Doctrine and Literature of the Kabalah
1903	*Obermann*, by Etienne Pivert de Senancour [tr. and ed.]
	The Cloud upon the Sanctuary, by the Councillor von Eckartshausen [ed.]
1904	*The House of the Hidden Light*, by the High Fratres Filius Aquarum [i.e. Arthur Machen] and Elias Artista [i.e. A. E. Waite]
1906	*Strange Houses of Sleep*
	Studies in Mysticism and certain aspects of the Secret Tradition
	Steps to the Crown
1909	*The Hidden Church of the Holy Graal*
1910	*Rituals of 'The Holy Order of the G∴D∴ under the obedience of the Independent and Rectified Rite'* [seven in number]
	The Tarot of the Bohemians, by Papus [ed.]
	Lumen de Lumine, or A New Magical Light, by Thomas Vaughan [ed.]
1911	*The Pictorial Key to the Tarot*
	The Book of Ceremonial Magic
	The Secret Tradition in Freemasonry
1912	*Some Characteristics of the Interior Church*, by I. V. Lopukhin [ed.]
	The Book of Destiny, by Grand Orient
1913	*The Secret Doctrine in Israel*
	The History of Magic, by Eliphas Lévi [tr. and ed.]
1914	*The Collected Poems*
1915	*The Way of Divine Union*
1916	*Rituals of the Fellowship of the Rosy Cross* [eight in number; additional texts and revisions appeared up to 1942]
1917	*The Harmonial Philosophy. A Compendium and Digest of the Works of Andrew Jackson Davis* [ed.]
1919	*The Works of Thomas Vaughan* [ed.]
1921	*A New Encyclopaedia of Freemasonry*
	The Book of the Holy Graal

1922 *Raymund Lully*
Saint-Martin the French Mystic

1923 *Lamps of Western Mysticism*
The Book of Formation (Sepher Yetzirah), by Rabbi Akiba ben Joseph [ed.]

1924 *The Brotherhood of the Rosy Cross*

1925 *Emblematic Freemasonry*

1926 *The Secret Tradition in Alchemy*
The Book of Life in the Rose [successive parts appeared up to 1928]

1927 *The Quest of the Golden Stairs*

1929 *The Holy Kabbalah*

1933 *The Holy Grail, its Legends and Symbolism*

1937 *The Secret Tradition in Freemasonry*

1938 *Shadows of Life and Thought*

(II)
THE WAITE PAPERS (PRINCIPAL CONTENTS)

Manuscripts

Diaries

(a) Annus Mirabilis Redivivus. Diary from 2 October 1902 to 2 October 1903. Bound in at the end are the records of The Rabelaisian Order of Tosspots, and the text of Machen's Hermetic Ritual.
(b) Business Diaries. 4 vols. 1900 to 1906. A record of Waite's activities on behalf of Messrs Horlick & Co. and of his work as private secretary to James Horlick. It includes carbon copies of the more important business letters written by Waite.
(c) Small diaries. Pocket diaries for the years 1909 to 1942. (Those for 1911 and 1914 are missing.)

Collectanea Metaphysica. A bound volume of miscellaneous notes, unpublished and discarded poems, and records of sittings with mediums *c.*1880–7.

The Secret Commonwealth of Rogues and Vagabonds. A bound volume of typescripts of unpublished sensational fiction *c.*1880–1900.

Esoteric Freemasonry. Notes on the esoteric history of Freemasonry, its doctrines, symbols, and science. Unpublished typescript *c.*1893.

Avalon. The original manuscript draft of the poem, in Waite's hand.

Diana Vaughan and the question of modern Palladism. Unpublished typescript of the sequel to *Devil-Worship in France* (1897).

The Sodality of the Shadows. Manuscript records of the society, bound up with two unpublished stories *c.*1900–10.

Dealings in Bibliomania. Unpublished typescript with MS corrections *c.* 1923.

The Independent and Rectified Rite of the Golden Dawn

(a) Manuscript rituals, 2 vols. *c.*1904–6.
(b) *R∴R∴ et A∴C∴ Convocations*. Typescripts and manuscripts of Waite's Addresses to the Order, together with copies of the Preliminary Report, Declaration of Independence, and circular letters 1903–8.
(c) Bound volume of completed Forms of Application for candidates for the Order, together with Order Summonses. 1904–13.
(d) *The Testimonies of Frater Finem Respice* (i.e. R. W. Felkin). Manuscript transcript of Waite's conversations with Felkin over the Third Order, the German Rosy Cross, and other matters concerning Felkin's Temple. 1915. (The conversations from 1906 to 1915.)

Fellowship of the Rosy Cross

(a) Minute Books of the F∴R∴C∴ and O∴S∴R∴ et A∴C∴ 5 vols., 1915–38.
(b) Register of Addresses, 1920–8.
(c) Forms of Profession for candidates for the Order. 2 vols. of completed forms, 1915–27.

Concerning Malted Milk. Typescript copies of two hundred promotional circular letters written by Waite for Horlick & Co.

Printed papers

Early Writings. 3 vols. Two contain prose contributions to periodicals; the third contains verse. 1876–81.
Reviews of early poetical works of Waite. 2 vols. 1878–9.
Miscellaneous Writings and Reviews. 23 vols. Periodical contributions by Waite and reviews of his work. 1884–1938.
Acta Latomorum. 4 vols. Printed ephemera relating to Waite's masonic career. 1901–38.
Announcements and Prospectuses. A volume of printed ephemera relating to Waite's published works. 1886–1911.

In addition to the above, the papers include revised texts of rituals; unbound manuscripts of lectures delivered by Waite; brief diary notes for part of the year 1901; notes and correspondence relating to the F∴R∴C∴; and a bound volume of portrait photographs and snapshots of Waite and his family.

According to the terms of Waite's will, his papers were ultimately to pass to the keeping of an institutional library; however, the institution in question declined to accept the papers and they are now dispersed between four private libraries, the owners of which do not wish to be identified. They are, however, willing to grant access to the papers to *bona fide* students, who are invited to communicate with the author via the publishers.

INDEX